British Folktales

BRITISH
FOLKTALES

KATHARINE BRIGGS

DORSET PRESS
New York

This edition published by Dorset Press,
a division of Marboro Books Corporation,
by arrangement with Pantheon Books,
a division of Random House, Inc., New York
1988 Dorset Press

ISBN 0-88029-288-1

Printed in the United States of America
M 9 8 7 6 5 4 3 2 1

ACKNOWLEDGMENTS

Grateful acknowledgment is made to the following for permission to reprint previously published material:

George Allen & Unwin Ltd. for "The Guardian Black Dog," "Croglin Grange," "The Dart of Death," "The Dream House," and "The Wooden Legs" from *In My Solitary Life* by Augustus Hare.

Mr. W. H. Barrett for "Flood Law in the Fens" from *Tales from the Fens* by W. H. Barrett, and for "Witches at Hallowe'en" from *More Tales from the Fens* by W. H. Barrett.

B. T. Batsford Ltd. and Miss Christina Hole for "John Rudall" from *English Folk-Lore*, and for "The Grateful Ghost" from *Haunted England* by Christina Hole.

Forge Books for "The Black Hen" from *The Devil in Devon* by J. R. W. Coxhead.

Mr. Frederick Grice for "The Longwitton Dragon" from *Folk Tales of the North Country* by Frederick Grice.

Miss Christina Hole and the Folk-Lore Society for permission to use the Society's publications.

Hutchinson & Co. Ltd. and the Earl of Airlie for "The Drummer of Airlie" from *Thatched with Gold* by Mabell, Countess of Airlie.

Mr. Peter Leather for "King Herla" and "The Shepherd and the Crows" from *Folk-Lore of Herefordshire* by Helen E. Leather.

In some cases, it has not been possible to trace the copyright owners.

To Katharine M. Law,
with many thanks for her unfailing interest
and for the help and advice she has given me
in the selection of the tales

CONTENTS

CONTENTS

CONTENTS

CONTENTS

CONTENTS

CONTENTS

CONTENTS

INTRODUCTION

As a child I was perhaps more fortunate than most because my father had collected three or four books on Folklore, so that, as well as the ordinary fairy stories which we had in our own nursery, Grimm, Hans Andersen, Perrault, Hauff's Fairy Tales, The Arabian Nights, two of Lang's coloured fairy books, Jack the Giant-Killer, The Babes in the Wood, and a few others, I had access to Hartland's *English Fairy and Folk Tales,* Yeats' *Irish Fairy And Folk Tales* and Douglas's *Scottish Fairy and Folk Tales,* all these in the Scott Publishing Library. There was besides *Celtic Folk Lore* by John Rhys, rather tougher reading because of all the Welsh scattered about it, but full of fascinating stories. I came across these four books when I was about nine years old, and they coloured my taste in Folk Narrative for the rest of my life. There were ordinary fairy stories in the books, but the tales which caught my fancy most were not the folk fictions, but the legends, short, factual-seeming accounts of Brownies and fairy changelings and women carried away into Fairyland to nurse the fairy babies, and, best of all, the anecdotes of little fairies captured by humans, such as the tale of Skillywidden, who happily got back to his parents and was not left to pine in captivity.

It was the memory of these small nuggets of tradition which made me when I was a grown woman rebel against the prettified, airy-fairy stories which were foisted upon children in the 1920s and 1930s, and told in so many schoolrooms and Brownie Pow-Wows, and which drove me into the Folk-Lore Society in an attempt to disentangle the strange muddle of Six names in the Brownie fairy lore. I may well be grateful to them, for it was the beginning of a life-long interest.

I have taken my *Dictionary of British Folk-Tales* (Part A, 2 volumes published in 1970 and Part B, 2 volumes published in 1971, 2558 pages in all) and selected a sampler of these fables, tales, legends and traditions to give the reader a conspectus of the riches of British Folklore. In this sampler, I have included the notes which are in the dictionary, particularly to indicate references to other stories, so that the interested reader can follow up ideas easily, and can then use the main dictionary. The cross references in *italic type* are to tales which are in this sampler; those in roman type are to be found in the dictionary.

MODERN FOLKLORE STUDY

The study of Folklore covers a wide area and touches a great number of disciplines. Professor Archer Taylor, one of the great Folklore scholars, used to describe it as a central study because it dealt with so many different aspects of scholarship: Sociology, Anthropology, Literature, Linguistics, Music, Drama, History, Archaeology. All these are of importance to Folklore, and Folklore is significant to them. So it will be seen that Narrative Research covers only a small part of Folklore Studies, though it has always been an important part to me personally because I have never lost my early love of stories and story-telling, and have found that those rooted in tradition are the best both to tell and to hear.

To run back over some of the contacts which Folklore has with other disciplines, Sociologists need to be aware of the regional Calendar Customs, deeply rooted in tradition, but with an increasing appeal for modern people, who are uneasily aware of their unrooted state. Many of these are celebrated all over Europe and spring from prehistoric attempts to control and stimulate the processes of Nature, to give strength to the New Year, to call on the Dead to help the growth of the buried crops, to reinforce the power of the Sun, and so on. Some of these celebrations were incorporated into the Christian Church, some, like the May Day celebrations, remained obstinately Pagan. Other Calendar Customs were more restricted in scope; civic rituals, like, for instance, the Lady Godiva Ride in Coventry, which had an earlier origin than the historical legends that it is supposed to celebrate. These festivals still meet a need, and they are investigated and chronicled by folklorists, as, for example in Dr Ellis Davidson's study of the Godiva Legend. The study of Industrial Folklore and of the traditional customs of civic institutions, of schools, colleges and other collective institutions are obviously of importance to Sociologists, as are expressions of Mob Psychology, witchhunts of all periods and racial prejudices. It is unnecessary to stress the close connection between Anthropology and Folklore: each subject was at one time a branch of the other. One of the most fascinating aspects of the study of Literature is to observe the way in which folk traditions, beliefs and legends are drawn up by poets and story-tellers from the common stock and shaped into literature, which in its turn enriches the common stream of tradition, is re-shaped as folk-tales, ballads and proverbial sayings, until these in their turn become the inspiration of a new poet. Linguistic studies, and particularly the study of dialects, deal with the very stuff of Folklore. Some of the best of our more recent folk-tales are to be found in the dialect publications.

Like poets, musicians drew much of their inspiration from folk-music —among modern composers Bartok is an outstanding example of this— and art music becomes popularized among the folk if it is sufficiently haunting and direct, and is used for ballad and broadside tunes, gradually undergoing those traditional variations which characterise folk-art. The same is true of Drama, which not only draws themes from folk-tales and folk-beliefs but may well spring from the folk-plays which still survive, though in a weakened form. Local anecdotes, handed down from father to son, sometimes throw a revealing light on historical events, and an observation of the processes of oral transmission may well make us wary of written reports. The use of some of the articles dug up by archaeologists may well be explained by the more recent use of similar artefacts in recent folk tradition: and so on. It is an enormous, many-branched subject, and folklorists meeting together at a generalized conference will be pursuing a great variety of specialized activities, and will have a great deal to teach each other.

One thing has to be remembered about the study of Folklore; it is, like History and the study of Literature, an inexact science; though all three may make use of technical aids it is still inexact, because there can be no controlled experiments. In the past it has collected around it—as Psychical Research is also apt to do—a fringe of quacks and cranks who have done nothing for the reputation of the study as a discipline. Serious scholars are, however, aware of this danger, and modern scientific aids to collection as well as a highly responsible attitude to research in general are now making their impact on the public estimation of Folklore, and the important part that the study can play in the evaulation of our environment is increasingly realized. Another danger to the serious study of the subject arises out of its growing popularity. Folklore is being invaded and captured by the mass media for commercialization. True traditions are coarsened and falsified. This is not the legitimate, spontaneous growth which we find in stories handed from father to son or in customs that alter as they are practised, it is an ignorant and wilful debasement for the sake of money. This danger is particularly present in America and England. Most of the European countries have a well-established, scholarly discipline in the Folklore field. Their chief danger would be from pedantry.

Professor R. D. Dorson, of Bloomington, Indiana, has waged a continuous war against this falsification, and has coined a name for it, "Fakelore", as opposed to "Folklore". He writes eloquently on the subject in his book, *American Folklore*. The book is useful too in outlining the general field of Folklore research. Professor Dorson points out that in England, America and the Romance nations of Europe "Folk-lore", the word coined by W. J. Thoms in 1846, dealt especially in oral traditions carried down the centuries, local customs, beliefs, vestigial rituals, tales, songs, festivals, while in the Teutonic nations the "*Volkskunde*" embraced as well all traditional artefacts.

Thoms in his first definition of the word gives its scope as "Comprising that department of the study of antiquities and archaeology which embraces everything relating to ancient observances and customs, to the notions, beliefs, traditions, superstitions, and prejudices of the common people." It will be seen that the scope of this, though quite wide enough to provide a lifetime's study, does not embrace anything like the ground covered by modern Folklore disciplines. By 1895 Marion Roalfe Cox in her admirable book, *An Introduction to Folk-lore*, covered a much wider area. The subjects she suggested as proper Folklore research include: magic, myths, beast-fables, giants, the distinction made between "*Märchen*" and Sagas, folk-tales, folk-songs, popular ballads, rhymes, traditional games, folk-drama, nursery rhymes and riddles, proverbs— almost all the material covered by modern Folklore studies, except for artefacts, which have lately been admitted, so that modern Folklore now covers both "Folklore" and "*Volkskunde*."

A further slight shift of emphasis in our own time allows for the inclusion of modern Folklore, still generally insisting on oral transmission but including newly invented tales, rhymes and rumours. The social range is also wider. The emphasis is no longer exclusively on peasant customs. Industrial Folklore and the customs of courts and colleges are now considered worthy of study.

THE DIVISIONS OF FOLK-TALES

When we come to the consideration of folk-tales we find that they can be broadly divided into two categories, Folk Narratives or Folk Fiction, and Folk Legends or "*Sagen*". Folk Narratives will probably deal with Folk beliefs actually held, but the whole story is frankly fictional, in the same way that a modern detective story must be accurate in its description of a motorcar, a revolver and the procedure of a law-court, but is yet frankly and avowedly fiction, probably with an announcement on the front that no reference is intended to any living person. To take a well-known German Fairy Tale, "Hansel and Grethel" was conceived in a society which ardently believed in witches and was ready to believe stories of their ritual cannibalism, in which the power of witches to transform one thing into another, or at least to create an illusion of transformation, was taken for granted, but there is no doubt that the story is a fictional one, invented to delight an audience. Folk Legend, on the other hand, is an account of something that was believed to have happened, historical, anecdotal, supernatural, curious. Broadly speaking it is easy to distinguish between these two categories, though all kinds of border cases arise. For instance, the story believed by the first narrator but picked up, retold and furbished by a sceptical collector, who cannot resist the temptation to improve on it, may become, after it has passed through several hands, a good example of a Folk Fiction. On the whole, however, the two genres can be distinguished without too much difficulty. There is a typical beginning and ending for the Fictional Tale. Usually it begins with some such formula as "Once upon a Time", and we are dismissed at the end by another formula, "They all lived happily ever after." Or a more farcical ending may mark the return to the everyday world, something like, "I was asked to the wedding, but by the time I got there there was nothing left but a peascod, so I jumped on it and tobogganed home."

A legend, on the other hand, will begin something like: "Well, it's a queer thing, but as my grandfather was going past the churchyard one night he saw an old chap coming out of the lychgate, who came right up to him, and then he saw he was an old neighbour of his who had been buried last week."

An example of a story of this kind, with a rather more humorous turn, is *Company on the Road*.

A Folk Narrative commonly forms a recognizable pattern, which is called a "Type". Folk Legends sometimes have Types of their own, but are generally made up of one or more "motifs", that is the strands that make up a tale. A Type should be made up of a cluster of motifs, though there are some stories so anecdotal that they consist of one motif only, and hardly deserve to have a Type assigned to them. The Aarne–Thompson Type Index is usually employed in the Folk-Tale Archives of the World. It was first laid down by the Finnish scholar, Antti Aarne, and afterwards twice enlarged and revised by Professor Stith Thompson of Bloomington, Indiana. Other suggestions for classification had been made earlier, some of them quite promising, but none had been laid out in detail, and though the Aarne–Thompson Index has been criticized on various points, it seems unlikely that it will be superseded. The *Motif-Index* is a massive work in six volumes for which Stith Thompson is alone responsible. It covers a much wider field than the Type Index which only catalogues Folk Narratives, while the *Motif-Index* has a mythological section and covers some literary treatment of Folklore themes as well as Legends. Ideally a list of the motifs occurring in a tale should give its plot, but this rarely happens except in such well-known stories as

"Cinderella". Even a selection of the motifs of this story gives one a plot of the whole, though in a rather ponderous style. "Cinderella" is Type 510. Among the motifs assigned to the French version are: S31 Cruel Stepmother; F311 Fairy Godmother; D813 Magic object received from fairy; D1050.1 Clothes produced by magic; F861.4.3 Carriage from pumpkin; D411.6.1 Transformation: mouse to horse; N711.6 Prince sees heroine at ball and is enamoured; C761.3 Tabu: staying too long at ball; H36.1 Slipper test: identification by fitting of shoe; F823.2 Glass slipper; L162 Lowly heroine marries Prince. (Peter Opie, however, in his *Classic Fairy Tales*, has pointed out that this last motif is not applicable to "Cinderella".)

This particular story is so well known that the motifs outline the whole plot. Two important monographs have been written on the "Cinderella" theme, an early one by Marion Roalfe Cox, and a later very full treatment by Anna Birgitta Rooth of Sweden. An example of a story with only one motif is Type 1030. This is the Crop Division, when the man and the bogie who both claim a field, take turns to take the top of the crops or the roots, and the man always wins. The motif assigned to this is K171. Many of the Ogre stories collected by Antti Aarne have only one motif. They are more properly parts of a long struggle between a man and a giant after the pattern of "Jack the Giant-killer".

FOLK NARRATIVES

There are many categories into which Folk Narratives can be divided. That used in the Aarne–Thompson *Types of the Folktale* is pretty generally followed. The general headings are: I Animal Tales, II Ordinary Folk-Tales (sub-divided into A Tales of Magic, B Religious Tales, C Novelle (Romantic Tales) D Tales of the Stupid Ogre). Then III Jokes and Anecdotes, IV Formula Tales, and there is one short section of Unidentified Tales. All except this last are sub-divided, generally to differentiate between the people of whom the stories are told. For instance, the Animal Tales are sub-divided into Wild Animals, Wild and Domestic Animals, Man and Wild Animals, Domestic Animals, Birds, Fish, Other Animals and Objects. This is in some ways an unsatisfactory division because it disregards the real differences between Animal Tales, some of which are fables after the manner of Aesop, which satirize human habits and characteristics under the disguise of animals, some primitive conceptions of animals as on an equality with Man and some Origin Myths. It is more successfully used in category III, Jokes and Anecdotes, as

Numskull Stories, Stories about Married Couples, Stories about a Woman, and so on.

LEGENDS

The Legends have no such over-all coverage as the Narratives, but are often dealt with on a more national basis. This is understandable because of the particularity of the Legend, believed to have happened at a definite time and place. Certain Legends, however, are set in many different places, either by the general resemblance of human nature or by transmission. Reidar Christiansen of Norway worked on the classification of these diffused Legends and produced the fruit of his work in *The Migratory Legends, A Proposed List of Types with a Systematic Catalogue of the Norwegian Variants*, of which the first version was published in Helsinki in 1951. This list he envisages as continuous with the Aarne–Thompson Type Index. He leaves a space for possible additions to the Type Index. Starting at the number 3000 he leaves a gap of four between each entry to allow for possible accretions later. Thus the first entry is "3000. Escape from the Black School of Wurtemberg", and the next is "3005. The Would-be Ghost". Professor Christiansen divides the Migratory Legends into eight categories: The Black Book of Magic, The Experts, Legends of the Human Soul, of Ghosts and Revenants, Spirits of Rivers, Lakes and the Sea, Trolls and Giants, The Fairies, Domestic Spirits, Nisse, Haugetusse, Tusse, Gobonden and lastly, Local Legends of Places, Events and Persons. He does not include unexplained supernatural happenings, glimpses into the past and similar strange experiences. Nor does he include sacred legends of Saints and Heroes, nor ecological legends; but on the whole he gives a pretty full account of the Matter of Legend.

Séan Ó'Súilleabhain, in his most excellent and encyclopaedic book, *A Handbook of Irish Folk-Lore*, devotes several chapters to the exposition of Irish legendary matter, though he does not arrange the legends as numbered types. His exploration covers some of the same ground as *The Migratory Legends* but gives full coverage to Mythological Legends, Origin Myths, Supernatural Beings, The Devil, Mythical Champions and Warriors, Supernatural Personages, Supernatural Places, Supernatural Phenomena, The Afterworld. In the chapter on Historical Traditions he writes of Individual Personages, Important Historical Events, Local Happenings, Ireland in Tradition, and Traditions about Foreign Countries. It will be seen that a great many aspects of Folk Legend and Folk

Tradition are touched on here, and though it deals with one particular country the book is in general of the greatest assistance to anyone who is taking up Folklore research for the first time.

THE BARDIC TRADITION AND STORY-TELLING

The body of tales from which we are taking our Sampler is much more fragmented than those in the Celtic-speaking areas of these Islands, where the shadow of the Bardic traditions survived the great days of the Bards for many generations, so that the heroic legends were held sacred, and in Ireland tales were found in oral tradition in the last century which reproduced, almost word for word, some of the very early written manuscripts, and these were told by unlettered people who could not possibly have read them. The same is true of some of the West Highland tales collected by Campbell of Islay.

Ireland and Wales were the two counties in which the Bards were specially revered. Lady Wilde, in *Ancient Legends of Ireland*, gives an eloquent account of the great learning and accomplishments of the Ollaves, Filés and Senachies who were trained in the Bardic College at Tara. The head of them was the *Ard-File*, or chief poet, who was given an almost royal state.

She describes these poets in action: "The Brehons, seated on a hill, intoned the laws to a listening people; the Senachies chanted the genealogies of the Kings; and the Poets recited the deeds of the heroes, or sang to their gold harps those exquisite airs that still enchant the world. . . . The chief poet was required to know by heart four hundred poems, and the minor bards two hundred. And they were bound to recite any poem called for by the kings at the festivals."

For these services the poets were paid an income by the state according to their eminence, besides the rich gifts given to them by the kings. Any king regarded by the poets as niggardly was cruelly satirized, so that blisters were raised on his face, and one king even went mad and died after a particularly cutting lampoon. At length the Bards became so intolerable in their greed and arrogance that the Brehons, or law-givers, were forced to make enactions against them, and at last their power went into decline. The influence of the Welsh Bards was sufficiently strong to give rise to the legend that Edward I was obliged to massacre them before he could conquer Wales. The Welsh Bards, however, continued with a diminished influence until the end of the seventeenth century, for Aubrey writes of how the wandering Bards had the gift of improvising verse, a gift which sometimes left them suddenly and never returned. The last descendants of the Bards were the wandering droll-tellers of Cornwall, from whom Hunt and Bottrell collected tales. Cornwall, of course, was another Celtic area; in England we might suggest that the last descendants of the Anglo-Saxon Minstrels and the Norman Troubadours were the wandering ballad-singers who carried ballads and chapbooks about with them, commending their wares by singing snatches of songs and telling stories from their chapbooks. Shakespeare's Autolycus is a specimen of them, and we find quite a number of references to them in seventeenth-century drama. Gipsies carried stories about with them, and gained a welcome at lonely farmhouses by their tale-telling. The same is true of the "Travelling Men", the Tinkers of Scotland, from whom a sympathetic collector can still obtain excellent fairy tales, drolls and memorats. A few generations ago, however, small, lonely communities did not even need wandering chapmen or Bards, for they could provide their own entertainment round their winter firesides or at local gatherings. The English Bluebeard story, "Mr Fox", shows how story-telling took its place even on such lively occasions as betrothal parties. But in the Highlands and Islands of Scotland the art of self-entertainment was raised to its highest pitch. Alexander Carmichael, whose *Carmina Gadelica*, the fruit of forty years' travel and research in the Hebrides, was published in 1900, gives a memorable account of a Highland *ceilidh*, a session of story-telling, ballads and riddles. It may appear slightly idealized, but Alexander Carmichael had travelled on foot through the Hebrides, and had been welcomed wherever he went. He was the colleague of Campbell of Islay, perhaps the greatest of the Highland collectors, and he was more qualified than most of us to speak of the inhabitants of the Hebrides. He tells us about the variation in methods of story-telling which is of prime importance for us to know in determining the methods of oral transmission.

In a crofting townland [he says] there are several story-tellers who recite the oral literature of their predecessors. The story-tellers of the Highlands are as varied in their subjects as are any literary men and women elsewhere. One is a historian narrating events simply and concisely; another is a historian with a bias, colouring his narrative according to his leanings. One is an inventor, building fiction upon fact, mingling his materials, and investing the whole with the charm of novelty and the halo of romance. Another is a reciter of heroic poems and ballads, bringing the different characters before the mind as clearly as the sculptor brings the figure before the eye. One gives the songs of the chief poets, with interesting accounts of their authors, while another, generally a woman, sings, to weird airs, beautiful old songs, some of them Arthurian.

He goes on to describe a *ceilidh*, one out of many which he had attended.

The house of the story-teller is already full, and it is difficult to get inside, and away from the cold wind and sleet without. But with that politeness native to the people, the stranger is pressed to come forward and occupy the seat vacated for him beside the houseman. The house is roomy and clean, if homely, with its bright peat fire in the middle of the floor. There are many present— men and women, boys and girls. All the women are seated, and most of the men. Girls are crouched between the knees of fathers or brothers or friends, while boys are perched wherever—boy-like—they can climb.... The houseman is twisting twigs of heather into ropes to hold down thatch, a neighbour crofter is twining quicken roots into cords to tie cows, while another is plaiting bent grass into baskets to hold meal. The housewife is spinning, a daughter is carding, another daughter is teasing, while a third daughter, supposed to be working, is away in the background conversing in low whispers with the son of a neighbouring crofter. Neighbour wives or neighbour daughters are knitting, sewing or embroidering. The conversation is general....

The stranger asks the houseman to tell a story, and after a pause the man complies.

The tale is full of incident, action and pathos. It is told simply yet graphically, and at times dramatically—compelling the undivided attention of the listener. At the pathetic scenes and distressful events the bosoms of the women may be seen to heave and their silent tears to fall. Truth overcomes craft, skill conquers strength, and bravery is rewarded. Occasionally a momentary excitement occurs when heat and sleep overpower a boy, and he tumbles down among the people below, to be trounced out and sent home. When the story is ended it is discussed and commented upon, and the different characters praised or blamed according to their merits and the views of the critics.

THE COLLECTION OF FOLK MATERIAL

The date of the *ceilidh* which Carmichael describes was 1861–2. Then any number of stories could be easily obtained, deriving from the beginning of the seventeenth century, told by entirely unlettered narrators in beautiful, polished, traditional language. By the time Carmichael published them they had become almost impossible to obtain because of the wholesale conversion of the population to a militant Puritanism, and the active discouragement of the Gaelic language by the Schoolmaster, the Minister and the elders had driven songs, music and proverbs underground. The people were still as courteous and hospitable as ever, but they had learnt to distrust their ancient riches. No such violent revolution happened in Ireland, where the stream of narrative continued unchecked. The present problem of the Irish folklorists is how to deal with the wealth of material they have obtained. Séan Ó'Súilleabhain's handbook gives much wise advice about the best methods to pursue so as to secure accuracy in recording and the best conditions for the performance of the stories, but at the time when he wrote the tape recorder was not in such general use. Advice which is applicable to our more sophisticated times in England as well as in America is to be found in Professor Kenneth Goldstein's book, *A Guide for Field Workers in Folklore*. Professor Goldstein is a skilled worker in the field and has collected in England and Scotland as well as in the USA. As an experienced and vital teacher he is well able to pass on his findings and to make his experience available to others. His is one of the best books to begin on, but there is no lack of reading material for anyone who really wishes to pursue the subject. A fuller list is to be found in the entire Dictionary.

Stories will be found in this Sampler which have been collected with the help of modern techniques and appliances, but there are also tales which have been written down hundreds of years ago and which depend for their vividness on the unsophisticated approach of the narrator. I have tried to select stories from different parts of the country, told by different kinds of people, some unusual and some familiar. Besides this I have picked out a few which illustrate folk-beliefs, or provide a link with far-spread stories. For instance, "Jack and the Giants" is the only remnant of "The Grateful Dead", of which the earliest example is in the Apocrypha, the often illustrated story of "Tobias and the Angel". There are several variants of this in Celtic tradition, and we come across it in Peele's *Old Wives Tale*, but "Jack and the Giants" is solitary in England. My chief criterion, however, has been my own enjoyment of the story and my pleasure in handing it on—an enjoyment which has endured since I browsed over Hartland's folk-tales at nine years old.

REFERENCES

Aarne, Antti and Thompson, Stith, *The Types of the Folktale: A Classification and Bibliography*, 2nd revision, Helsinki, 1961.
Carmichael, Alexander, *Carmina Gadelica*, 3 vols, Oliver & Boyd, Edinburgh, 2nd edition, 1928.
Christiansen, Reidar, *The Migratory Legends*, Helsinki, 1958.
Cox, Marion Roalfe, *Cinderella*, Folk-Lore Society, 1843.
Cox, Marion Roalfe, *An Introduction to Folk-lore*, David Nutt, London, 1895.
Dorson, R. D., *American Folklore*, University of Chicago Press, 1959.
Goldstein, Kenneth S., *A Guide for Field Workers in Folklore*, Folklore Associates,

Pennsylvania, and Jenkins, London, 1968.

Opie, Peter, *Classic Fairy Tales*, Oxford University Press, 1974.

Ó'Súilleabhain, Séan, *A Handbook of Irish Folk-Lore*, Jenkins, London, 1963.

Rooth, Anna Birgitta, *Cinderella*, Lund, 1961.

Thompson, Stith, *Motif-Index of Folk Literature*, 6 vols, revised and enlarged editions by Stith Thompson, Rosenkilde & Bagger, Copenhagen, 1955.

Wilde, Lady, *Ancient Legends of Ireland*, 2 vols, London, 1887.

British Folktales

PART 1
FABLES AND EXEMPLA

The Animal Tales collected in this group of folk narratives are not animal anecdotes, nor tales of magical animals such as we find in the Fairy Tales. They are fables after the manner of Aesop which carry a moral applicable to humanity, or animal tales with a moral or satiric intention, in which the characters are nominally animals but talk and behave like human beings. In the primitive tales, such as those told by the Australian aborigines, animals do indeed share human characteristics, but this is because they were believed to be gods, more powerful than men, or at least man's intellectual equals. The approach in the fables is more sophisticated, the so-called animals are humans wearing animal masks.

Aesop's fables had a great influence in early times. A study of their transmission may be found in the second volume of Bengt Holbek's reproduction of *Aesop's Leyned og Fabler*, printed from the manuscript of Christiern Pedersen, 1556. The earliest surviving collection is dated in the first century AD. A lost book of Alfred the Great introduced Aesop's fables into England, with some native additions. Avianus' fables (c. AD 400) in verse were the chief source of the medieval fables; in 1484 Caxton printed *The Boke of Subtyl Historyes and Fables of Esop*, and new versions of them continued to come out all through the sixteenth and seventeenth centuries.

This number of editions shows the respect in which the fables were held, and indeed they passed into common speech as proverbial wisdom, as we see for instance, in the nickname of "Archibald Bell-the-Cat" in Scottish history. There were many literary versions of which Henryson's "Tail of the Uplandis Mous and the Burges Mous" is one of the most charming, though Chaucer's *Nonnes Preests Tale* is even more attractive.

An excellent example of the extent to which fables were quoted in Courts and Council Chambers is to be found in a letter quoted in the appendix of the King's Classics edition of Roper's *Life of Sir Thomas More*. It was from Lady Alington, More's stepdaughter, to Margaret Roper. It retells two fables not now generally known, the first about a defiling rain that fell upon a country mainly inhabited by fools. The wise men of the land foresaw the rain, took refuge underground and so escaped it; but when they emerged, thinking to have gained added prestige, the bespattered fools thought themselves much improved by the dirt and mocked at the wise men, utterly refusing to be ruled by them. The second story was about the inequalities of the confessional and of how the lion was absolved for his slaughters, the ass put to penance for eating a blade of grass and the wolf left to judge for himself. Sir Thomas said that he had often heard the first story from Cardinal Wolsey in the King's Council Chambers. The second, as he pointed out, belonged to stories of the confessional and could not have been told by an early heathen slave like Aesop. Neither had any bearings on his plight. The incident shows how commonly these fables were cited in royal council chambers and places where matters of importance were debated, and the numbers which passed into proverbial phrases such as "dog in the manger", "sour grapes", and so on, proves that they were equally used by common men. The four tales chosen out of the twenty-nine to be found in the *Dictionary of British Folk-Tales* illustrate different kinds of Fables and Exempla. "Belling the Cat" is a true Aesop's fable, and the incident illustrates the use of the Fables in rhetoric and debate; "The Bum Bee" is a modern variant of Aesop's "The Ant and the Cricket" with an ending in which summary justice is done on the King of the Ants; "The Farmer and his Ox" is a terse jocular story of a talking beast which points the moral that the treatment a man receives is a mirror of his own behaviour and "The Yaller-Legg'd Cock'ril" shows more observation of animal behaviour than most of the earlier fables, but is none the less framed to point a moral. For want of space no origin myths have been included. A well-known one, "The Wren, King of the Birds" will be familiar to most people.

BELLING THE CAT

Many of the nobility and barons held a secret council in the church of Lauder, where they enlarged upon the evils which Scotland sustained through the insolence and corruption of Cochran and his associates. While they were thus declaiming, Lord Gray requested their attention to a fable. "The mice," he said, "being much annoyed by the persecution of the cat, resolved that a bell should be hung about puss's neck, to give notice when she was coming. But though the measure was agreed to in full council, it could not be carried into effect, because no mouse had courage enough to undertake to tie the bell to the neck of the formidable enemy." This was as much as to intimate his opinion that though the discontented nobles might make bold resolutions against the King's ministers, yet it would be difficult to find anyone courageous enough to act upon them.

Archibald, Earl of Angus, a man of gigantic strength and intrepid courage, started up when Gray had done speaking. "I am he", he said, "who will bell the cat"; from which expression he was distinguished by the name of Bell-the-Cat to his dying day.

From *Tales of a Grandfather*, Sir Walter Scott, first series, ch. XXII, p. 222.

¶ Aesop: Jacobs, *The Fables of Aesop* (New York, 1894), no. 67. Turkish, Wesselski, *Hodscha Nasreddin*, I, no. 213. American Negro, Joel Harris, *Nights with Uncle Remus* (Boston, 1883). Irish, seven examples.

This anecdote about the conspiracy of the Scottish nobles against the favourites of James III shows that the fable was familiar in Scotland as early as 1482.

THE BUM BEE [summary]

The Queen of the Bumble Bees went out one day to get food for her children, and she was overtaken by a terrible storm. When it was at its worst, she saw ahead of her the palace of the King of the Pismoules, so she knocked at the door. A maidservant came to the door and the Bum Bee said, "Will you ask the King if the Queen of the Bum Bees can get shelter for the night out of the storm?" The maid shut the door and went to ask the King of the Pismoules. "Oh no," said the King. "She'll not get shelter here. Tell her, 'Where you made your summer's honey, go and make your winter's quarters.'" So the maid took the King's message, and went and shut the door on her, and the poor Queen of the Bum Bees struggled on through the storm, and at long last, more dead than alive, she got home, and told her children how the King of the Pismoules had refused her shelter and said; "Where you made your summer's honey, go and make your winter's quarters." And she said, "If the King of the Pismoules comes here seeking hospitality when I'm out, mind and pour boiling water on him." So the next summer the King of the Pismoules was out hunting, and he was overtaken by a terrible storm of rain, and he lost his party and his horse threw him and he hurt his leg. So he went to the Queen of the Bum Bees' palace to ask for shelter. But when she looked out and saw who it was she said; "Do you mind how you told me when I was near dead in the storm, 'Where you made your summer's honey, there make your winter's quarters'?" And she had a big kettle of boiling water and she poured it over the King of the Pismoules. And for all I know, it killed him.

The School of Scottish Studies, Maurice Fleming, from Bella Higgins, Perthshire.
¶ No exact parallel to this can be found. See "The Fox and the Magpie".

THE FARMER AND HIS OX

There were a zurly old varmer and 'e 'ad a girt ox. One day 'e said to it, "Thee girt orkurd vule. Stupid vule thou be. I wonder who taught thee to be zo orkurd!"

And the ox 'e turn round to varmer, and 'e say, "Why, it were thee, tha' girt stupid vule!"

Ruth L. Tongue, *Folktales of England*, p. 140.
¶ Baughman records only American versions, the earliest in 1925. Text from South Carolina. This could be classified as a Shaggy Dog story, but the brevity and the moral both qualify it to be considered as a fable.

THE YALLER-LEGG'D COCK'RIL

He's a good hand at swaggerin' hissen off, he is. Bud it'll be happenin' to him as it happen'd to th' yaller-legg'd cok'ril, if he doesn't mind what he's aboot.

What soort'n a taale's that, do ye saay? Why, it's a peäce 'at my gran'-feyther offens tell'd me when I was a little lad at hoäme.

Yaller-legg's cock'ril liv'd i' frunt yard wi' owd white cock 'at was his feyther, an' red co`k liv'd o' steäm-hoose side o' yard. An' won daay,

16

when owd cock's sittin' crawin' upon crew-yard gaate, cock'ril gets up an' begins to craw an' all.

"Cock-a-doodle-doo," says owd cock. "Kick-a-ee-a-ee", says cock'ril: he couldn't craw plaain yit, he was ower yung. "Houd thy noise," says owd cock, as couldn't abeär to hear him skreelin' like yon. "Houd thy noise, bairns should be seän an' not heerd." Soä cock'ril, 'at thinks as he's doin' on it fo'st raate, has to get off gaate an' tek up wi' th' hens an' chickens agaan. An' owd cock craws an' craws, till at last cock fra t'uther side o' yard cums to knaw what's up. Bud when he seäs who it is 'at's makkin' all to-do, he reckons 'at he's nobbut dropp'd in by chanche, an' passes time o' daay: an' then says as how he mun goä and seä if garthman isn't sarvin' pigs, an' if he hasn't slatter'd a few taaties an' things 'at'll mak a dinner fer that theare last cletch 'at graay hen's browt off. An' soä he taks his hook back agaain to steäm-hoose yard.

Bud daay efter, when owd cock's gone a peäce o' waay doon sandy laane wi' a pullet 'at's lookin' fer a nest, cock'ril flies upo' gaate agaan, an' claps his wings an' craws till th' hens is o'most stoäne-deäf. Fo'st won on 'em tell'd him to cum doon, an' then anuther, bud it wasn't noa good: he was that setten upo' hearin' hissen 'at he niver hed noä time to listen to onybody else. Awiver, just when he reckon'd 'at he'd gotten to do it o'most as well as his feyther, or mebbe a bit better, up cums cock fra t'uther side o' yard wi' all his neck-feathers up, an' he says to cock'ril, "I thowt I heerd ye at it yesterdaay, an' noo I knaw I did: cum on." An' afoor cock'ril could get oot anuther craw, red cock hed him off gaate an' doon i' crew-yard. An' when he'd gotten him theare, he wasn't long afoor he'd made an end o' him. An' when owd cock cum'd hoäm he fun' pigs just finishin' cock'ril's yaller legs, an' he heerd red cock crawin' like mad upo' steäm-hoose wall. "A-deary-me", says he, "I knaw'd how it would be if he wouldn't keäp his tung still. Well, you uther chickens mun tak warnin' by him, an' mind what I tell ye; niver craw till yer spurs is grawn."

M. Peacock, *The Lindsey Folk-Speech*, p. 105.

PART 2
FAIRY TALES

In this group the term "Fairy Tales" are those folk-fictions of which magical or supernatural episodes are a necessary part. This is the real distinction made between the Novelle and the Fairy Tales. The theme may very often be similar, the dividing line is between the natural and magical machinery. The Type-Index calls them "Ordinary Folk-Tales".

Modern England is more sparsely provided with Fairy Tales than the rest of Europe. Literary references show that we were once rich in them and all the sub-divisions of this class which are recorded in the Aarne–Thompson Index are represented somewhere in the British Isles, though England is not so well supplied with them as the Celtic parts of these Islands. For instance, the last trace of The Grateful Dead (Type 505) is to be found in "Jack and the Giants", the Chapbook version of "Jack the Giant-killer", though there are many examples of it in Ireland and in the Highlands of Scotland. The Name of the Helper (Type 500) is richly represented in England by "Tom Tit Tot", in the Lowlands of Scotland by "Whuppity Stoorie" and in Cornwall by "Duffy and the Devil". There are many Cinderella stories, of which "Ashey Pelt" is a good and brief example of a version much older than the Cinderella of Perrault.

The Devil and Witches play quite a part in these stories. In "The Man who wouldn't go out at Night" the Devil gets the worst of it, as he often does. The medieval story "King Herla" is one of the best examples of the supernatural passage of time in Fairyland. There are good stories here, and many as good had to be omitted because they were too lengthy. I have chosen the tersest.

ALLISON GROSS [summary]

Allison Gross, "the ugliest witch i' the north country", lured a young man into her bower and with many fair speeches tried to persuade him to become her "lemman so true". He withstood all her bribes and blandishments, for first she promised him a scarlet embroidered mantle, then a "sark o' the saftest silk", wrought with pearls, then a cup of red gold. But he would not so much as give her one kiss, and at last she blew three blasts on a grass-green horn and, taking a silver wand in her hand, turned round three times, muttering words that chilled the blood till the youth fell down senseless and she changed him into a worm,

> "And gard me toddle about the tree."

Every Saturday night his sister Maisry came with a silver basin and silver comb, and took the worm's head on her knee and tended it. There seemed to be no remedy against the enchantment, until at last, on Hallowe'en, the fairy court rode by, and the queen, alighting near the tree where the worm lay coiled, took it up in her hand, and stroked it three times over her knee, and the worm was restored to its own shape.

Child, *The English and Scottish Ballads*, I, pp. 313–15.

¶ There is no motif in the Index for the turning of a man or woman into a monster, though this occurs in "The Loathly Lady" type. See also "The Laidly Worm of Spindlestone Heugh", "The Lailey Worm".

ASHEY PELT

Well, my Grandmother she told me that in them auld days a ewe might be your mother. It is a very lucky thing to have a black ewe. A man married again, and his daughter, Ashey Pelt, was unhappy. She cried alone, and the black ewe came to her from under the grey-stone in the field, and said, "Don't cry, go and find a rod behind the stone and strike it three times, and whatever you want will come." So she did as she was bid.

She wanted to go to a party. Dress and horses all came to her, but she was bound to be back before twelve o'clock or all the enchantment would go, all she had would vanish.

The sisters, they didna' like her, she was so pretty, and the stepmother, she kept her in wretchedness just.

She was most lovely. At the party the Prince fell in love with her, and she forgot to get back in time. In her speed a-running, she dropped her silk slipper, and he sent and he went over all the country, to find the lady it wad fit. When he came to Ashey Pelt's door he did not see her. The sisters was busy a-nipping and a-clipping at their feet to get on the silk slipper, for the king's son he had given out that he loved that lady sae weel he wad be married on whaever could fit on that slipper.

The sisters they drove Ashey Pelt out bye to be out of the road, and they bid her mind the cows. They pared down their feet till one o' them could just squeeze it on. But she was in the quare agony I'm telling you.

So off they rode away: but when he was passing the field, the voice of the auld ewe cried on him to stop, and she says, says she—

> "Nippet foot and clippet foot
> Behind the king's son rides,
> But bonny foot and pretty foot
> Is with the cathering hides."

So he rode back and found her among the cows, and he married her, and if they live happy, so may you and me.

Norton Collection, II, p. 78. *Folk-Lore*, VI (1895), pp. 305–6, contributed by M. Damant. "The following tale was told me by a woman now living, a native of Ulster, aged about 60."
¶ See "Ashpitel".

THE DEAD MOON [dialect modified]

Long ago the Lincolnshire Cars were full of bogs and it was death to walk through them, except on moonlight nights, for harm and mischance and mischief, Bogles and Dead Things and crawling horrors came out at nights when the moon did not shine. At length the Moon heard what things went on in the bog-land when her back was turned, and she thought she would go down to see for herself, and find what she could do to help. So at the month's end she wrapped a black cloak round her, and hid her shining hair under a black hood, and stepped down into the boglands. It was all dark and watery, with quaking mud, and waving tussocks of grass, and no light except what came from her own white feet. On she went, deep into the bogland and now the witches rode about her on their great cats, and the will-o'-the-wykes danced with the lanterns swinging on their backs, and dead folks rose out of the water, and stared at her with fiery eyes, and the slimy dead hands beckoned and clutched. But on she went, stepping from tuft to tuft, as light as the wind in summer until at length a stone turned under her, and she caught with both hands at a snag nearby to steady herself; but as soon as she touched it it twisted round her wrists like a pair of handcuffs and held her fast. She struggled and fought against it but nothing would free her. Then, as she stood trembling she heard a piteous crying, and she knew that a man was lost in the darkness, and soon she saw him, splashing after the will-o'-the-wykes, crying out on them to wait for him, while the Dead Hands plucked at his coat, and the creeping horrors crowded round him, and he went further and further from the Path.

The Moon was so sorry and so angry that she made a great struggle, and though she could not loose her hands, her hood slipped back, and the light streamed out from her beautiful golden hair, so that the man saw the bog-holes near him and the safe path in the distance nearly as clear as by day. He cried for joy, and floundered across, out of the deadly bog and back to safety, and all the bogles and evil things fled away from the moonlight, and hid themselves. But the Moon struggled in vain to free herself, and at length she fell forward, spent with the struggle, and the black hood fell over her head again, and she had no strength to push it off. Then all the evil things came creeping back, and they laughed to think they had their enemy the Moon in their power at last. All night they fought and squabbled about how best they should kill her, but when the first grey light before dawn came they grew frightened, and pushed her down into the water. The Dead Folk held her, while the Bogles fetched a great stone to put over her, and they chose two will-o'-the-wykes to guard her by turns, and when the day came the Moon was buried deep, until someone should find her, and who knew where to look?

The days passed, and folk put straws in their caps, and money in their pockets against the coming of the new Moon, and she never came. And as dark night after dark night passed, the evil things from the bogland came howling and screeching up to men's very doors, so that no one could go a step from the house at night, and in the end folk sat up all night, shivering by their fires, for they feared if the lights went out, the things would come over the thresholds.

At last they went to the Wise Woman who lived in the old Mill, to ask what had come of their Moon. She looked in the mirror, and in the brewpot, and in the Book, and it was all dark, so she told them to set straw and salt and a button on their door-sills at night, to keep them safe from the Horrors, and to come back with any news they could give her.

Well, you can be sure they talked, at their firesides and in the Garth and in the town. So it happened one day, as they were sitting on the settle at the Inn, a man from the far side of the bogland cried out all of a sudden, "I reckon I know where the Moon is, only I was so mazed I never thought on it." And he told them how he had been all astray one night, and like to lose his life in the bog-holes, and all of a sudden a clear bright light had shone out, and showed him the way home. So off they all went to the Wise Woman, and told what the man had said. The Wise Woman looked in the Book, and in the pot, and at last she got some glimmer of light and told them what they must do. They were to set out together in the darkness with a stone in their mouths and a hazel twig in their hands, and not a word must they speak till they got home; and they must search through the bog till they found a coffin, and a cross, and a candle, and that was where the Moon would be. Well, they were main feared, but next night they set out and went on and on, into the midst of the bog.

They saw nothing, but they heard a sighing and whispering round them and slimy hands touching them, but on they went, shaking and scared, till suddenly they stopped, for half in, and half out of the water they saw a long stone, for all the world like a coffin, and at the head of it stood a black snag stretching out two branches, like a gruesome cross, and on it flickered a tiddy light. Then they all knelt down and they crossed themselves and said the Lord's Prayer, forward for the sake of the cross, and backward against the Bogles, but all silently, for they knew they must not speak. Then all together they heaved up the stone. For one minute they saw a strange beautiful face looking up at them and then they stepped back mazed with the light, and with a great shrieking wail from all the horrors, as they fled back to their holes, and the next moment the full moon shone down on them from the Heavens, so that they could see their path near as clear as by day.

And ever since then the Moon has shone her best over the boglands, for she knows all the evil things that are hid there and she remembers how the Car men went out to look for her when she was dead and buried.

Mrs Balfour, "Legends of the Cars", *Folk-Lore*, II. An unusual mythological theme. The plot corresponds to an Indian motif, A.754.1.1; it is uncommon in European folk-tales.

THE FLIGHT OF BIRDS

There was once a farmer living in a wild part of the country, where strangers seldom came. His wife was very beautiful and a good wife to him, and her husband loved her so fondly and so jealously that he could hardly bear another man to set eyes on her. One night of great storm and wind a small boat was forced to seek shelter in the little bay near the farm, and a stranger came knocking at the door to ask for food and lodging. He was a fine-looking man, and as he sat warming himself by the fire, and glancing at the goodwife as she moved about the room, it came into the farmer's head that anyone who saw them would say that they would make a grand pair, and that he himself looked nothing beside them. A little thing is tinder to a jealous heart, and as he was thinking so, it chanced that the stranger yawned, and from the table where she was laying supper his wife yawned too. "Ah," thought the husband, "there is but one thought between them. Likely they are lovers from long syne, and he came here with no purpose but to lie with her."

No sooner did the thought pass through his head than he took it as proved, and all through supper he sat glowering there without a word to throw at a dog. If they had met on road or at market he would have fought the stranger and tried to kill him, but here he was a guest, and his life was sacred.

The stranger soon went into the bedroom they had left empty for him, and fell asleep; then the husband reached a hempen rope down from the rafters and took his wife by the wrist. "Come," he said, and led her out into the stormy night. "What's the matter? What are you wanting with me?" "I'm wanting to keep you an honest and true wife, and I see no way for it but to hang you. That'll be your old love, no doubt."

"I declare to God, I've never seen him till this day."

"Then the thought gaed quickly between you. What for did you gant when he ganted?" And for all his wife could say, she could not shake his belief, nor soften his heart. He put the rope round her neck, and led her towards the nearest tree. The wind was dropping, but it still blew hard, and they struggled against it towards a ragged wood that stood in a sheltered dean not far from the farm. As they went, a flock of small birds passed them, fluttering against the wind. The moon shone out fitfully as they reached the first tree, and the farmer threw up his rope over the lowest bough. It crossed it, but it did not lodge there, for the flight of birds landed on the branch, and it slid down over their beating wings.

He tried again, but with no better success. "We'll leave that tree to the birds," he said, "and gang on to the neist." They moved on, but the flight of birds went with them, and when the farmer threw up the rope, it slid down once more. Then his wife spoke for the first time since they had set out:

> "The birdies flee frae tree tae tree,
> Sae ganting gangs frae Man tae me," she said.

But the farmer was obstinate. "We'll try't again," he said, and he went on, and the birds went with them. Then again as his rope slipped down his wife said:

> "The birdies flee frae tree tae tree,
> Sae ganting gangs frae Man tae me."

But he was obstinate still, and tried one tree after another all through the wood, and still the birds went before him. At last he said, "This wood is o'er full of birdies, but I mind me of an old fir tree, that stands its lane on the hillside a twa-three mile off. And the wind blows sae snell through it that nae birdies will light on it. We will gang there."

So they set off on the long tramp, and the birds left the wood, and soared high up into the air, and for a while they did not see them.

They went on and on, struggling against the wind, until they reached the one lonely pine on its hill top, and it was the grey light before dawn.

"There are no birdies here to save you," said the farmer, and flung the rope up at the nearest branch, high above them. But as he threw, there was a grand whirr of wings, and the birds swept down from the sky again, and the rope fell to the ground. And the first rays of the sun fell on the farmer's wife, as she said again:

> "The birdies flee frae tree tae tree,
> Sae ganting gangs frae Man tae me."

At the sight and the sound, the farmer's heart was softened, and he burst into tears. He knew that his wife was true to him, and he knew that if he had murdered her in his jealous anger, the birds would have followed him night and day, and he would have known no rest. He took the rope from his wife's neck, and they went back hand in hand; and so long as he lived the farmer never mistrusted her again.

Miss Naismith, from her mother, heard in 1917, Berwickshire.

¶ The foundation story of this type is a jocular tale of a jealous husband, very different in mood from this. Examples have been found in Finland, Estonia, Livonia and Sweden. In its present form it was printed in *Von Prinzen, Trollen und Herrn Fro*, II (1957).

THE GOBBORN SEER

Once there was a man, Gobborn Seer, and he had a son called Jack.

One day he sent him out to sell a sheep-skin, and Gobborn said, "You must bring me back the skin and the value of it as well."

So Jack started, but he could not find any who would leave him the skin and give him its price too. So he came home discouraged.

But Gobborn Seer said, "Never mind, you must take another turn at it tomorrow."

So he tried again, and nobody wished to buy the skin on those terms.

When he came home his father said, "You must go and try your luck to-morrow," and the third day it seemed as if it would be the same thing over again. And he had half a mind not to go back at all, his father would be so vexed. As he came to a bridge, like the Creek Road out yonder, he leaned on the parapet thinking of his trouble, and that perhaps it would be foolish to run away from home, but he could not tell which to do; when he saw a girl washing her clothes on the bank below. She looked up and said, "If it may be no offence asking, what is it you feel so badly about?"

"My father has given me this skin, and I am to fetch it back and the price of it beside."

"Is that all? Give it here, and it's easy done."

So the girl washed the skin in the stream, took the wool from it, and paid him the value of it, and gave him the skin to carry back.

His father was well pleased, and said to Jack, "That was a witty woman; she would make you a good wife. Do you think you could tell her again?"

Jack thought he could, so his father told him to go by-and-by to the bridge, and see if she was there, and if so bid her come home to take tea with them.

And sure enough Jack spied her and told her how his old father had a wish to meet her, and would she be pleased to drink tea with them.

The girl thanked him kindly, and said she could come the next day; she was too busy at the moment.

"All the better," said Jack, "I'll have time to make ready."

So when she came, Gobborn Seer could see she was a witty woman, and he asked her if she would marry his Jack. She said, "Yes," and they were married.

Not long after, Jack's father told him he must come with him and build the finest castle that ever was seen, for a king who wished to outdo all others by his wonderful castle.

And as they went to lay the foundation-stone, Gobborn Seer said to Jack, "Can't you shorten the way for me?"

But Jack looked ahead and there was a long road before them, and he said, "I don't see, father, how I could break a bit off."

"You're no good to me then, and had best be off home."

So poor Jack turned back, and when he came in, his wife said, "Why, how's this you've come alone?" and he told her what his father had said, and his answer.

"You stupid," said his witty wife, "if you had told a tale you would have shortened the road! Now listen till I tell you a story, and then catch up with Gobborn Seer and begin it at once. He will like hearing it, and by the time you are done you will have reached the foundation-stone."

So Jack sweated and overtook his father. Gobborn Seer said never a word, but Jack began his story, and the road was shortened as his wife had said.

When they came to the end of their journey, they started building of this castle which was to outshine all others. Now the wife had advised them to be intimate with the servants, and so they did as she said, and it was "Good morning" and "Good day to you" as they passed in and out.

Now, at the end of a twelvemonth, Gobborn, the wise man, had built such a castle thousands were gathered to admire it.

And the king said: "The castle is done. I shall return to-morrow and pay you all."

"I have just a ceiling to finish in an upper lobby," said Gobborn, "and then it wants nothing."

But after the king was gone off the housekeeper sent for Gobborn and Jack, and told them that she had watched for a chance to warn them, for the king was so afraid they should carry their art away and build some other king as fine a castle, he meant to take their lives on the morrow. Gobborn told Jack to keep a good heart, and they would come off all right.

When the king had come back, Gobborn told him he had been unable to complete the job for lack of a tool left at home, and he should like to send Jack after it.

"No, no," said the king, "cannot one of the men do the errand?"

"No, they could not make themselves understood," said the Seer, "but

27

Jack could do the errand."

"You and your son stop here. But how will it do if I send my own son?"

"That will do."

So Gobborn sent by him a message to Jack's wife, "Give him *Crooked and Straight!*"

Now there was a little hole in the wall rather high up, and Jack's wife tried to reach up into a chest there after "crooked and straight", but at last she asked the king's son to help her, because his arms were longest.

But when he was leaning over the chest she caught him by the two heels, and threw him into the chest, and fastened it down. So there he was, both "crooked and straight!"

Then he begged for pen and ink, which she brought him, but he was not allowed out, and holes were bored that he might breathe.

When his letter came, telling his father he was to be let free when Gobborn and Jack were safe home, the king saw he must settle for his building, and let them come away.

As they left, Gobborn told him: Now that Jack was done with this work, he should soon build a castle for his witty wife far superior to the king's, which he did, and they lived there happily ever after.

Jacobs, *More English Fairy Tales*, p. 54.

❡ Collected by Mrs Gomme from an old woman at Deptford. "Gobborn Seer" comes from the Irish "Goban Saor", a travelling carpenter, a godlike character somewhat in the tradition of Wayland Smith. The tale is to be found in Ireland. "The Peasant's Wise Daughter", to which this tale bears some resemblance, occurs in Kennedy's *Fireside Stories*. A wise wife, who compensates for her husband's lack of intelligence, is to be found in "A Pottle of Brains".

THE GOLDEN BALL

There were two lasses, daughters of one mother, and as they came from the fair, they saw a right bonny young man stand at the house-door before them. They never saw such a bonny man before. He had gold on his cap, gold on his finger, gold on his neck, a red-gold watch-chain—eh! but he had brass. He had a golden ball in each hand. He gave a ball to each lass, and she was to keep it, and if she lost it, she was to be hanged. One of the lasses, 'twas the youngest, lost her ball. I'll tell thee how. She was by a park-paling, and she was tossing her ball, and it went up, and up, and up, till it went fair over the paling; and when she climbed up to look, the ball ran along the green grass, and it went right forward to the door of the house, and the ball went in and she saw it no more.

So she was taken away to be hanged by the neck till she was dead because she'd lost her ball.

But she had a sweetheart, and he said he would go and get the ball. So he went to the park-gate, but 'twas shut; so he climbed the hedge, and when he got to the top of the hedge, an old woman rose up out of the dyke before him, and said, if he wanted to get the ball, he must sleep three nights in the house. He said he would. .

Then he went up into the house, and looked for the ball, but could not find it. Night came on, and he heard bogles move in the courtyard; so he looked out of the window, and the yard was full of them.

Presently he heard steps coming upstairs. He hid behind the door, and was as still as a mouse. Then in came a big giant five times as tall as he, and the giant looked round but did not see the lad, so he went to the window and bowed to look out; and as he bowed on his elbows to see the bogles in the yard, the lad stepped behind him, and with one blow of his sword he cut him in twain, so that the top part of him fell in the yard, and the bottom part stood looking out of the window.

There was a great cry from the bogles when they saw half the giant come tumbling down to them, and they called out, "There comes half our master, give us the other half."

So the lad said, "It's no use of thee, thou pair of legs, standing alone at the window, as thou hast no eye to see with, so go join thy brother"; and he cast the lower part of the giant after the top part. Now when the bogles had gotten all the giant they were quiet.

Next night the lad was at the house again, and now a second giant came in at the door, and as he came in the lad cut him in twain, but the legs walked on to the chimney, and went up them. "Go, get thee after thy legs," said the lad to the head, and he cast the head up the chimney too.

The third night the lad got into bed, and he heard the bogles striving under the bed, and they had the ball there, and they were casting it to and fro.

Now one of them has his leg thrust out from under bed, so the lad brings his sword down and cuts it off. Then another thrusts his arm out at the other side of the bed, and the lad cuts that off. So at last he had maimed them all, and they all went crying and wailing off, and forgot the ball, but he took it from under the bed, and went to seek his true love.

Now the lass was taken to York to be hanged; she was brought out on the scaffold, and the hangman said, "Now, lass, thou must hang by the neck till thou be'st dead." But she cried out:

"Stop, stop, I think I see my mother coming!
   Oh, mother, hast brought my golden ball
      And come to set me free?"

"I've neither brought thy golden ball
      Nor come to set thee free,
   But I have come to see thee hung
      Upon this gallows-tree."

Then the hangman said, "Now, lass, say thy prayers, for thou must die."

"Stop, stop, I think I see my father coming!
   Oh, father, hast brought my golden ball
      And come to set me free?"

"I've neither brought thy golden ball
      Nor come to set thee free.
   But I have come to see thee hung
      Upon this gallows-tree."

Then the hangman said, "Hast thee done thy prayers? Now, lass, put thy head into the noose."

But she answered, "Stop, stop, I think I see my brother coming." And again she sang, and then she thought she saw her sister coming, then her uncle, then her aunt, then her cousin; but after this the hangman said, "I will stop no longer, thou'rt making game of me. Thou must be hung at once."

But now she saw her sweetheart coming through the crowd, and he held over his head in the air her own golden ball; so she said:

"Stop, stop, I see my sweetheart coming!
   Sweetheart, hast brought my golden ball,
      And come to set me free?"

"Aye, I have brought thy golden ball,
      And come to set thee free,
   I have not come to see thee hung
      Upon this gallows-tree."

And he took her home, and they lived happy ever after.

Jacobs, *More English Fairy Tales*, p. 12. Contributed by Baring-Gould to the first edition of Henderson's *Folk-Lore of the Northern Counties*.

¶ This appears to be a mixture of type 326A, a haunted house disenchanted by a man sleeping in it for a certain time, and the folk-song "A Maid Freed from the Gallows". The notion connecting the two has been often examined, for instance by M. Damant in his notes on "The Three Golden Balls", *Folklore*, VI, pp. 305–8, but the last word has probably been said by Tristram E. Coffin in "The Golden Ball and the Hangman's Tree", *Folklore International*, U.S.A. (1967), pp. 23–8. He established the unity of the theme.

JACK AND THE GIANTS

How King Arthur's son, going to seek his Fortune, met with Jack, etc.

King Arthur's only son desired of his father to furnish him with a certain sum of money, that he might go and seek his fortune in the principality of Wales, where a beautiful Lady lived, whom he heard was possessed with seven evil spirits; but the King his father advised him utterly against it, yet he would not be persuaded of it; so that he granted what he requested, which was one horse loaded with money, and another for himself to ride on; thus he went forth without any attendants.

Now after several days travel, he came to a market-town in Wales, where he beheld a large concourse of people gathered together; the King's son demanded the reason of it, and was told that they arrested a corpse for many large sums of money, which the deceased owed when he died. The King's son replied, "It is a pity that creditors should be so cruel. Go bury the dead," said he, "and let his creditors come to my lodging and their debts shall be discharged." Accordingly they came, and in such great numbers that before night he had almost left himself moneyless.

Now Jack-the-Giant-Killer being there, and seeing the generosity of the King's son, he was taken with him, and desired to be his servant; it was agreed upon, and the next morning they set forward, when, riding out at the town-end, an old woman called after him, crying out, "He hath owed me twopence these five years; pray sir, pay me as well as the rest!" He put his hand into his pocket, and gave it her; it being the last he had left, the King's son turning to Jack, said, "I cannot tell how I will subsist in my intended journey." "For that," quoth Jack, "take you no thought nor care. Let me alone, I warrant you we will not want."

Now Jack, having a small spell in his pocket, which served at noon to give them a refreshment, when done, they had not one penny left betwixt them; the afternoon they spent in travel and familiar discourse, till the sun began to grow low, at which time the King's son said, "Jack, since we have no money, where can we think to lodge this night?" Jack replied, "Master, we'll do well enough, for I have an uncle lives within two little miles of this; he's a huge and monstrous giant with three heads: he'll fight five hundred men in armour, and make them to fly before him." "Alas," quoth the King's son, "what shall we do there? He'll certainly chop us both up at one mouthful! nay, we are scarce enough to fill one of his hollow teeth." "It is no matter for that," quoth Jack, "I myself will go before, and prepare the way for you: therefore tarry here, and wait my return."

He waits, and Jack rides full speed, when coming to the gates of the castle, he knocked with such a force, that he made all the neighbouring hills to resound. The giant with a voice like thunder, roared out, "Who's there?" He answered, "None but your poor cousin Jack." Quoth he, "What news with my poor cousin Jack?" He replied, "Dear uncle, heavy news, God wot." "Prithee, what heavy news can come to me? I am a giant with three heads, and besides thou knowest I can fight five hundred men in armour, and make them fly like chaff before the wind." "O! but", quoth Jack, "here's the King's son coming with a thousand men in armour to kill you, and so to destroy all that you have!" "Oh! cousin Jack, this is heavy news indeed: I have a large vault under the ground, where I will immediately hide myself, and thou shalt lock, bolt, and bar me in, and keep the keys till the King's son is gone."

Now Jack having secured the giant, he soon returned and fetched his master, they were both heartily merry with the wine, and other dainties which were in the house: so that night they rested in very pleasant lodgings, while the poor uncle, the giant, lay trembling in the vault underground.

Early in the morning, Jack furnished his master with a fresh supply of gold and silver, and then set him three miles forward on his journey, concluding he was then pretty well out of the smell of the giant, and then returned to let his uncle out of the hole, who asked Jack what he would give him in reward if his castle was not demolished. "Why," quoth Jack, "I desire nothing but the old coat and cap, together with this old rusty sword and slippers, which are at your bed-head." Quoth the giant, "Thou shalt have them, and pray keep them for my sake, for they are things of excellent use. The coat will keep you invisible, the cap will furnish you with knowledge, the sword cuts in sunder whatever you strike, and the shoes are of extraordinary swiftness; these may be service-able to you, and therefore pray take them with all my heart." Jack takes them, thanking his uncle, and follows his master.

How Jack saved his Master's life, and drove the Spirits out of a Lady, etc.

Jack having overtaken his master, they soon after arrived at the Lady's house, who finding the King's son to be a suitor, she prepared a banquet for him, which being ended, she wiped his mouth with her handkerchief, saying, "You must shew me this one to-morrow morning, or else lose your head": and with that she put it into her own bosom.

The King's son went to bed very sorrowful, but Jack's cap of knowledge instructed him how to obtain it. In the middle of the night, she called on her familiar spirit to carry her to her friend Lucifer. Jack soon put on his coat of darkness with his shoes of swiftness, and was there as soon as her; by reason of his coat they could not see him. When she entered the place she gave the handkerchief to Old Lucifer, who laid it upon a shelf; from whence Jack took, and brought it to his master, who shewed it to the lady next day, and so saved his life.

The next night she saluted the King's son, telling him he must show her to-morrow morning the lips that she kissed last, this night, or else lose his head. "Ah," replied he, "if you kiss none but mine, I will": "'tis neither here nor there," said she, "if you do not death's your portion." At midnight she went as before, and was angry with Lucifer for letting the handkerchief go: "But now", said she, "I will be too hard for the King's son, for I will kiss thee, and he's to shew thy lips," which she did; Jack standing near him with his sword of sharpness, cut off the devil's head, and brought it under his invisible coat to his master, who was in bed, and laid it at the end of his bolster. In the morning, when the lady came up, he pulled it out by the horns, and shewed her the devil's lips which she kissed last.

Thus, having answered her twice, the enchantment broke, and the evil spirits left her; at which time she appeared in all her beauty, a beautiful and virtuous creature. They were married the next morning in great pomp and solemnity, and soon after they returned with a numerous company to the court of King Arthur, where they were received with the greatest joy, and loud acclamations by the whole court. Jack, for the many and great exploits he had done for the good of his country, was made one of the Knights of the Round Table.

Norton Collection, II, p. 66. *The History of Jack and the Giants* (Glasgow, 1807), pp. 8–12.

This tale is a thinly disguised version of "The Grateful Dead", only lacking the link between Jack and the dead man; the ransomed dead man in "The Old Wives' Tale" was also called Jack. The tale is more explicit and widely distributed in Celtic areas; it is therefore interesting to come across this practically complete version in an English tale.

¶ See also "Four Eggs a Penny", "The Red Etin". Celtic versions are: "Jack the Master" and "Jack the Servant", Kennedy; "The Barra Widow's Son", Campbell, XXXII.

THE KING OF THE BLACK ART
[condensed version]

There was once an old fisherman, and one day as he was fishing he drew out a long box, and inside was a baby boy. He took it home to his wife, and they brought it up as their own. When the boy was fourteen years old, a ship came to land, and on the bridge there was a man dressed as fine as a king, juggling with three poison-balls with spikes on them. The stranger came to shore, and seemed to take a great fancy to the boy; he offered to take him away for a year and day, and to teach the boy his art. He wheedled so that the fisherman and his wife agreed, and the boy went away with the stranger. In a year and day the a ship was back, and the boy was back, tossing seven poison-balls. The old couple were so pleased that they allowed the stranger to take the boy for another year and a day, but he did not come back. So the old wife sent the fisherman to look for him. The fisherman travelled on and on, until in a wee hut in a wood he saw an old, old man, who asked him in for the night. The fisherman told the old man his story, and the old man said, "There's little doubt that the King of the Black Art has your son, and there is no more I can tell you; but maybe my eldest brother can help you. He lives a week's journey from here. Tell him I sent you." So the next morning the fisherman set out, and he journeyed for a week to the older brother's house. And if the first old man was old, this was three times older. But he asked the fisherman in, and gave him food and lodging, and told him what to do. He was to go on to the King of the Black Art's castle, and ring the bell and ask for his son. They would laugh at him, and the King would tell him to choose his son from among fourteen pigeons that he would throw up into the air, and he was to choose a little, weak, raggety-winged one, that flew lower than the rest. The fisherman did as he was told, and chose the raggety-winged pigeon. "Take him, and be damned to you!" said the King, and his son stood beside him. They went away together.

"I'd never have got free if you'd not come for me," said the boy. "The

King of the Black Art and his two sons are at the head of all the wizards in the country. But I've learned something, and we'll get something back from them. Now, we're coming to a town where there is a market, and I'll change myself into a greyhound. All the lords and gentry will offer to buy me, but don't you sell me till the King of the Black Art comes. You can take five hundred pounds from him, but mind you, father, for your life, do not sell the collar and strap, but take it off me." So, in a moment, he'd turned himself into the finest greyhound dog that ever was seen, and the fisherman led him into the market. Knights and nobles were crowding round him to buy, but he would take no offers till the King of the Black Art and his two sons came into the place, and he would not let him have the dog under five hundred pounds. Then he took the strap from round the dog's neck, and tied a piece of string round it instead, and walked away. As soon as he was out of the town, there was his son beside him, for he had been the strap. They went on to another town, and the son turned himself into a grand stallion horse, but he warned his father not to sell the bridle with him, whatever he did. The knights and nobles came round him as before, for no such horse had ever been seen in those parts; but he would not sell him to anyone till the King of the Black Art and his two sons came, and he asked a thousand pounds from him. "He looks worth it," said the King of the Black Art, "and I'll give it if he is as good as his looks. But no man can buy a horse without trying it." The fisherman stood out for a while, but the King said, "Come to this wee house, and I'll show you the gold you'll get. But I must just ride him round the fair-ground." The glint of the gold was too much for the fisherman. He said, "Just ride him round the ground then," and the King leapt on the horse's back. The fisherman turned to look at the gold, and it turned to dung before his eyes, and when he looked back, the horse was gone.

The King of the Black Art rode the horse back to a stable where he was fastened up with other horses, and they were fed on salt beef, and not given a drop to drink till their tongues were swollen and coated. One day the King and his sons had gone hunting, and the boy spoke to the groom who brought their food, and begged to be given a drink. The groom was frightened, but the horse begged until he had compassion on it, and led it out to the stream. The horse begged him to loosen the bit so that he could drink, and when he did so it slipped its head out of the bridle, and slipped into the stream as a salmon. As he did so, all the bells of the castle rang, and the magicians dashed back from the hills, turned themselves into otters, and swam after the salmon.

35

They came closer and closer, until they were almost on him, then he leapt into the air, and turned into a swallow. The otters turned into hawks, and pursued him. The swallow saw a lady sitting in a garden, flew to her, and turned into a ring on her finger. The hawks swept round her and flew away. Then the ring spoke. It said, "Lady, in a few minutes three labourers will come here, and offer to build up your dyke. When they have done it, they will ask for the ring from your finger for payment. But say to them that you would rather throw it into that bonfire, and throw it as you speak." The lady said she would do as he told her, and in a few minutes the three labourers arrived. They built up the walls as if by magic, and when she offered them money, they asked for the ring, but she threw it into the fire. The labourers turned themselves into three blacksmiths, and began to blow up the fire, but the ring hopped out on the other side into a pile of corn, and turned itself into a grain in the pile. The magicians turned into three cocks, and began to eat the corn, but the boy turned into a fox, and snapped off the three cocks' heads as quick as thought. So the King of the Black Art was defeated, and the boy rejoined his father, and they lived prosperously all their days by his magic art.

School of Scottish Studies, Hamish Henderson, from John Stewart.

¶ This is a complete version of "The Magician and his Pupil", Grimm no. 68. It is widespread: Norwegian, Russian, French, Spanish, Greek, Highland and Irish versions are found, among others.

The English folk-song, "The Coal-Black Smith" (Baring-Gould), is an example of the contest.

See also "The Black King of Morocco".

KING HERLA

Herla was king of the Ancient Britons, and was challenged by another king, a pigmy no bigger than an ape, and of less than half human stature. He rode on a large goat; indeed, he himself might have been compared to Pan. He had a large head, glowing face, and a long red beard, while his breast was conspicuous for a spotted fawnskin which he wore on it. The lower part of his body was rough and hairy, and his legs ended in goats' hooves. He had a private interview with Herla, in which he spoke as follows: "I am lord over many kings and princes, over a vast and innumerable people. I am their willing messenger to you, although to you I am unknown. Yet I rejoice in the fame which has raised you above other kings, for you are of all men the best, and also closely connected with me both by position and blood. You are worthy of the honour of adorning your marriage with my presence as guest, for the King of France has given you his daughter, and indeed the embassy is arriving here to-day, although all the arrangements have been made without your knowledge. Let there be an everlasting treaty between us, because, first of all, I was present at your marriage, and because you will be at mine on the same day a year hence." After this speech he turned away, and moving faster even than a tiger, disappeared from his sight. The King, therefore, returned from that spot full of surprise, received the embassy, and assented to their proposals. When the marriage was celebrated, and the king was seated at the customary feast, suddenly, before the first course was served, the pigmy arrived, accompanied by so large a company of dwarfs like himself, that after they had filled all the seats at table, there were more dwarfs outside in tents which they had in a moment put up, than at the feast inside. Instantly there darted out from these tents servants with vessels made out of precious stones, all new and wondrously wrought. They filled the palace and the tents with furniture either made of gold or precious stones. Neither wine nor meat was served in any wooden or silver vessel. The servants were found wherever they were wanted, and served nothing out of the king's or anyone else's stores, but only from their own, which were of quality beyond anyone's thoughts. None of Herla's provisions were used, and his servants sat idle.

The pigmies won universal praise. Their raiment was gorgeous; for lamps they provided blazing gems; they were never far off when they were wanted, and never too close when not desired. Their king then thus addressed Herla: "Most excellent King, God be my witness that I am here in accordance with our agreement, at your marriage. If there is anything more that you desire, I will supply it gladly, on the condition that when I demand a return, you will not deny it." Hereupon, without waiting for an answer he returned to his tent and departed at about cock-crow with his attendants. After a year he suddenly came to Herla and demanded the observance of the treaty. Herla consented, and followed at the dwarf's bidding. They entered a cave in a very high cliff, and after some journeying through the dark, which appeared to be lighted, not by the sun or moon, but by numerous torches, they arrived at the dwarf's palace, a splendid mansion.

There the marriage was celebrated, and the obligations to the dwarf fittingly paid, after which Herla returned home loaded with gifts and offerings, horses, dogs, hawks, and all things pertaining to hunting and falconry. The pigmy guided them down the dark passage, and there gave them a (small) bloodhound (*canem sanguinarium*) small enough to be carried (*portabilem*), then, strictly forbidding any of the king's retinue to dismount until the dog leapt from his carrier, he bade them farewell, and returned home. Soon after, Herla reached the light of day, and having got back to his kingdom again, called an old shepherd and asked for news of his queen, using her name. The shepherd looked at him astonished, and said, "Lord, I scarcely understand your language, for I am a Saxon, and you a Briton. I have never heard the name of that queen, except in the case of one who they say was Herla's wife, queen of the earliest Britons. He is fabled to have disappeared with a dwarf at this cliff, and never to have been seen on earth again. The Saxons have now held this realm for two hundred years, having driven out the original inhabitants." The king was astonished, for he imagined that he had been away for three days only. Some of his companions descended from horseback before the dog was released, forgetful of the dwarf's commands, and were instantly crumbled to dust. The king then forbade any more of his companions to descend until the dog leapt down. The dog has not leapt down yet. One legend states that Herla for ever wanders on mad journeys with his train, without home or rest. Many people, as they tell us, often see his company. However, they say that at last, in the first year of our (present) King Henry (the second) it ceased to visit our country in pomp as before. On that occasion, many of the Welsh (*Wallenses*) saw it whelmed in the Wye, the Herefordshire river (*Waiam Herefordiae flumen*). From that hour, that weird roaming ceased, as though Herla had transferred his wandering (*Errores*, a pun containing the idea of error) to us, and had gained rest for himself. (A hit at contemporary politics.)

Folk-Lore of Herefordshire, E. M. Leather, p. 172. Derived from Walter Map's *De Nugis Curialium*.

❡ The Irish tale of the Return of Ossian is one of the most poetic of many stories about the miraculous passage of time in fairyland. A widespread Japanese version is "Urashima Taro" (*Folktales of Japan*, no. 32). Hartland devoted three chapters to the subject in *The Science of Fairy Tales*. The Welsh story of Shon ap Shenkin is one of many Celtic versions.

See also "The Noontide Ghost", "The Stonemason of the Charltons".

THE MAN WHO WOULDN'T
GO OUT AT NIGHT [dialect modified]

There was a farmer, a great upstanding chap, and he wouldn't go out after dark, not for anything. It was not so bad in the Summer, but when All Hallows was come and gone things grew terribly awkward. There might be stock to feed and cows to milk and lambs to help into this world, but he wouldn't put a foot outside the door after sunset, not if you begged him on your bended knees. What was worse, his wife was expecting a child and she asked him flat out if he'd fetch the doctor if her pains came on her at night, and he had to admit that he wouldn't. She knew there must be something far amiss there, because he fairly doted on her. So she begged and prayed him to tell her what was the matter, and at last it came out.

It seemed when he was a foolish youngster that he had sold his soul to the Devil, old Bogey, he called him, for prosperity on the farm, and now the time had come to pay. Old Bogey was hanging round the farm to snap him up if he set foot over the threshold after dark. The door was well guarded with horseshoes and a piece of mountain ash, but once beyond them and the farmer was a lost soul.

Well the poor wife was hard set to it to know what to do, but she made up her mind she must save her husband, and the farm and stock beside. So she took an iron plough colter and she made it red-hot in the fire, and she rolled out a great piece of pastry and made a deep cross in it, and filled the cross with salt; then she put the red-hot colter into the pie, with the cross turned inside so that it didn't show. When it was done she sent her man into the bed-chamber, and she opened the farm door and stretched out her hand with the pie.

"Are you there, sir?" she said. "My man's just a-getting ready to come, and here's a warm bite for you whilst you're a-waiting."

Bogey took the pie and bit into it hard, and he pretty near broke every tooth in his head, and the cross and the salt were like poison to him. Just then the wife cried out from her chamber, "We're a-coming, sir, we're a coming."

"Who's we?" said Bogey, anxious all of a sudden.

"Why, I'm a-coming with my dear man," she said, "to cook for the both of you."

With that they say old Bogey let out a yell that sunk two ships off

Lundy, and he took himself off to Taunton as fast as he could fly. And what I've seen of the Taunton folk, he stayed there for good and all.

Collected by Ruth L. Tongue. Recorded from her on 29 September 1963, as heard at Brampton Ralph Women's Institute in 1962. She knew other versions told between 1930 and 1940, by a blacksmith at Vellow, a cottage woman at Monkshields, and a farmer's wife at Elworthy. First published in *The Folktales of England*, 1965. Also in *Somerset Folklore*.

The Irish tale of Finn McCoole (Patrick Kennedy, *Legendary Fictions of the Irish Celts*, London 1866, pp. 303–5) uses the same theme.

❡ See also "Dule upon Dun", "Will the Smith".

THE OLD WOMAN WHO LIVED IN
A VINEGAR BOTTLE

Once upon a time there was an old woman who lived in a vinegar bottle. One day a fairy was passing that way, and she heard the old woman talking to herself.

"It is a shame, it is a shame, it is a shame," said the old woman. "I didn't ought to live in a vinegar bottle. I ought to live in a nice little cottage with a thatched roof, and roses growing all up the wall, that I ought."

So the fairy said, "Very well, when you go to bed to-night you turn round three times, and shut your eyes, and in the morning you'll see what you will see."

So the old woman went to bed, and turned round three times and shut her eyes, and in the morning there she was, in a pretty little cottage with a thatched roof, and roses growing up the walls. And she was very surprised, and very pleased, but she quite forgot to thank the fairy.

And the fairy went north, and she went south, and she went east, and she went west, all about the business she had to do. And presently she thought, "I'll go and see how that old woman is getting on. She must be very happy in her little cottage."

And as she got up to the front door, she heard the old woman talking to herself.

"It is a shame, it is a shame, it is a shame," said the old woman. "I didn't ought to live in a little cottage like this, all by myself. I ought to live in a nice little house in a row of houses, with lace curtains at the windows, and a brass knocker on the door, and people calling mussels and cockles outside, all merry and cheerful."

The fairy was rather surprised; but she said: "Very well. You go to bed to-night, and turn round three times, and shut your eyes, and in the morning you shall see what you shall see."

So the old woman went to bed, and turned round three times and shut her eyes, and in the morning there she was in a nice little house, in a row of little houses, with lace curtains at the windows, and a brass knocker on the door, and people calling mussels and cockles outside, all merry and cheerful. And she was very much surprised, and very much pleased. But she quite forgot to thank the fairy.

And the fairy went north, and she went south, and she went east, and she went west, all about the business she had to do; and after a time she thought to herself, "I'll go and see how that old woman is getting on. Surely she must be happy now."

And when she got to the little row of houses, she heard the old woman talking to herself. "It is a shame, it is a shame, it is a shame," said the old woman. "I didn't ought to live in a row of houses like this, with common people on each side of me. I ought to live in a great mansion in the country, with a big garden all round it, and servants to answer the bell."

And the fairy was very surprised, and rather annoyed, but she said: "Very well, go to bed and turn round three times and shut your eyes, and in the morning you will see what you will see."

And the old woman went to bed, and turned round three times, and shut her eyes, and in the morning there she was, in a great mansion in the country, surrounded by a fine garden, and servants to answer the bell. And she was very pleased and very surprised, and she learned how to speak genteelly, but she quite forgot to thank the fairy.

And the fairy went north, and she went south, and she went east, and she went west, all about the business she had to do; and after a time she thought to herself, "I'll go and see how that old woman is getting on. Surely she must be happy now."

But no sooner had she got near the old woman's drawing-room window than she heard the old woman talking to herself in a genteel voice.

"It certainly is a very great shame," said the old woman, "that I should be living alone here, where there is no society. I ought to be a duchess, driving in my own coach to wait on the Queen, with footmen running beside me."

The fairy was very much surprised, and very much disappointed, but she said: "Very well. Go to bed to-night, and turn round three times and shut your eyes; and in the morning you shall see what you shall see."

So the old woman went to bed, and turned round three times, and shut her eyes; and in the morning, there she was, a duchess with a coach of her own, to wait on the Queen, and footmen running beside her. And she was very much surprised, and very much pleased. BUT she quite forgot to thank the fairy.

And the fairy went north, and she went south, and she went east, and she went west, all about the business she had to do; and after a while she thought to herself: "I'd better go and see how that old woman is getting on. Surely she is happy, now she's a duchess."

But no sooner had she come to the window of the old woman's great town mansion, than she heard her saying in a more genteel tone than ever: "It is indeed a very great shame that I should be a mere Duchess, and have to curtsey to the Queen. Why can't I be a queen myself, and sit on a golden throne, with a golden crown on my head, and courtiers all around me."

The fairy was very much disappointed and very angry; but she said: "Very well. Go to bed and turn round three times, and shut your eyes, and in the morning you shall see what you shall see."

So the old woman went to bed, and turned round three times, and shut her eyes; and in the morning there she was in a royal palace, a queen in her own right, sitting on a golden throne, with a golden crown on her head, and her courtiers all around her. And she was highly delighted, and ordered them right and left. BUT she quite forgot to thank the fairy.

And the fairy went north, and she went south, and she went east, and she went west, all about the business she had to do; and after a while she thought to herself: "I'll go and see how that old woman is getting on. Surely she must be satisfied now!"

But as soon as she got near the Throne Room, she heard the old woman talking.

"It is a great shame, a very great shame," she said, "that I should be Queen of a paltry little country like this instead of ruling the whole round world. What I am really fitted for is to be *Pope*, to govern the minds of everyone on Earth."

"Very well," said the fairy. "Go to bed. Turn round three times, and shut your eyes, and in the morning you shall see what you shall see."

So the old woman went to bed, full of proud thoughts. She turned round three times and shut her eyes. And in the morning she was back in her vinegar bottle.

Camp-fire story, 1924.

¶ The motif of the spared fish and the greedy wife is absent. A lively version of "The Fisherman and his Wife" was heard in Oxfordshire in 1965, but the source could not be traced, and it seems likely that it was derived directly from Grimm, no. 19. The story has a wide distribution. Forty-one Irish versions are given in *Béaloideas*, XIV, pp. 273 ff.

TOM TIT TOT

Well, once upon a time there were a woman, and she baked five pies. And when they come out of the oven they was that overbaked, the crust were too hard to eat. So she says to her darter:

"Maw'r," says she, "put you them there pies on the shelf an' leave 'em there a little, an' they'll come agin." She meant, you know, the crust 'ud get soft.

But the gal she says to herself, "Well, if they'll come agin, I'll ate 'em now." And she set to work and ate 'em all, first and last.

Well, come supper time, the woman she said: "Goo you, and git one o' them there pies. I dare say they've come agin now."

The gal she went an' she looked, and there warn't nothin' there but the dishes. So back she come, and says she, "Noo, they ain't come agin."

"Not none on 'em?" says the mother.

"Not none on 'em," says she.

"Well, come agin or not come agin," says the woman, "I'll ha' one for supper."

"But you can't, if they ain't come," says the gal.

"But I can," says she, "Goo you an' bring the best of 'em."

"Best or worst," says the gal, "I've ate 'em all, an' you can't ha' one till that's come agin."

Well, the woman she were wholly bate, an' she took her spinnin' to the door to spin, and as she spun she sang:

"My darter ha' ate five, five pies to-day.
My darter ha' ate five, five pies to-day."

The King he were a' comin' down the street an' he hard her sing, but what she sang he couldn't hare, so he stopped and said:

"What were that you was a singin' of, Maw'r?"

The woman, she were ashamed to let him hare what her darter had been a doin', so she sang, 'stids o' that:

"My darter ha' spun five, five skeins to-day,
My darter ha' spun five, five skeins to-day."

"S'ars o' mine!" said the king, "I never heerd tell of anyone as could do that."

Then he said: "Look you here, I want a wife and I'll marry your darter. But look you here," says he, "'leven months out o' the year she shall have all the vittles she likes to eat, and all the gownds she likes to git, and all the cump'ny she likes to hev; but the last month o' the year she'll ha' to spin five skeins ev'ry day, an' if she doon't, I shall kill her."

"All right," says the woman, for she thowt what a grand marriage that was. And as for them five skeins, when te come tew, there'd be plenty o' ways o' gettin' out of it, an' likeliest, he'd ha' forgot about it.

Well, so they was married. An' for 'leven months the gal had all the vittles she liked to ate, and all the gownds she liked to git, an' all the cump'ny she liked to hev.

But when the time was gettin' oover, she began to think about them there skeins an' to wonder if he had 'em in mind. But not one word did he say about 'em, and she whoolly thowt he'd forgot 'em.

Howsivir, the last day o' the last month, he takes her to a room she'd nivir set eyes on afore. There worn't nothin' in it but a spinnin' wheel and a stool. An' says he, "Now, me dear, hare yow'll be shut in tomorrow with some vittles and some flax, and if you hain't spun five skeins by the night, yar hid'll goo off."

An' awa' he went about his business. Well, she were that frightened. She'd allus been such a gatless mawther, that she didn't so much as know how to spin, an' what were she to dew to-morrer, with no one to come nigh her to help her. She sat down on a stool in the kitchen, an' lork! how she did cry!

Howsiver, all on a sudden she hard a sort of a knockin' low down ont he door. She upped and oped it, an' what should she see but a small little black thing with a long tail. That looked up at her right kewrious, an' that said:

"What are yew a cryin' for?"

"Wha's that to yew?" says she.

"Nivir yew mind," that said. "But tell me what you're a cryin' for?"

"That 'oon't dew me noo good if I dew," says she.

"You doon't know that," that said, an' twirled that's tail round.

"Well," says she, "that oon't dew no harm, if that doon't dew no good," and she upped and told about the pies an' the skeins an' everything.

"This is what I'll do," says the little black thing. "I'll come to yar winder iv'ry mornin' an' take the flax an' bring it spun at night."

"What's your pay?" says she.

44

That looked out o' the corners o' that's eyes, an' that said:

"I'll give you three guesses every night to guess my name, an' if you hain't guessed it afore the month's up, yew shall be mine."

Well, she thowt she'd be sure to guess that's name afore the month was up.

"All right," says she, "I agree."

"All right," that says, an' lork! how that twirled that's tail.

Well, the next day, har husband he took her inter the room, an' there was the flax an' the day's vittles.

"Now there's the flax," says he, "an' if that ain't spun up this night off goo yar head." An' then he went out an' locked the door.

He'd hardly goon, when there was a knockin' agin the winder. She upped and she oped it, and there sure enough was the little oo'd thing a settin' on the ledge.

"Where's the flax?" says he.

"Here te be," says she. And she gonned it to him.

Well, come the evenin', a knockin' come agin to the winder. She upped and she oped it, and there sure enough was the little oo'd thing with five skeins of flax on his arm.

"Here te be," says he, an' he gonned it to her.

"Now what's my name," says he.

"What, is that Bill?" says she.

"Noo, that ain't," says he. An' he twirled his tail.

"Well, is that Ned?" says she.

"Noo, that ain't," says he. An' he twirled his tail.

"Well, is that Mark?" says she.

"Noo, that ain't," says he. An' he twirled harder, an' awa' he flew.

Well, when har husband he come in, there was the five skeins riddy for him.

"I see I shorn't hev for to kill you to-night, me dare," says he. "Yew'll hev yar vittles and yar flax in the mornin'," says he, an' awa' he goes.

Well, ivery day the flax an' the vittles, they was brought, an' ivery day that there little black impet used for to come mornin's an' evenin's. An' all the day the mawther she set a tryin' fur to think of names to say to it when te come at night. But she niver hot on the right one. An' as that got to-warts the ind o' the month, the impet that began for to look soo maliceful, an' that twirled that's tail faster an' faster each time she gave a guess.

At last te came to the last day but one.

The impet that come at night along o' the five skeins; an' that said:

"What, hain't yew got my name yet?"

"Is that Nicodemus?" says she.

"Noo, t'ain't," that says.

"Is that Sammle?" says she.

"Noo t'ain't," that says.

"A-well, is that Methusalem?" says she.

"Noo, t'ain't that norther," he says.

Then that looks at her with that's eyes like a cool o' fire, an' that says,

"Woman, there's only tomorrer night, an' then yar'll be mine!" An' awa' te flew.

Well, she felt that horrud. Howsomediver, she hard the King a comin' along the passage. In he came, an' when he see the five skeins, he says, says he:

"Well, my dare," says he, "I don't see but what you'll ha' your skeins ready tomorrer night as well, an' as I reckon I shorn't ha' to kill you, I'll ha' supper in here tonight." So they brought supper, an' another stool for him, and down the tew they sat.

Well, he hadn't eat but a mouthful or so, when he stops an' begins to laugh.

"What is it?" says she.

"A-why," he says, "I was out a-huntin' to-day, an' I got awa' to a place in the wood I'd never seen afore. An' there was an old chalk pit. An' I heerd a sort of a hummin' kind o'. So I got off my hobby, an' I went right quiet to the pit, an' I looked down. Well, what should there be but the funniest little black thing yew iver set eyes on. An' what was that dewin' on, but that had a little spinnin' wheel, an' that were spinnin' wonnerful fast, an' a twirlin' that's tail. An' as that span, that sang:

"Nimmy nimmy not,
My name's Tom Tit Tot."

Well, when the mawther heerd this, she fared as if she could ha' jumped outer her skin for joy, but she di'n't say a word.

Next day, that there little thing looked soo maliceful when he come for the flax. An' when night came, she heerd that a knockin' agin the winder panes. She oped the winder, an' that come right in on the ledge. That were grinnin' from are to are, an' Oo! that's tail were twirlin' round so fast.

"What's my name?" that says, as that gonned her the skeins.

"Is that Solomon?" she says, pretendin' to be afeard.

"Noo, t'ain't," that says, an' that come fudder into the room.

46

"Well, is that Zebedee?" says she agin.

"Noo t'ain't," says the impet. An' then that laughed, an' twirled that's tail, till yew cou'n't hardly see it.

"Take time, woman," that says; "next guess an' you're mine." An' that stretched out that's black hands at her.

Well, she backed a step or two, and she looked at it, an' then she laughed out, an' says she, a-pointin' of her finger at it,

> "Nimmy nimmy not,
> Yar name's Tom Tit Tot."

Well, when that hard her, that shruck awful, an' awa' that flew into the dark, an' she niver saw it noo more.

E. S. Hartland, *County Folk-Lore*, I, p. 43 (Suffolk section). (Told by an old servant to the writer when a child.) A.W.T., 'Suffolk Notes and Queries', *Ipswich Journal*, 15 January 1878.

Reprinted by Edward Clodd from *The Ipswich Journal*, 'Notes and Queries', edited by F. Hindes Groome, from a lady who had heard it from an old Suffolk nurse.
¶ Edward Clodd elaborated the article, "The Philosophy of Rumpelstiltskin" (*The Folk-Lore Journal*, 1889), into a book, *Tom Tit Tot, an Essay on Savage Philosophy in Folk-Tale* (1898), in which he examines the primitive name-tabus. "Rumpelstiltskin" (Grimm, no. 55), is the best known version of this widespread tale. It is most frequent in Ireland, Germany, Denmark and Finland.

See also "Duffy and the Devil", "Whuppity Stoorie", "Titty Tod".

This version is in the Suffolk dialect. "Maw'r" or "Mawther" means "daughter", or "girl"; "gatless", "heedless" or "careless".

The question of what happened at the end of the next eleven months is neatly answered in the appended sequel.

THE GIPSY WOMAN [sequel to "Tom Tit Tot"]

Well, the hool o' that yare, the mawther she'd the best o' livin' an' the best o' cump'ny, till the 'leventh month was nare oover.

An' then, her husban' says to her, says he: "Well, me dare, to-day, that's the end o' the month, an' to-morrer yow'll ha' to begin an' spin yare five skeins ivvery day."

She hadn't nivver given a thawt but what he'd clane forgotten about it; an' now, what to dew she did not know. She knew she couldn't reckon noo moor on Tom Tit Tot, an' she couldn't spin a mite herself: an' now har hid 'ud have to come off!

47

Well, pore Toad, she set herself down agin on a stule in the backhouse, an' she cried as if har heart 'ud break.

All at onst, she hared someone a knockin' at the door. Soo she upped an' onsnecked it, an' there stood a gipsy woman, as brown's a berry.

"A why, what's this to-dew hare?" sez she, "What a'ir yew a-cryin' for like that?"

"Git awa', yow golderin' mawther," says she. "Doon't yew come where yew ain't no good."

"Tell me yar trouble, an' maybe I *shorl* be some good," says the woman.

Well, she looked soo onderstandin' that the gal she upped an' toold her.

"Wha's that all?" sez she. "I ha' holped folks out o' wuss than this, an' I'll help you out o' this."

"Ah! but what de yew arst for dewin' of it?" sez the gal, for she thowt how she'd nare gonned herself awa' to that snaisty little black impet.

"I doon't ask nothun' but the best suit o' clothes yow ha' got," the gipsy said.

"Yow shall hev 'em, an' welcome," says the gal, an' she runned an' ooped the hutch where har best gownd an' things was, an' giv' 'em to the woman, an' a brooch o' gay goold. For she thowt to herself, "If she's a chate an' can't help me, an' may hid is cut off, that woon't make noo matters if I *hev* giv' awa' my best gownd."

The woman, she looked rarely plazed when she see the gownd: an' sez she: "Now then, yow'll ha' to ask all the fooks yew know to a stammin' grand partery, an' I'll come tew't."

Well, the mawther, she went to har husban' an' says she: "My dare, bein' that 'tis the larst night afoor I spin, I shud like to hev a partery."

"All right, me dare," sez he.

Soo the fooks wuz all arst, an' they come in their best cloothes; silk an' sattuns, an' all mander o' fine things.

Well, they all had a grand supper o' the best o' vittles, an' they liked theirselves rarely well. But the gipsy woman she niccer come nigh, an' the gal her heart was in her mouth.

One o' the lords as was right tired o' dancin', said that it wornt far from bull's noon, and te wus time te goo.

"Noo, noo, dew yew sta' a little longer," says the gal. "Le's hev a game o' blind man's buff fust." Soo they begun to play.

Just then the door that flew oopen, an' in come the gipsy woman. She'd woished herself, an' coomed her hair, an' whelmed a gay an' gah hankercher round har hid, an' put on the grand gownd, till she looked like a Queen come in.

48

"S'ars o' mine, whu's that?" says the King.

"Oo, that's a frind o' mine," saz the gal. An' she looked to see what the gipsy 'ud do.

"What, are yew a playin' blind man's buff?" sez she. "I'll jine in along on ye."

An' soo she did. But in her pocket what wuz there but a little gotch of cold cart-grease; an' as she run she dipped har hand in this hare grease, an' smudged it on the fooks as she run by.

That warn't long afore somebody hollered out. "Oo lork, there's some rare nasty stuff on my gownd."

"Why, soo there is on mine," sez another, "that must ha' come off o' yow."

"Noo, that that di'n't. Yow ha' put it onto me." An' then nigh ivvery-body began to holler an' quarrel with ache other, ache one a thinkin' that the tother had goon an' smirched 'em.

Well, the King he come forrerd an' he heerd what was the matter. The ladies was a cryin', an' the gentlemen was a shoutun', an' all their fine things was daubed oover.

"Why, wha's this?" he sah, for there was a great mark on his cootsleeve. He smelt of it an' then he turned up his noose, an' says he: "That's cart-grease."

"Noo, that ain't," sez the gipsy woman. "That's off my hand. Tha's spindle grease."

"Why, wha's spindle grease?" sez he.

"Well," says she, "I ha' bin a great spinner i' my time, an' I span an' span an' span five skeins a day. An' becos I span se much the spindle grease that worked inter my hands, and now woish 'em as often as I may, I naster every thing I touch. An' if yer wife spins like I, she'll ha' spindle grease like I."

Well, the King he looked at his coot sleeve, an' he rubbed it an' snuffed at it an' then he said: "Look yew hare, me dare, an' listen what I sa' to yew. If ivver I see ye with a spindle agin in yar hands, yar hid'll goo off." Soo she hadn't never to spin noo more.

An' tha's all.

Norton Collection, II, p. 42. *East Anglian*, VII (1897–8), sec. iii. Probably 1897. From Miss L. A. Fison and Mrs Walter Thomas, her sister, from their nurse. Also in *Merry Suffolk* (1899), pp. 102–3, where the spelling of the dialect is somewhat different. In the *Merry Suffolk* version "Tom Tit Tot" ends with the traditional sentence: "Lork! How she did clap her hands for joy. 'I'll warrant my master'll ha' forgot all about spinning next year,' says she."

PART 3
JOCULAR TALES

Jocular Tales are among those most alive in modern oral tradition, only to be rivalled by ghost stories. They are still handed from mouth to mouth in clubs and public houses, at dinner hour in works and harvest fields, at women's tea parties and in after-dinner speeches. They are as popular now as they were in the sixteenth century, and many of them are equally indecent. The "Shaggy Dog Story" is a comparatively modern development. It is already going rather out of fashion, but no doubt the wittiest examples will hold their place. "The Dog That Talked" is an example of one with a neat twist to it.

It is no easy matter to thread one's way through the mazes of the Jocular Tale, and only a small sample of them can be shown here. At first as we read one after the other there seems a great sameness about them, but there are actually many varieties of subject and treatment. They may be divided into: Local Taunts, Noodle Tales, Courtship Tales and Anti-feminist Taunts, Conflicts between Husband and Wife, Bawdy Tales, Tales of Trickery, Practical Jokes that Went Wrong, Exploits of Jesters, The Child or Simpleton Exposing the Wise, Jokes against Particular Classes or Professions, Jokes about Animals, Unexpected Twists or Quirks, Jokes that Depend on Puns, Nonsense Tales. And many more might be worked out.

A particularly large class in England, though it is not peculiar to England, is the Local Taunt, the Noodle Tale multiplied to cover a whole village. Gotham, whether in Nottingham or Sussex, is generally taken as the typical village of fools, though over fifty places can be found scattered through the different counties of England against whom the same sort of accusations are levelled. One of the commonest taunts is that they tried to wall in the cuckoo. This subject was dealt with by J. E. Field in some detail in *The Myth of the Pent Cuckoo*. Mr Field had an interesting thesis to advance; it is that the sites of cuckoo pens are always places where a stand was made by the Britons against the Saxons, and that the simpleton villages were pockets of Ancient Britons who kept their identity. A similar explanation can be advanced for simpleton villages in other countries. Mr Field derived "cuckoo" from the same root as the "cucking-stool" on which scolds were ducked, with the meaning of "scold" or "jabber". The pen is the high, fortified place which held out longest. There is, for instance, a cuckoo pen, with no story attached to it, near Wittenham Clumps in Oxfordshire, and another near Idbury, on the wold above Burford. Whether this conjecture be well grounded or no, there is no doubt that the Gothamite stories are of great antiquity. Some of them are told in a twelfth-century Latin poem published by Wright in one of his collections.

Both the Gothamite and the ordinary Noodle Tales are treated by Clouston in his well-known Book of Noodles. This is useful for comparison, but even more helpful is *The Fool, His Social and Literary History*, by Enid Welsford. She traces the medieval and Renaissance fools back to the classical parasites and buffoons, and indicates the connection between licensed fools and bards and the value attached to railing as a means of averting ill luck. The buffoons of the Italian Renaissance courts raised folly to a high art, and were many of them men of learning, such as Dominicus Ciaiesius, buffoon to Duke Ferdinand I of Florence. He taught the duke's children Latin, and also secretly obtained a doctorate of law at Pisa University. The tradition of these learned buffoons may explain why Skelton and George Buchanan were pressed into the part of Royal Jesters. The Khojah Nasr-ed-Din, the most famous of all noodles, was also accounted a preacher and a man of learning.

Another aspect of the buffoon studied by Enid Welsford is his connection with the simpleton or madman, the magical inspiration ascribed to madness and the good luck which is said to accompany deformity. She touches on, but does not fully explore, the part played by scurrilous jests in fertility rites. It is a matter which might well be further investigated. Nonsense Tales may also have a notion of magical efficacy behind them, apart from the pleasure which most people take in nonsense.

Another purpose of Jocular Tales is as social comment. They may be used either to repress and hold up to scorn undesirable behaviour or as a retaliation of the under-privileged against their superiors in wealth or learning. But whatever solemn purposes may be found underlying these tales it is to be hoped that most people tell them and listen to them because they find them funny.

There will always be new Jocular Tales to collect, though many of them will be old in form, however new in fashion, for so long as people meet together socially so long they will amuse each other with tales.

AUSTWICK CARLES: II [summary]

Once a farmer of Austwick, wishing to get a bull out of a field, called nine of his neighbours to his aid. For some hours they tried in vain to lift the animal over the gate, and at last sent one of them to find more helpers.

He opened the gate and went through, and only after he was out of sight did the others begin to think that the bull also might have been let out the same way.

W. A. Clouston, *The Book of Noodles*, p. 54, "The Bull in the Field".

Another Austwick farmer had to take a wheelbarrow to a certain town, and to save a hundred yards in following the ordinary road, he took it through the fields. This involved lifting the barrow over twenty-two stiles.

THE AUSTWICK CARLES AND
THE WATCH: V

Some of the [Austwick] carles had been over to Settle, and on returning, pot valiant, one of them was out-distanced by the others, when his attention was arrested by something alive, with a "lang tail", saying "Tack him, tack him."

"Hoo, hoy, chaps," he exclaimed to his companions, "stop, or he'll a me." His companions waited to hear what was the cause of alarm to him. When he reached them he told them, "There was a lile fella under t'wa' as said he'd a me." They all returned, and still found the sound repeating, "Tack him, tack him." And now commenced the tug-of-war. Armed with knob-sticks, they cavilled as to which should lead the attack on the "tick 'em, tack 'em fella". At last dispute was brought to an end by the whole body of companions advancing in abreast to the attack.

Smash went the knob-sticks, and soon silenced the "tick 'em tack 'em" voice. Not being able to find the remains of the still small voice in the dark, they resolved to search for him in the morning, when lo! and behold! the ghost, the robber, the kidnapper, was discovered to be a simple watch, and none of them had ever heard a watch tick before.

Norton Collection, IV, p. 129. From N. Dobson, *Rambles by the Ribble*, first series, p. 40.
¶ Tales of Local Follies are very common in England. The best known of them is "The Wise Men of Gotham". See also "The Borrowdale Follies", "Bolliton Jackdaws", "The Chiseldon Follies", "The Yabberton Yawnies".

THE BEST WAY TO DIE

There's the story of the three old miners—were retired—one was well over 70, the other one was 80 some odd, and the oldest was 96! and they were in the eventide of their life—summertime sitting on the council seat enjoying the sunshine—watching the traffic going back and forth...and they suddenly discussed how they'd like to die!...see...the youngest now of the trio was well over 70, he said, "Well, boys *bach*," he said, "I've been watchin' these red sports cars," he said, "that these youngsters have got travelling back and fore," he said, "I don't know nothing about cars," he said, "but I'd like to get into one of those," he said... "Rev up," he said, "that's what I think they call it...60–70–80 miles an hour—Bang into a lamp post—everything at an end...that's the way I'd like to die"—"What about you, John?" he said. Now the one who was over 80 now, the second oldest of the trio..."Well, boys," he said, "I'm a bit more modern than you are," he said, "I've been reading about these Sputniks," he said, "I would like to volunteer to go into one of these... Sputniks," he said. "They tell me they go up into the sky—thousands of miles," he said..."I'd like to be up there," he said, "10,000 miles up—something go wrong with the works—explosion—everything finish—that's the way I would like to go out," he said. Now the oldest of the trio of the old miners—he was ninety-six—so they said to him, "You're silent, Robert?"..."Ha, boys," he said, "I've been listening to you two," he said. "D'you know the way I'd like to go out?" he said. "No, Robert—which way would you like to die?" "Well, boys *bach*," he said, "to tell you the truth—I'd like to be shot by a jealous husband!"

Roy Palmer, from Ewan MacColl and Charles Parker.

¶ The literary reference to this in the Motif-Index is Tennyson's *Ulysses*. This recently collected anecdote is a livelier and more humorous illustration of the same theme: *Si vieillesse pouvait*.

BOX ABOUT

Sir Walter Raleigh's eldest son, Walter, was of a very quarrelsome disposition. One day, his father was invited to dinner with some great nobleman, and he was asked to bring his young son. He talked to the boy, and said that he was such a bear that he did not like to bring him into this good company. Mr Walter humbled himself, and said he would behave very discretely. His father therefore took him, but kept him at his side. Young Walter sat demurely for some time, but in a pause he made a very outrageous remark [*omitted by Aubrey*]. "Sir Walter being strangely surprised and putt out of countenance at so great a table, gives his son a damned blow over the face. His son, as rude as he was, would not strike his father, but strikes over his face the gentleman that sat next to him, and sayd, 'Box about, 'twill come to my father anon.' 'Tis now a common-used proverb."

John Aubrey, *Brief Lives*, II, p. 185.

¶ There are Russian and Lithuanian versions of this tale. None is listed in Norton or Baughman.

This young Walter Raleigh died in his father's lifetime, in America. Raleigh's poem "The Weed and the Wag" was addressed to him.

THE CUCKOO-PENNERS

Round April 15th they hold Cuckoo Fair Day down to Crewkerne, 'cos when cuckoo do come, they begins to think about putting in the 'arvest.

If 'e come early, they get a good 'arvest, but if 'e come late, well, then they don't 'ave much chance. Well, the Crewkerne wiseacres, they put their 'eads together, and they say, "Well, if us kept cuckoo, us 'ud get more 'n one 'arvest in one year." So they outs, and they vinds a young cuckoo in a dunnock's nest. Well, they veeds 'en, and while they keeps 'en ved and 'appy, the rest o' the Crewkerne men, they builds a 'edge right round 'en. "Now," say they, "Us'll 'ave three 'arvests this year. Look 'ow the 'edge be a-growing!" Cuckoo were growing too. Well, the 'edge grew nice and 'igh, and the cuckoo grew 'is wings, and 'e flied nice and 'igh. And 'e went!

Collected by Ruth L. Tongue from L. Wyatt in 1913; from Crewkerne, Somerset.
See "The Borrowdale Cuckoos", "The Wise Men of Gotham".

THE DOG THAT TALKED

A man was entering a village inn one day, when a large sheepdog lying beside the door looked up, and said to him, "Good morning, sir." The man stopped in astonishment, thinking he must be mistaken, but the dog said again, "Good morning, sir."

"Er—good morning," he managed to reply, and going indoors, he said to the landlord, "That's an extraordinary dog of yours just outside."

"Oh, I don't know, sir," answered the man, "I don't know there's anything special about him."

"Nothing special!" exclaimed the other. "He said 'Good morning, sir' to me as I came in."

"Impossible!" said the landlord. "But he did—he said it twice." "Oh, no, sir, you must be mistaken," said the man again. Then, after a pause, he asked, "Was there another dog there as well?" "I don't think so," said the guest; "but wait a minute. There was a little white terrier, but he was lying quite a way off."

"Ah! that'd be it," the landlord said. "He's a ventriloquist!"

Margaret Nash-Williams from J. D. K. Lloyd, Esq., C.B.E., Wales, c. 1960.

In J. H. Brunvand's *A Classification for Shaggy Stories*, *JAFL*, LXXVI (1963), this is numbered B.200. Eric Partridge examined this genre in *The Shaggy Dog Story: Its Origin, Development and Nature*.

¶ See also "The Horse that Played Cricket", "The Two Elephants", "The Tortoises' Picnic", "The Pious Lion".

DUTCH COURAGE

A man had been drinking after dinner, and he was sitting at the table with a few drops of whisky still at the bottom of his glass. Presently a mouse climbed up the tablecloth and ran about the table picking up crumbs. It climbed up the glass, fell inside, and sucked up all the whisky. Then it began dashing round the glass until it knocked it over, stood up unsteadily on its hind legs, brushed back its whiskers, clenched its front paws, and said: "Now, wher'sh that damned cat!"

K. M. Briggs, from Stella Pulling (college friend), Oxford, 1919.

AN EXORCISM

In a farre countrey there dwelled sometime a gentleman of good parentage, called Signor *Myʒaldo*, who had to his wife a verie faire and beautifull gentlewoman. And as the beastes most greedilie gaze at the Panther's skin, and the birds at the Peacock's plumes; so every fair feminine face is an adamant to draw the object of men's eyes to behold the beauties of women! experience proveth it true in the wife of *Myʒaldo*, for she being a woman of singular perfection and proportion, was generallie looked on and liked of al, but favoured and loved especiallie of a yong gentleman called *Peter*, dealing with such secrecie, that they continually satisfied their desires without giving Signor *Myʒaldo* the least occasion of suspition; and the meanes that they performed it with such secrecie was this. Everie weeke twice her husband rid from home, about certaine his affaires, and she very artificially neare to the highway that leads to the towne where *Peter* lay, had placed an asses head upon a tree, and when hir husband was gone forth, she tourned the head towards the town; but when he was at home, she alwaies had it looking to hir own house; using herein, as some thought, an Embleame, saying when she turned the Asses head forth, that the Asse hir husbande with the long horning eares was gone from home; and when it stood towards the house, that the Asse kept his chamber; but whatsoever in this hir conceit was, *Peter* alwaies knew when to come, and ever when *Myʒaldo* was from home resorted to his house. Now it chanced that certaine boyes coming by, and seeing the Asses head stand there, threw stones at it and hit it so often, that at last they turned the Asses head towards the town; which *Peter* walking abroad and spying, thought that *Myʒaldo* had gone from home; and therefore at night, walked towards his lovers house, and coming to the dore, finding it shut, according to his accustomed manner, knockt; the good wife awakt, heard him and was sore afraid that hir husband should hear him, and so lay still; by and by he knockt again mor lowd: *Myʒaldo* awoke, and hearing this, asked of his wife who it was that rapt at the dore, or what that knocking meant: Oh, husband, quoth she, be stil, it is a foule spirit that hauntes this house, and yet hitherto we never durst reveale it, and it hath, thanks be to God, bin your good fortune never to hear it before. *Myʒaldo*, richer by far than he was wise, beleeved his wife, and askt hir if it had done any harme: No, quoth shee, for I had learned a charme to send it home; frier Roland learned me it, and if it knocke again, you and I will goe down together, and I wil say my charme, and so we shall live at rest.

Peter that thought som other friend had bin with his Lemman, taking in scorn that hir husband (as he thought) being from home he should not be let in, knockt againe amaine. With that *Myʒaldo* and his wife arose, lighted a candle, and went down to the dore where *Peter* was: Then she wisht hir husband to kneele down upon his knees while she said the charme. With that she began thus:

> " Spirit, spirit, get thee hence,
> For here is no residence:
> Here thou maist not be
> This night to trouble me.

For my husband and I
Safe in our beds must lie,
Therefore from hence goe,
And trouble me no moe."

Now husband, quoth she, spit; and with that he spit, and *Peter* laught
hartily, and wisht he might spit out his teeth for being at home. This
charme said shee thrise over, and every time made him spit, that *Peter*
might be assuredly perswaded that hir husband was at home. Upon that
Myʒaldo and his wife went to bed, and heard the spirit no more; for *Peter*
went laughing home to his lodging.

From *The Cobbler of Caunterberie* (1590), pp. 61–2.
  Very probably borrowed from Boccaccio (VII, no. 1).
  See also the "Go from my Window" songs, such as that introduced into "The
Untrue Wife's Song".

GOOD AND BAD NEWS

Two friends who had not seen each other a great while, meeting by
chance, one asked the other how he did? He replied, that he was not very
well, and was married since they had last met. "That is good news
indeed." "Nay, not so very good neither, for I married a shrew." "That
is bad, too." "Not so bad, neither, for I had two thousand pounds with
her." "That is well again." "Not so well, neither, for I laid it out in sheep,
and they all died of the rot." "That was hard, in truth." "Not so hard,
neither, for I sold the skins for more than the sheep cost me." "Aye, that
made you amends." "Not so much amends, neither, for I laid my money
out in a house, and it was burned." "That was a great loss, indeed." "Not
so great a loss, neither—for my wife was burned in it."

Norton Collection, VI, p. 117. Glasgow.

THE MAN THAT STOLE THE
PARSON'S SHEEP

There was once a man that used to steal a fat sheep every Christmas. One
Christmas he stole the parson's sheep, and his son, a lad about twelve
years old, went about the village singing—

"My father's stolen the parson's sheep,
And a merry Christmas we shall keep,

We shall have both pudding and meat,
But you moant say nought about it."

Now it happened one day that the parson himself heard the boy singing these words, so he said, "My lad, you sing very well; will you come to church next Sunday evening, and sing it there?"

"I've no clothes to go in," said the boy. But the parson said, "If you will come to church as I ask you, I will buy you clothes to go in." The boy agreed, and at the end of the service, the parson said he wished all the people to stay and hear what the boy had to sing to them. But the boy sang,—

"As I was in the field one day,
I saw the parson kiss a may;
He gave me a shilling not to tell,
And these new clothes do fit me well."

S. O. Addy, *Household Tales*, p. 18. Collected in Calver, Derbyshire. Published in *The Folktales of England*, p. 117.

❡ This tale is scattered through Europe, and Baughman gives five United States references.

See also "The Parson's Sheep" and "The Wee Boy and the Minister Grey".

THE MILLER'S EELS

A certeine sir *John*, with some of his companie, once went abroad a jetting, and in a moone light evening robbed a millers weire, and stole all his eeles. The poore miller made his mone to sir *John* himselfe, who willed him to be quiet; for he would so cursse the theefe, and all his confederates, with bell, booke, and candell, that they should have small joy of their fish. And therefore the next sundaie, sir *John* got him to the pulpit, with his surplisse on his backe, and his stole about his necke, and pronounced these words following in the audience of the people.

All you that have stolne the millers eeles,
Laudate Dominum de coelis,
And all they that have consented thereto,
Benedicamus Domino.

Lo (saith he) there is sauce for your eeles my maisters.

Reginald Scot, *Discoverie of Witchcraft*, p. 151.

❡ At a date a little earlier than Scot the same story was told in *Tales and Quick Answers, A Hundred Merry Tales*, racily.

A variant of the tale is known in Finland and Sweden.

THE PAINSWICK ANCIENTS

'Twer ai nation long toime agone—'undreds o' years. Afore beer wur brewed when thur was nu'but waater ter drink, yer min'—not but oi be agun a quilt at times, nor a pipe o' bacca neither. Well, as oi wur a saayin', 'twur afore these things comm'd about, yer onderstan'...Well, some bloke as 'ad a bin hall over the world 'appened ter coom oop along this 'ere road one daay, an' 'e wur tired—a pilgrim, thaay call'd un. Oi dwon't knaaw what a pilgrim be, but 'owever, 'e wur tired, which caused un to set anunst a yep o' stwons, as might be wur we be now....Agen 'im wur squat a mon as looked like a livin' carpse, all shrivelled up, like, who were a blubberin' of 'is 'eart hout. This 'ere travellin' pilgrim, 'ad sid mony a hold man in 'is time, but 'e never coom'd athurt a cove o' t'likes o' this un. Bein' kind o' nesh in 'is 'eart, like, t'pilgrim 'e ups and axes t'bloke what's awry wi' 'e. T'old bloke—a shakin' an' a sobbin'—ses as 'is sheather 'ad bin a yutting of un...T'pilgrim axed un whur 'is sheather did bide, then ketched ault on t'old bloke an' carried un ter Pains'ick... Auter thaay coom'd ter t'sheather's 'ouse, another old mon come ter t'door, nation angered, wi' a dazzed girt stick purt nurly as big as 'issel', seein' as 'e wur bent neigh double, an' 'ad a girt long white beard, as swep' up t' groun'. T'pilgrim, 'e wur flummuxed wi' seein' of a older mon as 'im as 'e carried on 'is back. But bein' kinder venturesome, like, 'e ups an' ses: "Elekee, owd mon, dwon 'ee budge, an' kep thuck stick to theesel'." Then thuck sheather ups an' ses: "Oi'll gie my son a dazzed gurt larropin' if 'e dwon't stop a doin' what 'e 'ave bin adoin'. Cock thee eye oop in yon apple tree, guverner, ool't. 'Is gran'sheather 'ave bin an' rasked 'is old bwones a skinnin' oop thuck tree, auter t'fruit, an' this 'ere rascal 'ave bin a dubbin' of un wi' stones"...When t'pilgrim looked into the tree, 'e wur come over all scared, like, an' 'e cleared off wi' all t' power 'e wur ter able, a saayin' as folk lived for hever in Pains'ick.

Norton Collection, II, p. 211. Farmer, *A Wanderer's Gleanings*, pp 172–4. From an old man between Cranham and Painswick.

THE SECRET AGENT

An agent of a foreign power was sent to a village in mid-Wales, to make contact with another agent, who lived there. The houses had no names nor numbers; so, being at a loss, he knocked at a door at random. A woman put her head out of an upper window, and called down: "What do you want?"

"Does Mr Jones live here?" he asked.

"Yes, he does. What do you want with him?"

Looking uneasily about him, the man, as softly as possible, gave a secret code word.

"Oh, no, man!" in a loud clear voice. "Jones the Spy lives two doors further down."

Told to Margaret Nash-Williams at Oxford, about 1965.

There are various stories told about localities where everyone has the same name; as that about one of the Highland regiments where a stranger came enquiring for Ian MacGregor. "Which Ian MacGregor will you be meaning? There are twenty-five Ian MacGregors here." "It's Red Ian MacGregor I want." "Twenty of them are red.' "Well, the red Ian MacGregor I'm wanting has the itch." "Ach, man, twenty-four of them have the itch!"

THE THREE SILLIES

Once upon a time there was a farmer and his wife who had one daughter, and she was courted by a gentleman. Every evening he used to come and see her, and stop to supper at the farmhouse, and the daughter used to be sent down into the cellar to draw the beer for supper. So one evening she had gone down to draw the beer, and she happened to look up at the ceiling while she was drawing, and she saw a mallet stuck in one of the beams. It must have been there a long, long time, but somehow or other she had never noticed it before, and she began a-thinking. And she thought it was very dangerous to have that mallet there, for she said to herself: "Suppose him and me was to be married, and we was to have a son, and he was to grow up to be a man, and come down into the cellar to draw the beer, like I'm doing now, and the mallet was to fall on his head and kill him, what a dreadful thing it would be!" And she put down the candle and the jug, and sat herself down and began a-crying.

Well, they began to wonder upstairs how it was that she was so long drawing the beer, and her mother went down to see after her, and she found her sitting on the settle crying, and the beer running over the floor. "Why, whatever is the matter?" said her mother. "Oh, mother!" says she, "look at that horrid mallet! Suppose we was to be married, and was to have a son, and he was to grow up, and was to come down into the cellar to draw the beer, and the mallet was to fall on his head and kill him, what a dreadful thing it would be."

"Dear, dear! what a dreadful thing it would be!" said the mother, and she sat down aside of the daughter, and started a-crying too. Then after a bit the father began to wonder that they didn't come back, and he went down into the cellar to look after them himself, and there they two sat a-crying, and the beer running all over the floor. "Whatever is the matter?" says he. "Why," says the mother, "look at that horrid mallet. Just suppose, if our daughter and her sweetheart was to be married, and was to have a son, and he was to grow up, and was to come down into the cellar to draw the beer, and the mallet was to fall on his head and kill him, what a dreadful thing it would be!"

"Dear, dear, dear! so it would!" said the father, and he sat himself down aside of the other two, and started a-crying.

Now the gentleman got tired of stopping up in the kitchen by himself, and at last he went down into the cellar too, to see what they were after; and there they three sat a-crying side by side, and the beer running all over the floor.

And he ran straight and turned the tap. Then he said: "Whatever are you three doing, sitting there crying, and letting the beer run all over the floor?"

"Oh," says the father, "look at that horrid mallet! Suppose you and our daughter was to be married, and was to have a son, and he was to grow up, and was to come down into the cellar to draw the beer, and the mallet was to fall on his head and kill him!" And then they all started a-crying worse than before.

But the gentleman burst out a-laughing, and reached up and pulled out the mallet, and then he said: "I've travelled many miles, and I never met three such big sillies as you three before; and now I shall start out on my travels again, and when I can find three bigger sillies than you three, then I'll come back and marry your daughter." So he wished them goodbye, and started off on his travels, and left them all crying because the girl had lost her sweetheart.

Well, he set out, and he travelled a long way, and at last he came to a woman's cottage that had some grass growing on the roof. And the woman was trying to get her cow to go up a ladder to the grass, and the poor thing durst not go. So the gentleman asked the woman what she was doing. "Why, lookye," she said, "look at all that beautiful grass. I'm going to get the cow on to the roof to eat it. She'll be quite safe, for I shall tie a string round her neck and pass it down the chimney, and tie it to my wrist as I go about the house, so she can't fall off without my knowing it."

"Oh, you poor silly!" said the gentleman, "you should cut the grass and throw it down to the cow!" But the woman thought it was easier to get the cow up the ladder than to get the grass down, so she pushed her and coaxed her and got her up, and tied a string round her neck, and passed it down the chimney, and fastened it to her own wrist. And the gentleman went on his way, but he hadn't gone far when the cow tumbled off the roof, and hung by the string tied round her neck, and it strangled her. And the weight of the cow tied to her wrist pulled the woman up the chimney, and she stuck fast half-way, and was smothered in the soot.

Well, that was one big silly.

And the gentleman went on and on, and he went to an inn to stop the night, and they were so full at the inn that they had to put him in a double-bedded room, and another traveller was to sleep in the other bed. The other man was a very pleasant fellow, and they got very friendly together; but in the morning, when they were both getting up, the gentleman was surprised to see the other hang his trousers on the knobs of the chest of drawers and run across the room and try to jump into them, and he tried over and over again, and he couldn't manage it; and the gentleman wondered whatever he was doing it for. At last he stopped and wiped his face with his handkerchief. "Oh dear," he says, "I do think trousers are the most awkwardest kind of clothes that ever were. I can't think who could have invented such things. It takes me the best part of an hour to get into mine every morning, and I get so hot! How do you manage yours?" So the gentleman burst out a-laughing, and showed him to put them on; and he was very much obliged to him, and said he should never have thought of doing it that way.

So that was another big silly.

Then the gentleman went on his travels again; and he came to a village, and outside the village there was a pond, and round the pond was a crowd of people: And they had got rakes, and brooms, and pitchforks, reaching into the pond; and the gentleman asked what was the matter. "Why," they say, "matter enough! Moon's tumbled into the pond, and we can't rake her out anyhow!" So the gentleman burst out a-laughing, and told them to look up into the sky, and that it was only the shadow in the water. But they wouldn't listen to him, and abused him shamefully, and he got away as quick as he could.

So there was a whole lot of sillies bigger than them three sillies at home.

So the gentleman turned back home again, and married the farmer's daughter, and if they don't live happy for ever after, that's nothing to do with you or me.

Joseph Jacobs, *English Fairy Tales*, p. 9. From Burne and Jackson, *Shropshire Folklore*.

THE TWO PICKPOCKETS

There was a provincial pickpocket who was very successful at his work, and he thought he'd go up to London and see what he could do there. So he went up to London, and he was even more successful. One day he was busy in Oxford Street when he suddenly found that his own pocket-book had been taken. He looked round and saw a very attractive blonde girl walking away. He was sure that she was the one who had picked his pocket, so he followed her and got his pocket-book back from her. He was so much taken by her cleverness in robbing him that he suggested that they should go into partnership together. And so they did, and succeeded brilliantly. At length the provincial pickpocket thought: "We're the best pickpockets in London. If we married we could breed up a race of the best pickpockets in the world." So he asked the girl ,and she was quite agreeable, and they were married, and in due time a beautiful little baby boy was born to them. But the poor little fellow was deformed. His right arm was bent to his chest, and the little fist tightly clenched. And nothing they could do would straighten it. The poor parents were much distressed. "He'll never make a pickpocket," they said, "with a paralysed right arm." They took him at once to the doctor, but the doctor said he was too young, they must wait. But they didn't want to wait; they took him to one doctor after another, and at last—because they were very rich by this time—to the best child-specialist they could hear of. The specialist took out his gold watch, and felt the pulse on the little paralysed arm. "The flow of blood seems normal," he said. "What a bright little fellow he is for his age! He's focusing his eyes on my watch." He took the chain out of his waistcoat, and swung the watch to and fro, and the baby's eyes followed it. Then the little bent arm straightened out towards the watch, the little clenched fingers opened to take it, and down dropped the mid-wife's gold wedding-ring.

K. M. Briggs, from Ella Lowe, who heard it from her sister in London, some years before. Burford, February 1968.
¶ This type is known in India and Hawaii. See also "The Stolen Sheep".

YORKSHIRE FOLLIES

The considerate bandsman

Almost every village in the West Riding claims the story of the brass band which got back late at night after winning the band contest. So as not to wake the village they tiptoed up the main street in their stockinged feet; and, at the same time, to mark the triumphant occasion, they played *See the Conquering Hero Comes* at full blast.

Norton Collection, IV, p. 36 [extract]. From M. Wilson, Leeds.

PART 4
NOVELLE

Novelle may be called "Naturalistic Fairy Tales". The loutish simpleton of a hero gains the hand of the Princess, but without the help of a golden goose; the constancy and truth of the ill-used heroine win her happiness in the end but there is no fairy godmother to help her.

For the knowledge of most of these tales, though fortunately not all, we are dependent upon early literary sources; the matter not the manner is traditional. Many of these are linked with history as, for instance, the story of King Lear and Cordelia, a variant of "Cap O' Rushes", or King John and the Abbot of Canterbury, a widespread tale studied by Walter Anderson in *Kaiser und Abt*; or the equally travelled tale of "The Professor of Signs". Many have survived in Ballads, particularly the Outlaw tales, the Robin Hood stories or "Adam Bell, Clym of the Clough and William of Cloudesley". There are English Blue Beard stories of less sympathetic ruffians: "Mr Fox" was known to Shakespeare and Spenser and has survived orally in Somerset, and versions of it have also been preserved in the retentive memory of the Travelling People of these Islands. A particularly lively and entertaining version of the Chapbook Princess of Canterbury is "The King of the Liars" told to Hamish Henderson by Andra Steward in 1956. Type 910, Precepts Bought or Given Prove Correct, is to be found in all its forms. The one given here is "The Tale of Ivan" from Cornwall, of which again a more modern version is to be found in the Archives of the School of Scottish Studies. Many other plots, romantic, tragic and humorous, are to be found among the Novelle, of which this Sampler can give only a gleaning.

ADAM BEL, CLYM OF THE CLOUGH AND WILLIAM OF CLOUDESLEY

Merry and joyous it is in the green forest, when the leaves are full and broad, to walk beneath its breezy shade and hearken to the wild birds' song.

It is of three good yeomen of the north country that I seek at present to tell you all: Adam Bel, Clym of the Clough, and William of Cloudesley. Archers of approved skill were they, and outlawed for venison; and in the town of Carlisle where they dwelled, they sware brotherhood, and to the forest betook them. Whereof twain were single men; but Cloudesley had taken unto him a wife, and with moist eyes he brake from fair Alice, and the children clasped to his knee, to lead a strange new life in Inglewood with his two comrades, their hand against every man, and every man against them.

So they made such shift as they could, and passed their days amid the forest glades and lawns, sustaining themselves on the king's venison and the water of the brook; and ever and again a little boy, who had served Cloudesley as his swineherd, was sent to him privily, and brought him and the others victuals and raiment and news withal.

Till, after a certain space of time, Cloudesley waxed homesick, thinking often on his young wife Alice and his sweet little ones, whom he had left behind him; and he said to the others, that he would fain make his way to Carlisle, to gladden his eyes with the sight of them all once more. For Alice, while she caused the little swineherd to pass to and fro with meat for the foresters, held it unwise to charge the boy with any message praying Cloudesley to come unto her, seeing that she was so straitly observed.

Then said Adam Bel to him: "Ye go not, brother, by mine advice; for if ye be marked and the justice take ye, your life is even at an end. Stay, prythee, where ye are, and be content."

But Cloudesley replied: "Nay, wend thither I must; and if so I return not to you and Clym by noon, ye may augur that I am taken or slain."

And when his brethren saw that they might nowise prevail upon him they said no more, and he departed on his way, as it drew toward evening.

With a light step, and an anxious heart, he sped along till he came to the gates of Carlisle, and he passed in thereat disguised, that no man might discern who he was; and he paused not till he was at his own window, and called on Alice his wife to undo the door, for it was her own William who stood without.

Then when the joy of the meeting had a little abated, fair Alice gazed at him pensively, and said: "William, it is so that this house has been watched and beset for you this half-year or more."

But he replied to her: "Now I am here, bring me to eat and drink, and let us make good cheer while we may."

Now there was an old wife in the chimney corner, that Cloudesley had harboured for charity's sake some seven years, and that had not of long time set foot on ground. This shrew and cursed crone, albeit she had eaten his bread so long, seized her occasion, and crept privily to the sheriff, where he lived, and warned him that that very night William the outlaw had by stealth come into the town, and was even now securely at home, where they might have him.

The sheriff caused the bell to be rung, and the justice and the sheriff getting their men together, they soon encompassed the house round on every side. Then Cloudesley made all the doors fast, and took his sword and buckler and bow, and with his three children and fair Alice his wife mounted the stair to an upper chamber, where he imagined that he might withstand them all; and by his side his true wedded wife held a poleaxe in her hand.

Cloudesley bent his bow, and the arrow shivered in two against the justice's breastplate. "Beshrew the varlet," muttered Cloudesley, "that dressed thee in that coat; if it had not been thicker than mine, thou hadst not spoken more."

"Yield, Cloudesley," cried the justice, "and give up thy arms."

"A curse light on him," cried Alice, "who lendeth us such counsel!"

And they kept them all at a distance, for Cloudesley was at the window, with his bow ready bent, and none durst break the doors, so true an archer was he.

"Set fire on the house, since there is no other way," shouted the sheriff; and they did as he bad, and the flames quickly rose. Cloudesley opened a back window, and let down his wife and his children, and said to the sheriff, "For Christ's love, hurt them not, but wreak all your ire on me." And he kept his bow busy till all his arrows were spent and the fire nigh burnt his bowstring in twain.

"This is a coward's death," he exclaimed, "and liever had I fallen sword in hand than thus." And he cast down his bow, and taking his sword and buckler, leaped down among the throng, and smote them on every side, till only by hurling doors and windows at him could they make prisoner that stout and bold yeoman.

Then they bound him hand and foot, and led him to prison and the justice commanded that he should be hanged the next morning, and that the gates should be shut, so that none might enter thereat. For the justice doubted that Adam Bel and Clym of the Clough might gain tidings of their fellow, and might essay to rescue him from the gallows.

"Not Adam Bel, nor Clym, nor all the devils in Hell," quoth the justice, "shall save thee from the rope this time."

Early in the morning a pair of new gallows was erected in the market place, nigh the pillory, and the gates of Carlisle were locked.

Now Alice, seeing no other remedy, had that same night that Cloudesley was taken despatched with all speed to Inglewood the little swineherd, who crept unobserved through a crevice in the wall after dusk, and lost not a moment in finding the two foresters, where they lay under the greenwood shade.

"Too long, too long," cried he, "tarry ye here, ye good yeomen. Cloudesley is taken, and tomorrow betimes he shall be hanged on a new gallows in the market-place."

"He might have dwelled with us in peace," said Adam Bel, "as I prayed him heartily to do, and now here is a shrewd pass." And he took his bow in his hand, and a buck that bounded by was stretched suddenly on the ground. "That will serve us for our breakfast," said he, "ere we go. Fetch me my arrow again, boy, for we shall have need enough."

Now when these yeomen had eaten their meal hastily, they girded on their swords, and took their bows and arrows and bucklers, and sped on their way, for time pressed, and it was a fair May morning when they reached the gates of Carlisle.

II

"We must devise some sleight," said Clym of the Clough, "to get in. Let us say that we are messengers from the king."

"I have a fair letter," quoth the other; "we will declare that we have the king's signet; the porter is, I warrant, no clerk."

They beat hard at the door, and when the porter heard that they had the king's seal, he unlocked the gate, and let them enter.

"Now we are in," whispered Adam Bel; "but by Heaven! I do not know how we shall make our way out again."

"Let us seize the keys," whispered Clym.

They beckoned the porter to them, and wrang his neck, and cast his body into a corner.

"Now am I porter in his room," cried Adam, "the worst they have had here in Carlisle this hundred year."

And without more ado they hastened to the market-place, placing themselves where they might not be noted. They espied the gallows, and the justice with his inquest, that had ajudged Cloudesley to die, and Cloudesley hard by in a cart, bound hand and foot, with a rope round his neck.

The justice called a boy, and promised him the outlaw's clothes, if he would dig his grave against the time for despatch. Cloudesley cast his eye aside, where his two brethren stood, and he said to the justice: "Such wonders have happened ere now as that a man who diggeth a grave for another lieth in it himself."

But the justice answered and said: "Ah! thou talkest proudly. I will hang thee, fellow, with my own hand."

Scarce had the words fallen from him, when an arrow pierced his breast, and a second the sheriff's; the rest began to scatter, and Adam, running up to the cart, loosed Cloudesley, who wrenched an axe from a man near him. There was a panic; the bells were rung backward, the outhorns were blown, and the mayor with a strong force behind him arrived with their bills and their swords.

The foresters, when they saw them, were dismayed by their numbers, and retreated towards the gate; and when they could no longer use their bows, they cut down all that came near with their swords, till at last they reached the gate, and unlocked it; and when they were without, Adam Bel threw the keys at the heads of the mayor's men, and cried: "I give up my office. Prythee, elect a new porter." And they waited not to see what further befell but took their way back to Inglewood, where Cloudesley found fair Alice and his children three, that had thought him dead; and there was great rejoicing among them all and they feasted to their heart's ease.

Then, when those three bold foresters, with Alice and her children three, had supped merrily together, and they had rested somewhat after that notable work at Carlisle, quoth Cloudesley to the others: "Brethren mine, let us even go straightway to London to our king to seek his grace, ere the tidings come to his ear, how the justice and sheriff be slain, with many more; and Alice and two of my children shall repair to a nunnery hereby, and my eldest son I shall take with me."

So, when they came to London, they sought our lord the king, pushing bluffly past the porter at the palace gate, and the usher, and all, who pressed after them in a body to know what they would have; and they said they had travelled far to obtain from the king a charter of peace.

When they were brought into the presence of our lord the king, they fell on their knees, as the law of the land was, and each held up his hand;

and they said: "Lord, we beseech thee to grant us grace, for we have slain your highness's deer."

"What are your names?" asked the king.

"Adam Bel, Clym of the Clough, and William Cloudesley."

"Ah! ye be those thieves," returned the king, "that men have reported so oft to me? Gramercy, sirs, I shall see well that ye be hanged without more ado."

"We pray your highness," said they again, "that you will suffer us to leave you with our arms in our hands till we are out of this place, and we will seek no farther grace."

"You talk rather proudly," quoth the king. "Nay, nay; ye shall be of a surety hanged all three."

Now the queen, hearing the news of these archers having made so long a journey to see her lord the king, came to him, praying him, as he had made promise to her on their marriage to grant the first boon she should ask, to yield unto her the lives of those three yeomen; and the king, albeit he was wroth that she should have begged so mean a thing, when she might have had market-towns, castles and forests to her use and pleasure, said unto her: "I depart not, madam, from my word; they are yours."

"My lord," she said, "much thanks. I undertake that they shall become to your grace good men and true. But, prythee, speak a word to them, that they may know your bounty to them."

"You are pardoned, fellows," our lord the king said thereupon. "Go now, wash, and sit to meat."

A crafty man was William of Cloudesley, who thought of fair Alice and his sweet children, and wist well that the men of Carlisle would send messengers to London without delay to apprise our lord the king of what had there befallen; and, certes, scarcely were those three yeomen assoiled by our lady the queen's favour, when, as they sat at meat in the king's kitchen, there came a post from the north country to disclose the whole thing as it was.

The messengers kneeled, and presented their letters, saying, "Lord, your officers of Carlisle in the north country greet you well." And when our lord the king brake the seal, he was a sad man; for he found that those three yeomen, to whom he had granted grace, and leave to wash and eat at his board, had slain three hundred and more, with the justice and the sheriff, and the mayor and many other, and had ravaged his parks, and killed his deer, and by all that country were held in dread.

"Take away the meat," cried the king. "I can touch no more. What archers be these, that can do such feats with their bow? Marry, I have none such. Methinks I will see them shoot." And his grace commanded that his bowmen, and the queen's, should forthwith hold a meeting, and set up butts. Whereto Adam Bel, Clym of the Clough and William of Cloudesley were summoned to come.

They all took their turns, and the king's bowmen, and the queen's, put out their whole strength and skill before those three yeomen of the north country; but those three yeomen carried everything; and there was much marvelling at such archery.

But William of Cloudesley spake and said: "Gramercy, I hold him no archer that shooteth at such wide butts."

"What wouldest thou, then?" demanded the king.

"Such a butt, lord," he answered, "as men use in my country."

And the king gave him leave that he should shew his meaning.

Then Cloudesley took two hazel wands in his hand, and set them up two hundred paces apart, and said to the king: "Whoso cleaveth them both in twain, I hold him an archer indeed."

No man that was with the king raised his voice or made a sign, but all were still and silent; and the king said: "There is none here who can do such a thing."

"I shall try then," said Cloudesley, stepping forward suddenly; and fixing a bearing arrow in his bow, he drew it to the head, and split both the wands in two.

"Thou art the best archer," exclaimed the king, delightedly, "that I ever beheld."

"Wait a moment, lord," said Cloudesley," and I will shew your grace even more. Here is my little son, seven years old; dear enough to his mother and to me he is. Grieved in our hearts were we if any misadventure should befall him; yet, lo! I will bind him to a stake, and place an apple on his head, and at sixscore paces I will cut the apple in two."

None believed that even Cloudesley had the courage and steadfastness to achieve such a deed. But he called his son to him and fastened him with his back towards him, lest he might wince, to a post, and the apple was laid upon the child's head, and sixscore paces were measured out. Cloudesley stood motionless for an instant, not a breath was heard throughout all that meeting, and many prayed for the yeoman that God would protect him in his task, and some wept. He drew out a broad shaft, fixed it in his good bow, and the next moment the apple fell from the child's head, and not a hair was stirred.

"God forbid," cried the king, "that thou shouldest shoot at me! I perceive how my officers in Carlisle sped so ill when they had such a foe. But I have tried thee sorely, William, and thou art an exceeding good archer. I give thee eighteenpence a day, and thy clothing, and make thee a gentleman, and chief forester of my north country; and thy brethren twain shall be yemen of my chamber. Thy little son, whom thou so lovest, I will place in my wine cellar, and when he cometh to man's estate, he shall be farther preferred."

So said the king; and our lady the queen commanded that Alice should be brought to London to the court, and should be set over her nursery.

So fared these three yeomen excellently well through the mastery of William of Cloudesley and the gracious offices of our lady the queen; and when they had gone on pilgrimage to Rome, to our holy father the pope, to obtain remission of their sins against God, they returned to their own land, and lived ever after in ease and worship.

W. Carew Hazlitt, *National Tales and Legends*, p. 324. Cf. Child, III, p. 174, no. 116.

CAP O' RUSHES

Well, there was once a very rich gentleman, and he'd three darters. And he thought to see how fond they was of him. So he says to the first, "How much do you love me, my dear?" "Why," says she, "as I love my life." "That's good," says he. So he says to the second, "How much do you love me, my dear?" "Why," says she, "better nor all the world." "That's good," says he.

So he says to the third, "How much do *you* love me, my dear?" "Why," says she, "I love you as fresh meat loves salt," says she. Well, he were that angry. "You don't love me at all," says he, "and in my house you stay no more." So he drove her out there and then, and shut the door in her face.

Well, she went away, on and on, till she came to a fen. And there she gathered a lot of rushes, and made them into a cloak, kind o', with a hood, to cover her from head to foot, and to hide her fine clothes. And then she went on and on, till she came to a great house.

"Do you want a maid?" says she.

"No, we don't," says they.

"I hain't nowhere to go," says she, "and I'd ask no wages, and do any sort o' work," says she.

"Well," says they, "if you like to wash the pots and scrape the saucepans, you may stay," says they.

So she stayed there, and washed the pots and scraped the saucepans, and did all the dirty work. And because she gave no name, they called her Cap o' Rushes.

Well, one day there was to be a great dance a little way off, and the servants was let go and look at the grand people. Cap o' Rushes said she was too tired to go, so she stayed at home.

But when they was gone, she offed with her cap o' rushes, and cleaned herself, and went to the dance. And no one there was so finely dressed as her.

Well, who should be there but her master's son, and what should he do but fall in love with her, the minute he set eyes on her. He wouldn't dance with anyone else.

But before the dance were done, Cap o' Rushes she stepped off, and away she went home. And when the other maids was back, she was framin' to be asleep with her cap o' rushes on.

Well, next morning, they says to her:

"You did miss a sight, Cap o' Rushes!"

"What was that?" says she.

"Why the beautifullest lady you ever see, dressed right gay and ga'. The young master, he never took his eyes off of her."

"Well, I should ha' liked to have seen her," says Cap o' Rushes.

"Well, there's to be another dance this evening, and perhaps she'll be there."

But, come the evening, Cap o' Rushes said she was too tired to go with them. Howsumdever, when they was gone, she offed with her cap o' rushes, and cleaned herself, and away she went to the dance.

The master's son had been reckoning on seeing her, and he danced with no one else, and never took his eyes off of her.

But before the dance was over, she slipped off and home she went, and when the maids came back, she framed to be asleep with her cap o' rushes on.

Next day they says to her again:

"Well, Cap o' Rushes, you should ha' been there to see the lady. There she was again, gay an' ga', and the young master he never took his eyes off of her."

"Well, there," says she, "I should ha' liked to ha' seen her."

"Well," says they, "there's a dance again this evening, and you must go with us, for she's sure to be there."

Well, come the evening, Cap o' Rushes said she was too tired to go, an do what they would, she stayed at home. But when they was gone, she offed with her cap o' rushes, and cleaned herself, and away she went to the dance.

The master's son was rarely glad when he saw her. He danced with none but her, and never took his eyes off her. When she wouldn't tell him her name, nor where she came from, he gave her a ring, and told her if he didn't see her again he should die.

Well, afore the dance was over, off she slipped, and home she went, and when the maids came home she was framing to be asleep with her cap o' rushes on.

Well, next day they says to her: "There, Cap o' Rushes, you didn't come last night, and now you won't see the lady, for there's no more dances."

"Well, I should ha' rarely liked to ha' seen her," says she.

The master's son, he tried every way to find out where the lady was gone, but go where he might, and ask whom he might, he never heard nothing about her. And he got worse and worse for the love of her, till he had to keep his bed.

"Make some gruel for the young master," they says to the cook, "he's dying for love of the lady." The cook she set about making it, when Cap o' Rushes came in.

"What are you a' doin' on?" says she.

"I'm going to make some gruel for the young master," says the cook, "for he's dying for love of the lady."

"Let me make it," says Cap o' Rushes.

Well, the cook wouldn't at first, but at last she said yes; and Cap o' Rushes made the gruel. And when she had made it, she slipped the ring into it on the sly, before the cook took it upstairs.

The young man, he drank it, and saw the ring at the bottom.

"Send for the cook," says he. So up she comes.

"Who made this here gruel?" says he.

"I did," says the cook, for she were frightened, and he looked at her.

"No, you didn't," says he. "Say who did it, and you shan't be harmed."

"Well, then, 'twas Cap o' Rushes," says she.

So Cap o' Rushes came.

"Did you make the gruel?" says he.

"Yes, I did," says she.

"Where did you get this ring?" says he.

"From him as gave it me," says she.

"Who are you then?" says the young man.

"I'll show you," says she. And she offed with her cap o' rushes, and there she was in her beautiful clothes.

Well, the master's son he got well very soon, and they was to be married in a little time. It was to be a very grand wedding, and everyone was asked, far and near. And Cap o' Rushes' father was asked. But she never told nobody who she was.

But afore the wedding she went to the cook, and says she, "I want you to dress every dish without a mite o' salt."

"That will be rarely nasty," says the cook.

"That don't signify," says she. "Very well," says the cook.

Well, the wedding day came, and they was married. And after they was married, all the company sat down to their vittles.

When they began to eat the meat, that was so tasteless they couldn't eat it. But Cap o' Rushes' father, he tried first one dish and then another, and then he burst out crying.

"What's the matter?" said the master's son to him.

"Oh!" says he, "I had a daughter. And I asked her how much she loved me. And she said, 'As much as fresh meat loves salt.' And I turned her from my door, for I thought she didn't love me. And now I see she loved me best of all. And she may be dead for aught I know."

"No, father, here she is," says Cap o' Rushes.

And she goes up to him and puts her arms round him. And so they was happy ever after.

E. S. Hartland, *County Folk-Lore*, I. Suffolk, p. 40 (told by an old servant to the writer when a child); A.W.T., "Suffolk Notes and Queries", *Ipswich Journal* (1877).
    See also "Catskin", (A, II), *Ashy Pelt*, (A, II), "Mossycoat", (A, II).

THE KING OF THE LIARS [transcription from tape]

Well, this was a king, and he was very ill. His wife was deid, ye see, and he'd one daughter, and he sent in for the daughter one day, and he says, "Look here", he says, "ye can prepare yoursel' for a shock," he says. "In about a year's time, the doctor's told me," he says, "I might pass away, maybe before it. Now I think," he said, "ye should get up the Good Advisers here to me, and I'll tell them what I'm going to do with my kingdom, ye see, before I die. I want ye," he says," to go down for them now and take them up."

So anyway the girl went out and she was aafie forlorn-like about her father dyin', and took the three Wise Men (as they cry them) up to the side of the King's bed, ye see. So the king told them that he was dyin' jist any time, the doctor said, and he wanted a man to reign as king, ye see. (Are ye listenin', Toby?)

"I've made up my mind," says the king, he says, "the man that can make me call him a liar will get my daughter's hand in marriage, and my kingdom, ye see."

"Well, that soonds fair enough," says the Good Adviser, he says, "if ye want to do that, fair enough," he says, "but it could go on for years, this carry-on."

"No, no," he says, "I think if the right man comes in, a clever man that can trap me, that I can call him a liar, he'll get my daughter's hand in marriage."

"Very well," said the Good Advisers, "we'll leave it at that."

Well, for the first nine months, there was knights, nobles, tramps off the road, earls and dukes, and all these Knights of the Round Stables, come to tell the King that—to see if they could make him a liar—tell him the story, you see. But none of them succeeded in making the king cry him a liar.

Now, to make a long story short, Toby, at the bottom of the old wood there was a wee, what they call a toll-hoose, and there was a lazy laddie in there—they cried him Silly Jeck the Water Cairrier. He done nothing but cairried water to the servants in the castle—carried water to his mother, and he lay and slep' amongst the cinders, and he scraped the pots—for meat, ye see, when he was hungry.

So the mother got on to him one day—she was an auld wummin and she was milkin' the coo, and she says, "Jeck," she says, "wil ye no break a wee bit of stick for the mornin's fire?"

"Ach, mother," he says, "I'm tired," he says, "I want a sleep."

"A sleep," she says, "ye've duin nothing aa day," she says, "but lie, aboot that barn oot there," she says. "Ye'll no dig the gairden," she says, "ye'll do nothing. Ye'll no take the coo oot to the field."

"Ach, well," says Jeck, "if that's the way o't," he says, "I'm goin' away up to the king's castle," he says, "and I'm goin' to tell him a story, anyway," he says.

"You tell him a story!" she says. "If you go up near the King's castle," she says, "ye'll get shot."

"Well," he says, "I was speakin' tae a man in the toon the day," he says, "oniebody can go up," he says, "tramps off the road can go, and I'm jist as good to go," he says, "and tell him a story, as the next yin."

"Oh well," she says, "laddie, please yersel," she says, "but I hope ye win," she says.

"Ach, well, mother," he says, "I'll go up and see, onieway."

Well, Jeck had nae sword, but when he was goin' into a place like that—he was half-daft—he tied a scythe-blade wi' a big string at the side of his —— roon his waist, to let on he had a sword, ye see, tied to his side, a scythe-blade. He took this wi' him for protection. He marches doon this big drive, ye see, throu' the gates, and here a soldier—a guard—stopped him at the gate, ye see, one of the soldiers, and he says,

"Hullo," he says, "Jeck, where are you goin'?" he says,—aa the sodgers kent Jeck, ye see—aa the guardsmen kent Jeck—Jeck says,

"I'm goin' in," he says, "to see the King."

"Haw, haw, haw," he says, "you goin' to see the King, Jeck. Man," he says, "dinnae be silly," he says; "if you go in there," he says, "the sodgers 'll chase ye oot," he says. "Ye'll be the laugh at ye."

"No, no," says Jeck, "I don't think you've onie right to stop me," he says, "ye'd better let me by."

"Oh, well," he says—the sodger bowed to Jeck, makin' a fool of—he says, "all right," he says, "in you go," he says, "away you go."

So, anyway, Jeck marches in, thought he was a sodger, ye see, and the scythe-blade was swinging' back and forrit frae his side—and he goes up to the door, and aa the sodgers and the guards in the castle's laughin' at him passin'.

Up, and he knocks at the big knocker on the door, ye see, and the butler's come oot—man wi' a red coat, swallow-tail coat, cam oot, and he says—everybody kent him well, ye see—

"Jeck," he says, "what are ye doin here?" he says, "I hope ye're not thinkin'," he says, "the cow's roon about the castle here," he says; "you lookin' for your coo?"

"Naw," said Jeck, "I'm up to see the King."

"Well," says the ——, says, "What are ye up to see the King aboot?"

He says, "I'm up," he says, "to see," he says, "if I can cry him a liar."

"Oh, ye are! Oh well," says the butler, he says, "ye're jist as well to have a go as well as any other body," he says, "Jeck, I cannae keep ye back," he says. "It's free to all comers."

·Jeck went, ye see, and the maids is lookin' at Jack, inside, and laughin' at Jeck, at his old guttery boots, ye know, and his old torn trousers—he hadnae a patch on the airse o' his troosers—his shirt-tail was hingin' oot. So, anyway, up he goes on this plush carpets, red carpets, up the stair, ye see, and he goes up to the King's Castle, and they rang a bell, ye see, at the door, and the Good Advisers invited Jeck in. So Jeck saluted the King, ye see, and he says,

"How ye gettin' on, King," he says; "ye've been a long time lyin' in bed?"

"Aye," says he, "Jeck, I have. I havenae seen you," he says, "for years."

"No," he says, says Jeck, "and I don't like comin' to visit oniebody," he says, "in a state of this kind," he says, "seein' ye're no-weill in bed. For", he says, "I cam' up," he says, "King," he says, "to win your daughter's hann in marriage."

So the King looks at him, ye see—weighs him up and doon. The Good Advisers gied a wee-bit smile t'each other, so the King gien a wave wi' his hann for them to g'ootside, ye see. So the Good Advisers turns and walks oot of the room.

So this great big stately room, ye see, and Jeck wi' his guttery boots, and he lookit terrible-lookin', stannin' aside the King in the bed; and he startit tellin' the King the story.

Noo, this is the story that Jeck tell't the King, ye see.

He says, "You have knew my father," he says, "King," he says, "before he died?"

"Yes, a fine man," he says, "your father was, Jeck."

"Ah, but," says Jack, "he wasna good as me."

"Was he no?" said the King.

"No," says Jeck. "D'ye mean to cry me a liar?"

"Oh, no," said the King.

"Well," he says, "my father turned very ill," he says.

"Yes," said the King.

"And," he says, "I was left to run the wee-bit land doon there mysel'."

"Oh, I see," says the King. He says, "What did ye dae, Jeck?"

"Well," he says, "when my father died," he says, "I had to cut corn," he says, "cut wheat," he says, "and dae aa this things, and," he says, "d'ye ken what I cut it wi'?"

The King looked at his side, and he says, "Wi' your scythe-blade," he says, "I mean that sword you've got at your side," the King says tae him.

"Naw, naw," he says, "it wisnae the sword," he says, "it was wi' a heuk." (Noo a heuk's a wee thing ye cut grass wi'—ye see roadmen usin' it, at the side of the roads—a wee hookit thing like a big knife, like a knife. No, something like a neap-shar, but no a neap-shar—it's a heuk, for cuttin' grass.)

So, anyway, Jeck says, "I've cut," he says, "forty acre of wheat," he

80

says, "or corn," he says, "in two hours."

"God bless us!" says the King, he says. "Ye must hae been goin'—jist yerself', Jeck?"

"Jist mysel'," says Jeck. "D'ye mean to cry me a liar?"

"Oh, no," said the King. "I'll no cry you a liar."

"Well," he says, "I started, it was a bonnie morn," he says, "and the birds was whistlin', and I started cuttin' the corn, and," he says, "jist when I was goin' away to start," he says, "what comes oot of the corn," he says, "but a broon hare. And," he says, "wi' the excitement I ran eftir the hare," he says, "I'm aye fond of stewed hare," he says, "and rabbits," he says, "and I'd nae dog or nothin'," he says, "I was jist a herd, and I took the heuk and I threw it eftir the hare. And," he says, "it stuck, and then the heuk whirlt throu the air, and it stuck in the hare's back-end—the hannle of the heuk. Noo," he says, "the hare went roon the corn, and went roon the corn and went roon the corn," he says, "aboot forty mile-an-hour, and the heuk stickin' in its —— here. Roon the corn, and roon the corn it went, till it flattened every taste of corn in the field," he says, "less nor an hour."

"God bless us," says the King. "I never heard the like of that before, Jeck."

"D'ye mean to cry me a liar?" says Jeck.

"Oh, no," said the King.

"Well," he says, "now," he says, "there was a great famine," he says, "started," he says. "That was a poor year," he says, "for corn and wheat," he says. "What you know," he says, "the famine."

"What famine?" said the King.

"The big famine," he said, "before my father died."

The King says, "I never seen nae famine."

"D'ye mean to cry me a liar?"

"Oh, no," says the King. "I'll no cry ye a liar."

"Well," he says, "it was the year of the big famine," he says, "and here," he says, "nobody in Britain," he says, "England or Scotland," he says, "had wheat. The boats," he says, "were stormy", he says, "stormy in the sea," he says, "at that time. There were gale eftir gale," he says, "for aboot six weeks, and the boats couldnae get across," he says, "tae other countries, to get wheat or corn or meal owre to this country."

"I cannae mind of that," says the King.

"Ah, well," says Jeck, "I can mind it," he says, "and I dint think I'm a liar, am I, King?"

"No," he says, "ye're nae liar," he says.

"Well," he says, "what are ye speakin' aboot?" he says to the King.

"Well, that's aa right," says the King, he says. "Carry on. What happent?"

So the King's gettin' interested in this, ye see. He thocht Jeck was silly, but he's no so silly: he didnae think what to make of him.

"But anyway," he says, "well," he says, "there were no boats, but I went up," he says, "to tell aa the heid men," he says, "in the toon, that I would get wheat and corn back," he says, "in aboot a day's time. So they looked at me," he says, "and they laughed at me." He says, "Ye needna laugh," says he to them, he says, "I'll get wheat and corn," he says, "back," he says, "in nae time t'ye," he says, "jist maybe aboot a day."

Says the King, "Where was ye to get wheat and corn?"

Jeck says, "I was going to hae two jumps," he says, "and three leaps," he says, "and I was goin to cross the Mediterranean," he says, "into Africa or France or these countries; and I was goin' to load mysel'," he says, "and jump back again."

"Jump the sea!" says the King, he says, "how could—no human bein', Jeck," he says, "could jump the sea."

"Aye, but," he says, "I could jump the sea," he says, "and quay and aa," he says, "I could clear the toon and everything," he says, "wi' a jump." He says, ' D'ye mean to cry me a liar?"

"Oh, no," says the King. "I'll no cry ye a liar." he says, "How did ye dae't?"

"Well," he says, "I took two runnin' leaps," he says, "a hop, step and leap," he says, "what they dae at the games. And," he says, "I flew throu the air," he says, "and I landed in Africa. And the first man that come to see me," he says, "was a big chief," he says, "wi' feathers stickin' in his heid," he says. "He did the Rumba roon aboot me," he says, "dancin'", he says, "like a whale dancin' aboot me wi' feathers stickin' in his heid. So," he says, "I spoke in Gaelic tae him."

"Gaelic!" says the King.

"Yes," he says, "I spoke in Gaelic tae him."

"And did he ken Gaelic?"

"Aye," he says, "he kent Gaelic," he says.

"God bless us! I never heard o' onieone, either an African or a savage speakin Gaelic before."

"D'ye mean to cry me a liar?" says Jeck.

"No, no," says the King, "I'll no cry ye a liar."

Well, he has the King trementit to daith—the King didnae ken what to make of him—he'd the King a raigl't.

But, anyway, here, now, to make a long story short, he goes and tells—he gets throu the savages and that, he gets throu the savages to tell what happent aboot the corn and they were stervin—this country was stervin.

Well, now, "How are ye goin' to get the wheat and that back?" the savages says tae him.

Jeck says, "I'll get the wheat and that back."

Noo, there was something bitin' the back of his neck, and Jeck put his hand doon the back of his neck, cried—he caught a flea, and he turns the skin ootside-in, for a bag. He says, "Fill that."

So the King started laughin', "Haw, haw—." Says Jeck, "Whar are ye laughin' at, man?"

"Fill a flea-skin," he says, "with wheat and corn," he says, "that's ridiculous!"

"D'ye mean to cry me a liar?" says Jeck.

"Well—oh, no, oh, no," said the King. I'll no cry ye a liar." (He was gettin' a bit stupid noo, ye see.)

"Well," he says, "they pit four-hundred and fifty thoosand ton," he says, "of wheat," he says, "in the flea-skin."

"God bless us!" said the King; "that's an aafie corn," he says, "and wheat," he says, "tae pit in a, intil a flea-skin. And," he says, "how did ye get it ower?"

"Ah," he says, "that was the bloomin' trouble," he says, Jeck says. "I was in a mess noo," he says, "I startit trailin' it and humpin' it on my back."

"Thoosands of tons on your back, Jeck?"

"Aye," says Jeck, "thoosands of tons. D'ye mean to cry me a liar?"

"Oh, no," said the King.

"Well," he said, "what cam owre but a flock of geese? And," he says, "the sky," he says—"I thought there were going to be a thunderstorm," he said, "there were so many geese," he said, "it blackent the sun. And," he says, "they cam doon lower, and cam doon lower, and when they cam doon lower, the first of them says to me, 'Jeck, are ye in a bit of trouble?' he says. 'We were flyin away to Scotland,' he says, 'and we seen you doon ablow us,' he says, 'and some of them says, "There's Jeck doon there, we'll hae to go doon and help him."' 'It was very kind of ye,'" Jack says to the geese.

He says, "The geese spoke t'ye and cam doon to help ye, Jeck?"

"Aye," says Jeck.

He says, "What did they dae?"

"Ah, that is what I'm gaun to tell ye," said Jeck. "They tell't me to get

83

on, on their back. And they spread oot their wings, flat on the grund, just like a big sheet—like a big blanket," he says, "over this wide area," he says, "of desert."

"And what happent?" says the King.

"Well," he says, "I humphed and plowtered," he says, "till I got the corn and the wheat", he says, "owre on top of the seagulls's back. And I sat doon beside the corn," he says, "and I fell fast asleep. But," he says, "when I wakent up," he says, "I'm fleean owre the North Sea, and I'm lookin' doon at wee ships," he says, "gettin' wrecked in the gale. And," he says, "I could dae nothin' to help them. And," he says, "I'm lookin' owre the side—"

"How did ye look owre the side?" he says. "How monie geese were they?"

He says, "They were five hundert and fifty million."

"Five hundert and fifty million!" says the King—"God bliss!"

"D'ye mean to cry me a liar?" says Jeck.

He says, "How did ye see doon throu the geese, Jeck?"

He says, "I jist opent the feathers up like that," he says, "and lookt throu a hole," he says, "throu them. And," he says, 'I could see everything," he says, "like a telescope," he says, "doon throu the geese's belly," he says, "doon throu their stomicks, the wings."

"God bliss us!" said the King. "I never heard the like of that before."

"Naw," says he, "and it will be a while before ye hear't again," says Jeck. "D'ye mean to cry me a liar?"

"Oh, no," said the King.

Well, Toby, it went on like that. They were comin' across the North Sea, and they were near the Scottish coasts, when aa the geese startit to speak to each other, and, aw, there was an aafie noise, wi' them kecklin' and cairryin'-on. They got tired, wi' the weight of corn on their back, this thoosans of ton of wheat and corn on their back—they got tired.

So here now, when they [were] fleean owre, they said, "Jeck, we'll hae to let ye go." He says: "We can dae nothing. We're on Scotland, the ground of Scotland now, and," he says, "we're tired," he says. 'Ye'll need to let us go."

"And the geese done a dirty thing, King."

"What did they dae?" said the King. (The King's interested noo, ye see.) "What did they dae?" said the King.

"They opent up their wings, and put me and the corn and the wheat, cam doon," he says, "they cam mountin'—the noise," he says, "frae the heavens," he says, "like a thunderbolt or thunderstorm," he says, "of hailstones, the corn and the wheat comin' throu the sky, and I'm comin' doon along wi'd."

"Gode bliss us!" says the King, "did ye get kilt, Jeck?"

"Ah," says Jeck, "haud on till ye hear what happent. I cam' doon that fast," he said, "I thought I'd land," he says, "at my mother's back-door," he says, "but instead of me landin' at the back-door," he says, "I went on to a big rock," he says, "that was sittin' beside the shore," he says, "up to the neck," he says, "into a big whinstane rock."

"Up to the neck—wis ye not kilt?" says the King.

"Naw," says Jeck, "I was stuck in the rock and I couldnae get oot. And," he says, "all I could dae," he says, "was to move my heid back and forrit like that," he says, "and I couldnae get oot, my body's disappeart into the rock."

"Och," says the King, "I wadnae believe that, Jeck."

"Ye wadnae believe—d'ye mean to cry me a liar?"

"Oh, no," says the King. "I wadnae cry ye a liar."

"Well," he says, "I didnae know what to dae," says Jeck, he says, "and I'd only aboot two hundert yairds or three hundert yairds," he says, "to go hame," he says, "to my mother's hoose. And all the corn," he says,—"covert the wud," he says, "there were nae trees to be seen," he says—"so much corn and everything. And", he says, "in the excitement of the birds comin pickin' the corn and everything," he says, "I didnae ken what to do. I tried to shove mysel' oot of the rock, and I couldnae. And," he says, "the best thing I can dae is try and manoeuvre my sword—" he'd this old sword—he says, "I have it at my side here," he says, "this sword here,"—he says, "it cost me a few thoosan' pound, that sword."

The King looked at the scythe-blade, and he says,

"That a sword?" he says. "That's a scythe-blade."

"That a scythe-blade!" says Jeck. "It's a better sword," he says, "than monie guid men," he says, "has doon in the courtyaird doon there."

"Ach! That's a scythe-blade."

"D'ye mean to cry me a liar?" says Jeck.

"No, no," says the King, he says. "That's a good gold sword you've got." (See!)

"Well," he says, "I plowtert," he says, "and I moved my airm back and forrit," he says, "and I cut my heid off."

"Ye cut your heid off!" says the King.

"Yes," he says, "and it was the only wey I could get away," he says. "I tellt my heid to run hame and tell my mother to come wi' help, to get me oot of the rock."

"Ye tellt your heid," he says, "to run hame! How did ye manage that, Jeck?" he says, "when ye'd nae heid on?"

"D'ye mean to cry me a liar?" says Jeck.

"Oh, no," says the King. "I'll no cry ye a liar."

"Well," he says, "my heid rowellt hame," he says, "and I tellt it to hurry up, and the heid startit rowellin' like a big baa," he says, "along this dusty track. But," he says, "as my heid was goin' on the road," he says, "here there was a fox," he says, "stole my mother's hens—I hatit this fox," he says. "I'd two or three shots at it and I missed it. But," he says, "the fox started to chase my heid. And it's efter it," he says. "And I'm sayin', 'Run, heid, run!' I'm sayin'. 'Run, heid, run!' I'm shoutin'."

"How could ye shout," he says, "like that, Jeck," he says, "without a heid," he says. "How did your heid get on?"

"Just a minute," he says. "D'ye mean to cry me a liar?" says Jeck.

"Oh, no," said the King. "I'll no cry ye a liar."

"Well," he says, "the fox was catchin' up on my heid—catchin' up on my heid," he says, "and jist when the fox was goin' to catch up on my heid—goin' to bounce my heid," he says, "wi' the excitement I cried, 'Hooch!' and I jumped richt oot of the rock. And when I jumped oot of the rock, I ran efter the fox," he says, "whan it's got a grip of my heid in its mouth. And," he says, "I kickit the fox, and I kickit the fox, and I kickit the fox, and I kickit siven young foxes oot of the fox," he says. "And," he says, "d'ye ken this, King?"

"No, it's what?" says the King (and the King's gettin' excited, and he's sittin' up in his bed by this time, ye see—he feels right, too)—he says, "I kickit siven young foxes oot of the fox," he says, "and," he says, "*the worst fox's shite was better'n you.*"

"YE'RE A LIAR!" says the King. "Well," he says, "for that," he says, "I'll get your daughter's haund in marriage, and your castle," and the king faintit and dee'd.

And he's there yet, Toby, and he's mairrit to the lassie. That was a good story, Toby, eh?

School of Scottish Studies. Told to Hamish Henderson by Andra Stewart, 1956.

¶ This is a widespread tale. It is in Grimm (no. 112), and is spread all over Europe, and in Africa, America, India, and Indonesia. 228 Irish versions are cited (*Béaloideas*, IV, pp. 151ff.) and even more are cited in *The Types of the Irish Folktale* (Ó'Súilleabhain and Christiansen).

For rather similar tales see also "Daft Jack and the Heiress", "The Princess of Canterbury".

MR FOX

Lady Mary was young, and Lady Mary was fair. She had two brothers, and more lovers than she could count. But of them all, the bravest and most gallant was a Mr Fox, whom she met when she was down at her father's country house. No one knew who Mr Fox was; but he was certainly brave, and surely rich, and of all her lovers, Lady Mary cared for him alone. At last it was agreed upon between them that they should be married. Lady Mary asked Mr Fox where they should live, and he described to her his castle, and where it was, but, strange to say, did not ask her, or her brothers, to come and see it.

So one day, near the wedding-day, when her brothers were out, and Mr Fox was away for a day or two on business, as he said, Lady Mary set out for Mr Fox's castle. And after many searchings, she came at last to it, and a fine strong house it was, with high walls and a deep moat. And when she came up to the gateway, she saw written on it:

BE BOLD, BE BOLD

But as the gate was open, she went through it, and found no one there. So she went up to the doorway, and over it she found written:

BE BOLD, BE BOLD, BUT NOT TOO BOLD

Still she went on, till she came to the hall, and went up the broad stairs till she came to a door in the gallery, over which was written:

BE BOLD, BE BOLD, BUT NOT TOO BOLD,
LEST THAT YOUR HEART'S BLOOD SHOULD RUN COLD

But Lady Mary was a brave one, she was, and she opened the door, and what do you think she saw? Why, bodies and skeletons of beautiful young ladies all stained with blood. So Lady Mary thought it was high time to get out of that horrid place, and she closed the door, went through the gallery, and was just going down the stairs, and out of the hall, when who should she see through the window, but Mr Fox dragging a beautiful young lady along from the gateway to the door. Lady Mary rushed downstairs, and hid herself behind a cask, just in time, as Mr Fox came in with the young lady, who seemed to have fainted.

Just as he got near Lady Mary, Mr Fox saw a diamond ring glittering on the finger of the young lady he was dragging, and he tried to pull it off. But it was tightly fixed, and would not come off, so Mr Fox cursed and swore, and drew his sword, raised it, and brought it down upon the hand of the poor lady.

The sword cut off the hand, which jumped up into the air, and fell of all places in the world into Lady Mary's lap. Mr Fox looked about a bit, but did not think of looking behind the cask, so at last he went on dragging the young lady up the stairs into the Bloody Chamber.

As soon as she heard him pass through the gallery, Lady Mary crept out of the door, down through the gateway, and ran home as fast as she could.

Now it happened that the very next day the marriage contract of Lady Mary and Mr Fox was to be signed, and there was a splendid breakfast before that.

And when Mr Fox was seated at table opposite Lady Mary, he looked at her. "How pale you are this morning, my dear." "Yes," she said. "I had a bad night's rest last night. I had horrible dreams." "Dreams go by contraries," said Mr Fox; "but tell us your dream, and your sweet voice will make the time pass till the happy hour comes."

"I dreamed," said Lady Mary, "that I went yestermorn to your castle, and I found it in the woods, with high walls, and a deep moat, and over the gateway was written:

BE BOLD, BE BOLD"

"But it is not so, nor it was not so," said Mr Fox.

"And when I came to the doorway over it was written:

BE BOLD, BE BOLD, BUT NOT TOO BOLD"

"It is not so, nor it was not so," said Mr Fox.

"And then I went upstairs, and came to a gallery, at the end of which was a door, on which was written:

BE BOLD, BE BOLD, BUT NOT TOO BOLD,
LEST THAT YOUR HEART'S BLOOD SHOULD RUN COLD"

"It is not so, nor it was not so," said Mr Fox.

"And then—and then I opened the door, and the room was filled with the bodies and skeletons of poor dead women, all stained with their blood."

"It is not so, nor it was not so, and God forbid it should be so," said Mr Fox.

"I then dreamed that I rushed down the gallery, and just as I was going down the stairs, I saw you, Mr Fox, coming up to the hall door, dragging after you a poor young lady, rich and beautiful."

"It is not so, nor it was not so. And God forbid it should be so," said Mr Fox.

"I rushed downstairs, just in time to hide myself behind a cask, when you, Mr Fox, came in dragging the young lady by the arm. And, as you passed me, Mr Fox, I thought I saw you try and get off her diamond ring, and when you could not, Mr Fox, it seemed to me in my dream, that you out with your sword and hacked off the poor lady's hand to get the ring."

"It is not so, nor it was not so. And God forbid it should be so," said Mr Fox, and was going to say something else as he rose from his seat, when Lady Mary cried out:

"But it is so, and it was so. Here's hand and ring I have to show," and pulled out the lady's hand from her dress, and pointed it straight at Mr Fox.

At once her brothers and her friends drew their swords and cut Mr Fox into a thousand pieces.

Joseph Jacobs, *English Fairy Tales*, p. 148. Contributed by Blakeway to Malone's *Variorum Shakespeare*.

See "Mr Fox's Courtship" (below), with notes.

See also *The Oxford Student*, (B, VIII), "The Brave Maid Servant", (B, IX), "The Cellar of Blood".

THE PROFESSOR OF SIGNS [summary]

A famous Professor of Learning once came to England to examine all the scholars there. He went to Oxford, and it fared so badly that the students of Cambridge began to be anxious, and hit on a plan to raise the reputation of the place. So when the professor was expected some of the most learned dressed up as labouring men, and went to mend the roads. Presently the professor drove along, and his coachman called out to ask if he was on the right road. The road-man answered him in Latin. They rode on a little further and met another party who answered them in Greek. The professor thought to himself: "This must be a learned place, since the very road-men talk Latin and Greek. I must hit on some other subject to examine the students in."

So, when he got to Cambridge, he announced that he would test them in the Language of Signs. At this there was great consternation in the University, and none was more distressed than the best scholar of them all, a poor, one-eyed student, who had hoped for preferment from this examination. Whilst the others were preparing themselves, he wandered gloomily along the banks of the Cam, where he met a friend of his, a one-eyed miller, who asked why he was so sad. The student told him everything, and the miller suggested that *he* should try his luck, for he was a hardy fellow, and feared nothing, and since the test was to be silent, his speech would not betray him. They changed clothes, and the student waited anxiously outside the Examination Hall.

At first all was silent, but presently there was a great burst of applause, and the miller came slipping out. "Here, change quickly," he said, "they say I've won." The student pulled on his gown, and got into the Hall just in time to hear the Professor explaining.

"It was remarkable," he said. "Never would I have believed that a man could follow every turn of my thought. First I held up an apple, to signify that by the apple Mankind had fallen. But quick as thought he held up a piece of bread, to show that by the Bread of Life we were all redeemed. Then I held up one finger, to show there is but one God, but he held up two, to signify that we must not forget Christ, so I held up three, to remind him of the Trinity, and he very quickly clenched his fist, to show that three are yet one. He never faltered nor mistook, and richly deserves the Prize."

The scholar was delighted, but he wondered very much how the poor miller had gained such knowledge, so, as soon as he could slip away from the congratulations of his friends, he went to ask the miller's side of the disputation.

"He was a quarrelsome old fellow," said the miller, "but I gave as good as I got. First he scrabbled in his pocket, and he took out a green apple, and shook it under my nose, as much as to say he'd throw it at my head if I didn't watch out. So I felt in my pocket, but all I could find was an old bit of crust, so I shoved that under his nose, as much as to say, 'You throw the apple, and I'll throw the crust.' With that, he put away the apple, and poked his finger at me, as much as to say, 'I'll thrust out your eye!' So I poked my two fingers at him, to say, 'If you do, I'll put out your two!' Then he scrabbled at me with his three fingers, to show he'd scratch my face. And I wasn't going to stand that, so I doubled up me fist and shook it at him, to show I'd knock him down. And at that he clapped me on the back, and said I'd won."

Norton Collection, II, pp. 281–2. *Folk-Lore Record*, II (1879), pp. 173–6.

¶ Norton has made copious notes on this tale, pointing out that it consists of two parts: (*a*) the students posted along the road; and (*b*) the discussion in sign language.

Straparola is an early source of (*a*); Anthony à Wood gives a version of it which dates from the sixteenth century, and differs a good deal from Straparola. The (*b*) story is earlier known, the first written version being in *The Gloss of Accursius* (c. 1260). It is also found among the Nasr-el-Din stories. It was used by various writers, among them Rabelais. A Dutch version from Utrecht is the only example beyond these islands of the combination of (*a*) and (*b*). In this an Indian prince, on his way to Leyden, is greeted in Latin and Hebrew by students dressed as rustics. He is so impressed that he decides to examine the university in the sign language of which he is master. He is answered by a one-eyed gypsy. See also "The Miller at the Professor's Examination", "George Buchanan", "King John and the Abbot of Canterbury", "The Independent Bishop", "The Two Little Scotch Boys".

THE TALE OF IVAN

There were formerly a man and a woman living in the parish of Llanlavan, in the place which is called Hwrdh. And work became scarce, so the man said to his wife, "I will go search for work, and you may live here." So he took fair leave, and travelled far toward the east, and at last came to the house of a farmer and asked for work.

"What work can ye do?" said the farmer.

"I can do all kinds of work," said Ivan.

Then they agreed upon three pounds for the year's wages.

When the end of the year came round his master showed him the three pounds.

"See, Ivan," said he, "here's your wage; but if you will give it me back I'll give you a piece of advice instead."

"Give me my wage," said Ivan.

"No, I'll not," said the master; "I'll explain my advice."

"Tell it me, then," said Ivan.

Then said the master, "Never leave the old road for the sake of a new one."

After that they agreed for another year at the old wages, and at the end of it Ivan took instead a piece of advice, and this was it: "Never lodge where an old man is married to a young woman."

The same thing happened at the end of the third year, when the piece of advice was: "Honesty is the best policy."

But Ivan would not stay longer, but wanted to go back to his wife.

"Don't go to-day," said his master; "my wife bakes to-morrow, and she shall make thee a cake to take home to thy good woman."

And when Ivan was going to leave, "Here," said his master, "here is a cake for thee to take home to thy wife, and, when ye are most joyous together, then break the cake, and not sooner."

So he took fair leave of them, and travelled towards home, and at last he came to Wayn Her, and there he met three merchants from Tre Rhyn, of his own parish, coming home from Exeter Fair. "Oho! Ivan," said they, "come with us; glad are we to see you. Where have you been so long?"

"I have been in service," said Ivan, "and now I'm going home to my wife."

"Oh, come with us! You'll be right welcome."

But when they took the new road, Ivan kept to the old one. And robbers fell upon them before they had gone far from Ivan as they were going by the fields of the houses in the meadow. They began to cry out, "Thieves!" and Ivan shouted out "Thieves!" too. And when the robbers heard Ivan's shout, they ran away, and the merchants went by the new road and Ivan by the old one till they met again at Market Jew.

"Oh, Ivan," said the merchants, "we are beholding to you; but for you we would have been lost men. Come, lodge with us at our cost, and welcome."

When they came to the place where they used to lodge, Ivan said, "I must see the host."

"The host," they cried, "what do you want with the host? Here is the hostess, and she is young and pretty. If you want to see the host, you'll find him in the kitchen."

So he went into the kitchen to see the host; he found him a weak old man turning the spit.

"Oh! oh!" quoth Ivan, "I'll not lodge here, but will go next door."

"Not yet," said the merchants. "Sup with us and welcome."

Now it happened that the hostess had plotted with a certain monk in Market Jew to murder the old man in his bed that night while the rest were asleep, and they agreed to lay it on the lodgers.

So while Ivan was in bed next door, there was a hole in the pine-end of the house, and he saw a light through it. So he got up and looked, and heard the monk speaking. "I had better cover this hole," said he, "or people in the next house may see our deeds." So he stood with his back against it while the hostess killed the old man.

But meanwhile Ivan out with his knife, and putting it through the hole, cut a round piece off the monk's robe.

The very next morning the hostess raised the cry that her husband was murdered, and as there was neither man nor child in the house, but the merchants, she declared they ought to be hanged for it.

So they were taken and carried to prison, till at last Ivan came to them.

"Alas! Alas! Ivan," cried they, "bad luck sticks to us; our host was killed last night, and we shall be hanged for it."

"Ah! tell the justices," said Ivan, "to summon the real murderers."

"Who knows," they replied, "who committed the crime?"

"Who committed the crime!" said Ivan. "If I cannot prove who committed the crime, hang me in your stead."

So he told all he knew, and brought out the piece of cloth from the monk's robe, and with that the merchants were set at liberty, and the hostess and the monk were seized and hanged.

Then they all came together out of Market Jew, and they said to him: "Come as far as Coed Carrn y Wylfa, the Wood of the Heap of Stones of Watching, in the parish of Burman." Then their two roads separated, and though the merchants wished Ivan to go with them, he would not go with them, but went straight home to his wife.

And when his wife saw him she said: "Home in the nick of time. Here's a purse of gold that I've found; it has no name, but sure it belongs to the great lord yonder. I was just thinking what to do when you came."

Then Ivan thought of the third counsel, and he said: "Let us go and give it to the great lord."

So they went up to the castle, but the great lord was not in it, so they left the purse with the servant that minded the gate, and then they went home again and lived in quiet for a time.

But one day the great lord stopped at their house for a drink of water, and Ivan's wife said to him: "I hope your lordship found your lordship's purse quite safe with all its money in it."

"What purse is that you are talking about?" said the lord.

"Sure, it's your lordship's purse that I left at the castle," said Ivan.

"Come with me and we will see into the matter," said the lord.

So Ivan and his wife went up to the castle, and there they pointed out the man to whom they had given the purse, and he had to give it up and was sent away from the castle. And the lord was so pleased with Ivan that he made him his servant instead of the thief.

"Honesty's the best policy!" quoth Ivan, as he skipped about in his new quarters. "How joyful I am!"

Then he thought of his old master's cake that he was to eat when he was most joyful, and when he broke it, lo and behold inside it was his wages for the three years he had been with him.

Jacobs, *Celtic Fairy Tales*, p. 195, from Lluyd, *Archaeologia Britannia* (1707). Cornish.

¶ See also *The Three Good Advices*, "The Tinner of Chyannor", "Yalla-britches".

THE THREE GOOD ADVICES
[transcription of tape]

Oncet upon a time there was a man and a woman lived in a wee cottage, away up about the north of Scotland somewhere, ye see, and this man was a baker to trade, but in the village he was stayin' in, the old man of the baker's shop died, and this man was thrown out of a job—there were no baker's shop there. But he stuck his place for about two year, and things was gettin' very hard wi' him, ye see, so one day he says to the wife, he says, "I think", he says, "I'll go and look for a job," he says. "Things are very tight," he says—"nae work comin' into the hoose," he says, "and the two lassies at school," he says, "I've got to go and look for a job, ye see."

So his wife says, "Where are yė goin' 'a go?"

"I don't know," he says; "if ye jist make me up a piece," he says, "gie me a blanket wi' me," he says, "I'll march the road, and I'll try and get a job in some toon," he says; "I'll surely get a job somewhere, ye see. Doesnae maitter what it is."

So anyway, in the mornin' she gies him a piece and gies him a blanket—made her man as comfortable as she could for the long journey. And he's waved his kiddies farewell, and kissed his wife, and off he went—sets off, ye see. So anyway, on he goes—oh, he marched on till he was aboot six weeks on the road, till he comes marchin' intae a village. In the village, there was four cross-roads in this village in the street, a cross-roads. An he comes in—he looks up the one street and he looks doon the ither street, and he's standing at the corner—it was kinda well on in the night. An across the street was a baker's shop; it was shut.

In the front of the baker's shop there was a stoot man stannin', like the wan, the boss of the shop, was stannin'. An this man of the shop was matchin' this other man across the street,—the baker—stannin' watchin' the man that was lookin' for the job, ye see.

So he comes marchin' owre to the baker to ask where there was a lodgin'-hoose or anything where he could sleep for the night, and the man directed him where he could get lodgings. He says, "What are ye doin'?" he says—"Ye're a stranger here," says the man of the shop.

"Yes," he says, "I'm a stranger," he says. "I'm looking for a job."

He says, "What kinna job are ye lookin' for?"

"Well," says the man, "it's a funny thing," he says, "you asked me that," he says—"jist the same kinna job you are," he says. "I'm a baker. I'm a baker to trade."

"Well," says the man, "I could do wi' a man for a baker,—a man to make pastries."

They've come to an agreement, an' asked the wages, and the man tellt him.

"Well," he says, "ye'll get your lodgings," he says. "I'll gie ye a good pay, and everything."

So he was there for aboot six month, and he could make the loveliest pastries ever, the man—he was aboot the best baker this man had—the boss of the baker's shop—told him he was a good baker. And he got so much wi' his keep—got his food and his bed, but at the end of the year he got so much of his wages, a lump sum for goin' away.

Now he was wearied for his wife and two wee lassies—see—so he says to the man, "I'm goin' home," he says, "the day after to-morrow," he says, "I'm goin' back home," he says—"I want to see the wife and kiddies. And," he says, "I'll be liftin' aa my wages," he says, "I don't know what might happen me, for I've a long road to go home."

"That's all right," says the man, he says, "but," he says, "there's one thing," he says, "I'm goin' to ask ye," he says. "I jist cam in to see ye, man," he says, "before ye were goin' away up to your bed," he says, "whether wad ye take your year's wages, or take three good advices."

So the baker looked at him, says, "What d'ye mean, Boss?"

"Well," he says, "I'm only askin'," he says, "Whether wad ye take three good advices," he says, "or wad ye take your year's pay?"

"Well," he says, "ye've got me noo," he says, "ye see, I cud dae wi' my week's pey. An'," he says, "wi' three good advices I could walk oot in the road there and get killed," he says, "or something like that." And he says, "Wad ye gie me up to the morn's mornin' to think it owre?"

So the man says, "Yes, that'll do," he says. "If you wait till the morn's mornin' ye're gaun away to-morrow," he says, "I'll—ye can decide then which of the things ye want to take—your money or your three advices.'

So away, thinkin' in bed—he could hardly sleep. An' he says—whan he cam doon for his breakfast in the mornin', the Boss says, "Well," he says, "George," he says, "did ye make up your mind what ye're goin'to take," he says, "your money", he says, "there's your wages; there's your packet," he says, "there's a fair lump of money in it—I know you could be daein' wi' the money. And," he says, "I've got three good advices to gie ye," he says. "Have ye made up your mind which o'm ye're gonnae take?"

"Well," says the man, "I could dae wi the money," he says, "but I think I've made up my mind," he says, "to take the three good advices."

"Well," he says, "you took a wise decision," the man says.

"Well," he says, "the best advice is: Never take a near-cut!" He says, "Never get into a hoose," he says, "where there's a red-heidit man, a red-heidit wumman, a red-heidit—an auld red-heidit man, an auld red-heidit wumman, an' a red-heidit son."

"Oh," says the man, "I'll mind that."

"And," he says, "your third advice is," he says, "There's a half-loaf, an' don't break that half-loaf," he says, "till ye break it in your wife's apron. Get her to haud oot her apron," he says, "and break the half-loaf in your wife's apron—see?"

"Very good," says the man.

"But," he says, "there's your week's pey to ye. It will cairry ye hame."

So he bid his boss farewell, and said, "You were very good to me," and bid his family farewell, and away he set off for home.

In them days it was mail-coaches—there were nae motor-cars, an' buses —horseback and mail-coaches. He's marchin' the road back, and his feet were sore, travellin'. Well, he came to a near-cut, and across this near-cut, across the fields, was takin' aboot three mile off him, off his journey, see.

He forgot aboot the advice, and he says, "Well," he says, "I'm goin' owre this near-cut," he says, "and it'll cut three mile off me. And," he says, "my feet's sore, I'll have to go across this field."

Well, he went owre the stile, and he's marchin' through this field—it was a moonlight's night—and the frost was on everything. When he's comin' over the field, he hears the scream of a man, and this was Burkers cuttin' a packman's throat, in the middle of the field, jist as he was comin' owre the brae of the hill. The screams over the roads were something terrible. He backs back, and he backs back, and he ran for his life till he got on to the road, and he ran doon the road, and wi' the excitement— he ran doon the road—he ran to a wee crofter's hoose at the side of the road, and when he ran in oot the road, there was a red-heidit man, an auld red-heidit wumman, and a red-heidit son. And he knew he'd done wrong. The man said, "What is it?" "Ah", he says, "I'm tired—I got chased there and I cam in," he says, "to see if ye could pit me up for the night."

"Well," says the man, he says, "I'll tell ye," he says, "ye can gie him some parritch," he says, "and milk there—gie him a feed."

So he mindit on the three advices noo; he says, "I'm goin' 'a be murdered here the night," says, "this is a Burker's hoose. Well," he says, "listen," he says, "before ye gie me a wee bite of meat and that," he says, "and before ye's pit me in the byre," he says, "will ye let me oot for a minute—I want to do something, see?"

The man says, "Aye, aye," he says, "jist gang oot there, and dinnae be long."

And here, when he went oot, he went into the reed—that's where they keep the manure—coo's manure and horse-manure—he went into the reed, and he sat in a corner of the reed; he never cam back in again. An' they're searchin' for him up and doon, here and there, and they couldnae fin' him; they searched byre, stacks and everything, but they hadnae an idea tae gaun into the reed where the dung was, where he was sittin'—see?, he was hidin' in there.

He bade there tae aboot the break of day-light, and here was the mail-coach comin', wi' the mail and two horses. The man had a gun on top of the thing, and his two dogs, and the horses comin' trottin' along the road. He jumps owre and he held his hand up to the man like that, and tellt the man to gie him a lift. And he still had his parcel. He got on to the mail-coach, and he tells the man goin' along the road what happened.

"Well," he says, "if they come eftir ye," he says, "I'll gie them an unce of leid," he says, "oot of my gun, wi' this blunderbuss, I've got," he says, "and I'll put my dogs on them," he says. "Ye should watch what ye're daen, man." But when he got to the wife's hoose, the wife was glad to see him, and the wee lassie; she throwed her arms aroond her man and tellt him to come in.

"God", she says, "you look fagged oot," she says, and she says, "Have ye got the money?"

"No," he says, "I've only got this, what' I've got left,' 'he says, "aboot three pound," he says.

"Did ye no get nae mair nor that," she says, "for your year's workin'?"

"Naw," he says, "that's aa I've got," he says, but he started tellin' her aboot the three good advices. He says, "My first good advice was no to take a near-cut through the field, and whan I went through the field," he says, "there was a man gettin' murdered. An'," he says, "the other yin was no to gaun intae a hoose where there was red-heidit folk. But," he says, "that's what I done," he says, "and I sat in the reed aa night. An'," he says, "my third good advice," he says to his wife, "was this wee half-loaf. The baker told me," he says—"the boss at the baker-shop told me for to haud oot your apron. Now," he says, "haud oot your apron until I break the half-loaf."

An' the wife held oot the apron, like that, and he broke the half-loaf.

It was full of gold sovereigns. "Jingle, jingle, jingle, jingle," the gold sovereigns fell intae her apron, and they lived happily ever after, and she was glad to see her man—he was near killed. So the three good advices peyed him, didn't it?

That's the finish of it, and that's the end of my story.

My mother told us that story, years ago, when I was a wee boy.

School of Scottish Studies. Collected by Hamish Henderson from Andrew Stewart, 1955.

¶ See *The Tale of Ivan*, "The Tinner of Chyannor", "Yalla-britches". See also "The Reid-Heidit Family" among the Burker Tales.

THE UNGRATEFUL SONS

They have a tradition at Winterton that there was formerly one Mr Lacy, that lived there and was a very rich man, who, being grown very aged, gave all that he had away unto his three sons, upon condition that one should keep him one week, and another another. But it happened within a little while that they were all weary of him, after that they got what they had, and regarded him no more than a dog. The old man perceiving how he was slighted, went to an attorny to see if his skill could not afford him any help in his troubles. The attorny told him that no law in the land could help him nor yield him any comfort, but there was one thing onely which would certainly do, which, if he would perform, he would reveal to him. At which the poor old man was exceeding glad, and desired him for God's sake to reveal the same, for he was almost pined and starved to dead, and he would willingly do it rather than live as he did. "Well," says the lawyer, "you have been a great friend of mine in my need, and I will now be one to you in your need. I will lend you a strong box with a strong lock on it, in which shall be contained £1000; you shall on such a day pretend to have fetched it out of such a close, where it shall be supposed that you hid, and carry it into one of your sons' houses, and make it your business every week, while you are sojourning with such or such a son, to be always counting of the money, and ratleing it about, and you shall see that, for love of it, they'll soon love you again, and make very much of you, and maintain you joyfully, willingly and plentifully, unto your dying day." The old man having thanked the lawyer for this good advice, and kind proffer, received with a few days the aforesayd box full of money, and having so managed it as above, his graceless sons soon fell in love with him again, and made mighty much of him, and perceiving that their love to him continued stedfast and firm, he one day took it out of the house and carry'd it to the lawyer, thanking him exceedingly for the lent thereof.

But when he got to his sons he made them believe that (he) had hidden it again, and that he would give it to him of them whome he loved best when he dyd. This made them all so observant of him that he lived the rest of his days in great peace, plenty and happiness amongst them, and dyed full of years. But a while before he dyd he upbraded them for their former ingratitude, told them the whole history of the box, and forgave them.

County Folk-lore, v, Lincolnshire (Gutch and Peacock), p. 362. From the diary of Abraham de la Pryme, pp. 162–3.

¶ This type is given literary treatment by Ernest Seton Thompson in *Two Little Savages*.

PART 5
NURSERY TALES

The Nursery Tales are perhaps those that have the greatest chance of survival amongst us, for small children will always demand them, and if mothers no longer tell them they are likely to hear them on the wireless. People also commonly remember longest what they have heard earliest. There is one type of Nursery Tale which is not likely to be told to the very small, though it will be popular among older children. This is the alarming story, ending with a shout that is meant to startle the listener, such as "The Old Man at the White House", very popular with school-children. Such animal tales as "The Three Bears" and "The Three Wee Pigs" are suitable for very young children, and are perennially popular. "The Three Bears" has no type number, probably because it was long regarded as being the invention of Robert Southey, who actually only retold it. Even if he had been the originator, it has gone through enough changes in the course of transmission to qualify it as a late folk-tale.

Nonsense tales and jingles are popular with the very young, and keep their popularity as the children grow up. Some, like "Sir Gammer Vans", are pure nonsense; some, like "The Cattie sits in the Kiln-Ring Spinning", had probably originally a satiric intention and have been adopted by children. It is possible that some of them may have originated in thieves' cant, like the nursery rhyme,

> As I went over Humber-Jumber,
> Humber-Jumber, Jiney O!

and have been innocently adopted, as it has, for their pretty rhythm.

THE CATTIE SITS IN THE KILN-RING SPINNING

The cattie sits in the kiln-ring,
    Spinning, spinning;
And by came a little wee mousie,
    Rinning, rinning.

"O what's that you're spinning, my loesome,
    Loesome lady?"
"I'm spinning a sark to my young son,"
    Said she, said she.

"Weel mot he brook it, my loesome,
    Loesome lady."
"Gin he dinna brook it weel, he may brook it ill,"
    Said she, said she.

"I soopit my house, my loesome,
    Loesome lady."
"'Twas a sign we didna sit amang dirt then,"
    Said she, said she.

"I fand twall pennies, my winsome,
    Winsome lady."
"'Twas a sign ye warna sillerless,"
    Said she, said she.

"I gaed to the market, my loesome,
    Loesome lady."
"'Twas a sign ye didna sit at hame then,"
    Said she, said she.

"I coft a sheepie's head, my winsome,
    Winsome lady."
"'Twas a sign ye warna kitchenless,"
    Said she, said she.

"I put it in my pottie to boil, my loesome,
    Loesome lady."
"'Twas a sign ye didna eat it raw,"
    Said she, said she.

"I put it in my winnock to cool, my winsome,
  Winsome lady."
"'Twas a sign ye didna burn your chafts then,"
  Said she, said she.

"By came a cattie, and ate it a' up, my loesome,
  Loesome lady."
"And sae will I you—Worrie, worrie—guash, guash,"
  Said she, said she.

Chambers, *Popular Rhymes of Scotland*, p. 53.

❡ Versions of this tale are known in Finland, Norway, Denmark, Belgium, Russia, Greece, Indonesia and America. Lewis Carroll's "Fury said to a Mouse" is on something the same theme.

The usual tale is of a vain attempt to escape death by a captured mouse. In this version the mouse takes the initiative and seeks for reparation.

THE ENDLESS TALE

Once upon a time there was a king who had a very beautiful daughter. Many princes wished to marry her, but the king said she should marry the one who could tell him an endless tale, and those lovers that could not tell an endless tale should be beheaded. Many young men came, and tried to tell such a story, but they could not tell it, and were beheaded. But one day a poor man who had heard of what the king had said came to the court and said he would try his luck. The king agreed, and the poor man began his tale in this way: "There was once a man who built a barn that covered many acres, and that reached almost to the sky. He left just one little hole in the top, through which there was only room for one locust to creep in at a time, and then he filled the barn full of corn to the very top. When he had filled the barn there came a locust through the hole in the top and fetched one grain of corn, and then another locust came and fetched another grain of corn." And so the poor man went on saying "Then another locust came and fetched another grain of corn" for a long time, so that in the end the king grew very weary, and said the tale was endless, and told the poor man he might marry his daughter.

S. O. Addy, *Household Tales*, p. 15.

❡ This is the most complete of the English versions of "The Endless Tale", having the romantic suitor's task element.

THE OLD MAN AT THE WHITE HOUSE

There was once a man who lived in a white house in a certain village, and he knew everything about everybody who lived in the place.

In the same village there lived a woman who had a daughter called Sally, and one day she gave Sally a pair of yellow gloves and threatened to kill her if she lost them.

Now Sally was very proud of her gloves, but she was careless enough to lose one of them. After she had lost it she went to a row of houses in the village and inquired at every door if they had seen her glove. But everybody said "no", and she was told to go and ask the old man that lived in the white house.

So Sally went to the white house and asked the old man if he had seen her glove. The old man said: "I have thy glove, and I will give it thee if thou wilt promise me to tell nobody where thou hast found it. And remember, if thou tells anybody I shall fetch thee out of bed when the clock strikes twelve at night."

So he gave the glove back to Sally.

But Sally's mother got to know about her losing the glove, and said: "Where did you find it?"

Sally said: "I daren't tell, for if I do the old man will fetch me out of bed at twelve o'clock at night."

Her mother said: "I will bar all the doors and fasten all the windows and then he can't get in and fetch thee;" and she made Sally tell her where she had found her glove.

So Sally's mother barred all the doors and fastened all the windows, and Sally went to bed at ten o'clock that night and began to cry. At eleven she began to cry louder, and at twelve o'clock she heard a voice saying in a whisper, but gradually getting louder and louder:

"Sally, I'm up one step."
"Sally, I'm up two steps."
"Sally, I'm up three steps."
"Sally, I'm up four steps."
"Sally, I'm up five steps."
"Sally, I'm up six steps."
"Sally, I'm up seven steps."
"Sally, I'm up eight steps."
"Sally, I'm up nine steps."

"Sally, I'm up ten steps."
"Sally, I'm up eleven steps."
"Sally, I'm up twelve steps!"
"Sally, I'm at thy bedroom door!!"
"SALLY, I HAVE HOLD OF THEE!!!"

Reprinted from S. O. Addy, "Four Yorkshire Folk-Tales", *Folk-Lore*, VIII (1897), pp. 393–4, told by Richard Hirst, aged 18, of Sheffield.
¶ A literary version of this tale is Mark Twain's "The Man with the Golden Arm". See also "The Golden Arm", *Teeny-Tiny*, "The Bone", etc. Also "The Strange Visittor", "The Lady that Went to Church", "Peggy with the Wooden Leggy".

SIR GAMMER VANS

Last Sunday morning at six o'clock in the evening as I was sailing over the tops of the mountains in my little boat, I met two men on horseback riding on one mare: so I asked them, "Could they tell me whether the old woman was dead yet who was hanged last Saturday week for drowning herself in a shower of feathers?" They said they could not positively inform me, but if I went to Sir Gammer Vans he could tell me all about it.

"But how am I to know the house?" said I.

"Ho, 'tis easy enough," said they, "for 'tis a brick house, built entirely of flints, standing alone by itself in the middle of sixty or seventy others just like it."

"Oh, nothing in the world is easier," said I.

"Nothing *can* be easier," said they: so I went on my way.

Now this Sir G. Vans was a giant, and bottle-maker. And as all giants who *are* bottle-makers usually pop out of a little thumb-bottle from behind the door, so did Sir G. Vans.

"How d'ye do?" says he.

"Very well, I thank you," says I.

"Have some breakfast with me?"

"With all my heart," says I.

So he gave me a slice of beer, and a cup of cold veal; and there was a little dog under the table that picked up all the crumbs.

"Hang him," says I.

"No, don't hang him," says he; "for he killed a hare yesterday. And if you don't believe me, I'll show you the hare alive in a basket."

So he took me into his garden to show the curiosities. In one corner there was a fox hatching eagle's eggs; in another there was an iron apple-tree, entirely covered with pears and lead; in the third there was the hare which the dog killed yesterday alive in the basket; and in the fourth there were twenty-four *hipper switches* threshing tobacco, and at the sight of me they threshed so hard that they drove the plug through the wall, and through a little dog that was passing by on the other side. I, hearing the dog howl, jumped over the wall; and turned it as neatly inside out as possible, when it ran away as if it had not an hour to live. Then he took me into the park to show me his deer: and I remembered that I had a warrant in my pocket to shoot venison for his majesty's dinner. So I set fire to my bow, poised my arrow, and shot among them. I broke seventeen ribs on one side, and twenty-one and a half on the other; but my arrow passed clean through without ever touching it, and the worst was I lost my arrow: however, I found it again in the hollow of a tree. I felt it; it felt clammy. I smelt it; it smelt honey.

"Oh, ho," said I, "here's a bees' nest," when out sprang a covey of partridges. I shot at them; some say I killed eighteen; but I am sure I killed thirty-six, besides a dead salmon which was flying over the bridge, of which I made the best apple-pie I ever tasted.

Jacobs, *More English Fairy Tales*, p. 39.

⁋ There is a seventeenth-century version of this tale printed in *Penny Histories* (Bodleian, Wood, 704). It is an interesting example of the way in which tales are whittled down in oral tradition. It is called "A Strange and Wonderfull RELATION of an Old Woman that was Drowned at RATCLIF High-way a Fortnight Ago."

The beginning is not unlike the traditional story: "It was last Sunday morning, at four o'clock in the afternoon, before Sun-rise, going over Highgate-Hill in a Boat, I met a Man I overtook. I asked him, If the Old Woman was dead that was drowned at *Ratcliff Highway* a fortnight ago? He told me he could not tell; but if I went a little further, I should meet with two men a Horseback, upon a Mare, in a blew Jerkin and a pair of Freestone Breeches, and they would give me true intelligence."

After various *non sequiturs*, the narrator arrives at Sir John Vang's house. "At last I arrived at Sir John Vang's house, 'tis a little House all alone, encompassed with forty or fifty other Houses, having a brick Wall made of flint stones round about it, knocking at the door, Gammer *Vangs* (his wife) appeared: Gammer *Vangs*, said I, is Sir John Vangs within? Walk in, said she, and you shall find him in the little, great, round three-square Parlour. This Gammer Vangs had a little Old Woman to her Son, her Mother was a Church-Warden of a Troop of Horse, and her Grandmother was a Justice of the Peace; but when I came into the little, great, round, long three-square Parlour, I could not see Sir *John Vangs*, for he was a Gyant, but I espied abundance of wicker-bottles, and just as I was going out he call'd me, asking what I would have. So looking back I espied him just creeping out of a Wicker-bottle. (It seems by profession he was a Wicker-Bottle-Maker), and after he had made them he crept out of the stopper-holes."

The tale ends in a traditional way with a rhyme:

> Awake, arise, pull out your eyes,
> And see what time of day,
> And when you have done pull out your tongue,
> And see what you can say.

These *non sequiturs* were very popular in the seventeenth century. Corbet wrote two; an earlier one is to be found in Chambers' *Early English Lyrics*, "My Lady went to Canterbury" (c, li).

See "Five Men", "A Lying Tale", "Mother Shipton's House".

TEENY-TINY

Once upon a time there was a teeny-tiny woman lived in a teeny-tiny house in a teeny-tiny village. Now one day this teeny-tiny woman put on her teeny-tiny bonnet, and went out of her teeny-tiny house to take a teeny-tiny walk. And when this teeny-tiny woman had gone a teeny-tiny way, she came to a teeny-tiny gate; so the teeny-tiny woman opened the teeny-tiny gate, and went into a teeny-tiny churchyard. And when this teeny-tiny woman had got into the teeny-tiny churchyard, she saw a teeny-tiny bone on a teeny-tiny grave, and the teeny-tiny woman said to her teeny-tiny self, "This teeny-tiny bone will make me some teeny-tiny soup for my teeny-tiny supper." So the teeny-tiny woman put the teeny-tiny bone into her teeny-tiny pocket, and went home to her teeny-tiny house.

Now when the teeny-tiny woman got home to her teeny-tiny house, she was a teeny-tiny tired; so she went up her teeny-tiny stairs to her teeny-tiny bed, and put the teeny-tiny bone into a teeny-tiny cupboard. And when this teeny-tiny woman had been to sleep a teeny-tiny time, she was awakened by a teeny-tiny voice from the teeny-tiny cupboard, which said, "Give me my bone!"

And this teeny-tiny woman was a teeny-tiny frightened, so she hid her teeny-tiny head under the teeny-tiny clothes, and went to sleep again. And when she had been to sleep again a teeny-tiny time, the teeny-tiny voice again cried out from the teeny-tiny cupboard, a teeny-tiny louder, "Give me my bone!" This made the teeny-tiny woman a teeny-tiny more frightened, so she hid her teeny-tiny head a teeny-tiny further under the teeny-tiny clothes. And when the teeny-tiny woman had been to sleep again a teeny-tiny time, the teeny-tiny voice from the teeny-tine cupboard said again a teeny-tiny louder, "Give me my bone!" And this teeny-tiny woman was a teeny-tiny bit more frightened, but she put her teeny-tiny head out of the teeny-tiny clothes, and said in her loudest teeny-tiny voice, "TAKE IT!"

Halliwell, *Nursery Rhymes and Popular Tales*, p. 148.

THE THREE BEARS

Once upon a time there were Three Bears, who lived together in a house of their own, in a wood. One of them was a Little, Small, Wee Bear; and one was a Middle-sized Bear; and the other was a Great, Huge Bear. They had each a pot for their porridge; a little pot for the Little, Small, Wee Bear; and a middle-sized pot for the Middle Bear; and a great pot for the Great, Huge Bear. And they had each a chair to sit in; a little chair for the Little, Small, Wee Bear; and a middle-sized chair for the Middle Bear; and a great chair for the Great, Huge Bear. And they had each a bed to sleep in; a little bed for the Little, Small, Wee Bear; a middle-sized bed for the Middle Bear; and a great bed for the Great, Huge Bear.

One day, after they had made the porridge for their breakfast, and poured it into their porridge-pots, they walked out into the wood while their porridge was cooling, that they might not burn their mouths by beginning too soon to eat it.

And while they were walking, a little girl named Silver-hair came to the house. First she looked in at the window, and then she peeped in at the keyhole; and seeing nobody in the house, she lifted the latch. The door was not fastened, because the Bears were good Bears, who did nobody any harm, and never suspected that anybody would harm them. So little Silver-hair opened the door, and went in; and well pleased she was when she saw the porridge on the table. If she had been a good little girl she would have waited till the Bears came home, and then, perhaps, they would have asked her to breakfast; for they were good Bears—a little rough or so, as the manner of Bears is, but for all that, very good-natured and hospitable.

So first she tasted the porridge of the Great, Huge Bear, and that was too hot for her. And then she tasted the porridge of the Middle Bear, and that was too cold for her. And then she went to the porridge of the Little, Small, Wee Bear, and tasted that; and that was neither too hot nor too cold, but just right; and she liked it so well that she ate it all up.

Then little Silver-hair sate down in the chair of the Great, Huge Bear, and that was too hard for her. And then she sate down in the chair of the Middle Bear, and that was too soft for her. And then she sate down in the chair of the Little, Small, Wee Bear, and that was neither too hard, nor too soft, but just right. So she seated herself in it, and there she sate till the bottom of the chair came out, and down she came, plump upon the ground.

Then little Silver-hair went upstairs into the bed-chamber in which the Three Bears slept. And first she laid down upon the bed of the Great, Huge Bear; but that was too high at the head for her. And next she lay down upon the bed of the Middle Bear; and that was too high at the foot for her. And then she lay down upon the bed of the Little, Small, Wee Bear; and that was neither too high at the head nor at the foot, but just right. So she covered herself up comfortably, and lay there till she fell fast asleep.

By this time the Three Bears thought their porridge would be cool enough; so they came home to breakfast. Now little Silver-hair had left the spoon of the Great Huge Bear standing in his porridge. "SOMEBODY HAS BEEN AT MY PORRIDGE!" said the Great, Huge Bear, in his great, rough, gruff voice. And when the Middle Bear looked at his, he saw the spoon was standing in it too.

"*Somebody has been at my porridge!*" said the Middle Bear, in his middle voice.

Then the Little, Small, Wee Bear looked at his, and there was the spoon in the porridge-pot, but the porridge was all gone.

"Somebody has been at my porridge, and has eaten it all up!" said the Little, Small, Wee Bear, in his little, small, wee voice.

Upon this, the Three Bears, seeing that someone had entered their house, and eaten up the Little, Small, Wee Bear's breakfast, began to look about them. Now little Silver-hair had not put the hard cushion straight when she rose from the chair of the Great, Huge Bear.

"SOMEBODY HAS BEEN SITTING IN MY CHAIR!" said the Great, Huge Bear, in his great rough, gruff voice.

And little Silver-hair had squatted down the soft cushion of the Middle Bear.

"*Somebody has been sitting in my chair!*" said the Middle Bear, in his middle voice.

And you know what little Silver-hair had done to the third chair.

"Somebody has been sitting in my chair, and has sate the bottom of it out!" said the Little, Small, Wee Bear, in his little, small, wee voice.

Then the Three Bears thought it necessary that they should make further search; so they went upstairs into their bed-chamber. Now little Silver-hair had pulled the pillow of the Great, Huge Bear out of its place.

"SOMEBODY HAS BEEN LYING IN MY BED!" said the Great, Huge Bear, in his great, rough, gruff voice.

And little Silver-hair had pulled the bolster of the Middle Bear out of its place.

"*Somebody has been lying in my bed!*" said the Middle Bear in his middle voice.

And when the Little, Small, Wee Bear came to look at his bed, there was the bolster in its place; and the pillow in its place on the bolster; and upon the pillow was little Silver-hair's pretty head—which was not in its place, for she had no business there.

"Somebody has been lying on my bed—and here she is!" said the Little, Small, Wee Bear, in his little, small, wee voice.

Little Silver-hair had heard in her sleep the great, rough gruff voice of the Great, Huge Bear; but she was so fast asleep that it was no more to her than the roaring of wind, or the rumbling of thunder. And she heard the middle voice of the Middle Bear; but it was only as if she had heard someone speaking in a dream. But when she heard the little, small, wee voice of the Little, Small, Wee Bear, it was so sharp, and so shrill, that it awakened her at once. Up she started; and when she saw the Three Bears on one side of the bed, she tumbled out of the other and ran to the window. Now the window was open, because the Bears, like good, tidy Bears, as they were, always opened their bedroom window when they got up in the morning. Out little Silver-hair jumped; and away she ran into the wood; and the Three Bears never saw anything more of her.

Joseph Cundall, *A Treasury of Pleasure Books for Young People* (1856).
¶ The first widely known version of "The Three Bears" is that given by Southey in 1837 in *The Doctor*, IV, pp. 318–26. This was exactly copied by Jacobs in *English Fairy Tales*, p. 93. The heroine was an old woman. The story was not, however, originated by Southey, for a metrical manuscript version had been written by Eleanor Muir in 1831, for her godson. She described it as "the celebrated Nursery Tale of the Three Bears put into verse". This is in the Osborne Collection in The Toronto Public Library, and has now been published by the Oxford University Press.

N.G., in *The Three Bears and their Story* (1841), describes the author of *The Doctor* as the "original concocter" of the tale, but Joseph Cundall, whose version is given here, said that it had been often told, but never better than by Southey. In *Mother Goose's Fairy Tales* (Routledge, 1878) the three bears for the first time become Father, Mother, and Baby, and the little girl is Silver Locks. In 1889 she has become Little Golden-Hair, and very shortly after that, if not before, she took final shape as Goldilocks. In Dickens' reference to the tale in *Our Mutual Friend*, it is three hobgoblins, not three bears, who own the house.

In *More English Fairy Tales* (p. 87) Jacobs published "Scrapefoot", which he had lately discovered, in which the intruder was not a human being, but a fox. Jacobs thought it probable that this was a much earlier version, in which case the tale belongs to the early Bear and Fox tale-cycle.

See "Scrapefoot".

THE THREE WEE PIGS

There was once a pigs' house where they were getting thick on the ground. The old sow had a younger family, so one day she sent out Dennis and Biddy and Rex to find their fortunes for themselves. They wandered on and on, till they got up by the Devil's Elbow and Glenshee, and the wind was blowing, and it was snowing and raining at once, and oh! but their trotters were sore! So they sat down by the roadside, under the shelter of a wood. They sat for an hour. They had but one pipe and one match between them, and Dennis lent his pipe to Rex, and Rex dried the match in his hair, for it was soaked, and he sat and smoked the wee cuttie pipe. Presently they heard a cart coming along, and it was loaded with straw. Biddy thought she's build herself a house, if the man would give her some straw. And the man was very kind and obliging, for he was sorry for them, turned out of their Mother's house on such an awful day, just because Dennis had trod on one of the wee piglets by mistake.

So he gave them the straw, and some matches too, and Biddy built herself a cosy wee house. The other two were sitting a bittie longer, when they heard a cart coming up with slats of wood on it, and who should be driving it but Jimmie McLauchlan, who was at school with Dennis. So Dennis asked him for some of the slats of wood, to build himself a wee wooden housie. And Jimmie gave it him and welcome. Well, Dennis had hardly set to work when a lorry from Fife came up the road, with a load of bricks on it. Rex cried to the man, and he stopped, and threw out as many bricks as Rex needed to build himself a brick house. And there they were all settled for the night. But as Biddy was sitting in her cosy wee house, she heard someone knocking. "Is that you, Dennis?" she said. "Oh, no, it's an old friend," said a voice that she knew well. "Just let me in and have a news with you." "Oh, no, I'll not let you in," said Biddy, for she knew the wolf's voice when she heard it. "Then I'll puff and I'll blow, and I'll blow your house in," said the wolf, and he blew so hard that all the straw scattered. But just as he got in at the front door, Biddy ran out at the back, and went to Dennis's house. "He'll not blow this down," said Dennis. And that moment they heard the wolf at the door. "Let me in, I've a great piece of news for you." "No, we'll not let you

in," they said. "Then I'll puff and I'll blow, and I'll blow your house in."
And he blew so hard that he blew all the slats apart, and Biddy and Dennis
had only time to get out of the back door, and scamper to Rex's house
before the wolf was in at the front.

He raced on after them to Rex's house, but though he puffed and he
blew, he couldn't blow it down. So he crept up on to the roof to jump
down the lum. But Biddy had given Rex some straw to make a bed, and
when they heard the wolf on the roof he threw all the straw on the fire,
and it blazed up, and burnt him to death. So they hooked him down the
chimney, and cut him up into collops, and roasted him for their supper.
But there are no houses up in the wood now, for the pigs were all taken
to the old people's houses, and there they died.

School of Scottish Studies. Hamish Henderson, from Bella Higgins. Heard from her
mother.

❡ In version I the two first pigs are eaten by the wolf, and there is a further trial of
wits between the third pig and the wolf, reminiscent of the Brer Rabbit stories. The
same is true of the doggerel version printed by Joseph Cundall of "The Fox and the
Geese".

Version II, found by Andrew Lang, gives a happy ending to all three pigs, and the
same is true of III, the delightful "Three Wee Pigs", collected by Hamish Henderson.
See "The Fox and the Geese".

THE WEE, WEE MANNIE

Once upon a time when all big folks were wee ones and all lies were true,
there was a wee, wee Mannie that had a big, big Coo. And out he went to
her one morning, and said:

> "Hold still, my Coo, my hinny,
> Hold still, my hinny, my Coo,
> And ye shall have for your dinner,
> What but a milk-white doo."

But the big, big Coo wouldn't hold still. "Hout!" said the wee, wee
Mannie—

> "Hold still, my Coo, my dearie,
> And fill my bucket wi' milk,
> And if ye'll no' be contrairy
> I'll gi'e ye a gown o' silk."

But the big, big Coo wouldn't hold still. "Look at that now!" said the wee, wee Mannie.

> "What's a wee, wee Mannie to do,
> Wi' sic a big contrairy Coo!"

So off he went to his mother at the house. "Mother," he said, "Coo won't stand still, and wee, wee Mannie can't milk big, big Coo."

"Hout!" says his mother, "take stick and beat Coo." So off he went to get a stick from the tree, and said —

> "Break, stick, break,
> And I'll gi'e ye a cake."

But the stick wouldn't break, so back he went to the house. "Mother," says he, "Coo won't hold still, stick won't break, wee, wee Mannie can't beat big, big Coo."

"Hout!" says his Mother, "Go to the butcher and bid him kill Coo." So off he went to the Butcher, and said—

> "Butcher, kill the big, big Coo,
> She'll give me no more milk noo."

But the Butcher wouldn't kill the Coo without a silver penny, so back the Mannie went to the house. "Mother," says he, "Coo won't hold still, stick won't break, Butcher won't kill without a silver penny, and wee, wee Mannie can't milk big, big Coo."

"Well," said his mother, "go to the Coo and tell her there's a weary, weary lady with long yellow hair weeping for a sup of milk."

So off he went and told the Coo, but she wouldn't hold still, so back he went and told his mother.

"Well," said she, "tell the Coo there's a fine, fine laddie from the wars sitting by the weary, weary lady with the golden hair, and she weeping for a sup of milk."

So off he went and told the Coo, but she wouldn't hold still, so back he went and told his mother.

"Well," said his mother, "tell the big, big Coo there's a sharp, sharp sword at the belt of the fine, fine laddie from the wars who sits beside the weary, weary lady with the golden hair, and she weeping for a sup o' milk."

And he told the big, big Coo, but she wouldn't hold still.

Then said his mother, "Run quick and tell her that her head's going to be cut off by the sharp, sharp sword in the hands of the fine, fine laddie, if she doesn't give the sup of milk the weary, weary lady weeps for."

And the wee, wee Mannie went off and told the big, big Coo.

And when the Coo saw the glint of the sharp, sharp sword in the hand of the fine, fine laddie come from the wars, and the weary, weary lady weeping for a sup of milk, she thought she'd better hold still; so wee, wee Mannie milked the big, big Coo, and the weary, weary lady with the golden hair hushed her weeping and got her cup o' milk, and the fine, fine laddie new come from the wars put by his sharp, sharp sword, and all went well that didn't go ill.

Jacobs, *More English Fairy Tales*, p. 177.

A version of this, "There was a wee, wee wumman, who had a wee, wee coo", is printed in *JAFL*, XLVI, p. 81, no. 2016.

This tale is both more amusing and more poetic than "The Old Woman and her Pig", but it does not follow the same logical sequence.

See also "The Old Woman and Her Pig", "The Wife and Her Bush of Berries".

PART 6
BLACK DOGS

There are traditions of Black Dogs, good and evil, all over England, but they have received very little attention from the international index-makers. They are not entirely indigenous to Britain, for black dogs are known in Brittany and in Scandinavia. The *Motif-Index* mentions the black dogs that lead the wild hunt (E. 501, 4. 1.5). In the classification of E. T. Kristensen, *Danske Sagn*, devilish dogs and spectral dogs are given their places. On the Continent, the black dog is usually the witch's familiar, such as the black dog that accompanied Faustus. In Scotland the "Muckle Black Tyke", which presided at the Witches' Sabbats was supposed to be the Devil himself; the fairy dog was dark green. Occasionally in Scotland black dogs are treasure-guardians, like the dogs in Hans Andersen's "Tinder Box". Near Murthly, Perthshire, there is a standing stone, and it is rumoured that the man bold enough to move it will find a chest with a black dog sitting on it guarding it. It is said that the schoolmaster's sons once shifted the stone with gunpowder, but they took fright at the dog and put the stone back again. (This is on the authority of the Rev. Routledge Bell, who had it from one of his parishioners.)

The best studies of the Black Dogs are two articles in *Folk-Lore*: "The Black Dog", by Ethel Rudkin (*Folk-Lore*, June 1938), who gives various first-hand accounts of the black dog of Lincolnshire; and "The Black Dog", by Theo Brown (*Folk-Lore*, September 1958), who gives a systematic and generalized account of the black dog beliefs all over the country, with a map showing distribution.

She divides the dogs into three types: (A) the Barguest, which is a shape-shifting demon dog; (B) the black dog, which is uniform in type, about the size of a calf, generally shaggy and intensely black; (C) a rare type which occurs in certain parts of the country in conjunction with a calendar cycle.

Three other divisions might be made: the demon dogs; the ghosts of human beings; and the black dogs which appear to exist in their own right, some of them ghosts of dogs. They might also be divided into dangerous and benevolent dogs.

There are a great many accounts of the appearances of these dogs; many of whom are thought to be ghosts, some of dogs, some of humans, though others are thought to be devils and bogies. There are, however, several tales of guardian black dogs. Many, however, are accounts of appearances and can hardly be said to have stories attached to them.

THE BLACK DOG OF TRING

T. F. Thistleton Dyer, *The Ghost World*, p. 107.

Within the parish of Tring, Hertford, a poor old woman was drowned in 1751 for suspected witchcraft. A chimney-sweeper, who was the principal perpetrator of this deed, was hanged and gibbeted near the place where the murder was committed; and while the gibbet stood, and long after it had disappeared, the spot was haunted by a black dog. A correspondent of the *Book of Days* (ii, 433) says that he was told by the village schoolmaster, who had been "abroad", that he himself had seen this diabolical dog. "I was returning home," said he, "late at night in a gig with the person who was driving. When we came near the spot, where a portion of the gibbet had lately stood, he saw on the bank of the roadside a flame of fire as large as a man's hat. 'What's that?' I exclaimed. 'Hush!' said my companion, and suddenly pulling in his horse, made a dead stop. I then saw an immense black dog just in front of our horse, the strangest-looking creature I ever beheld. He was as big as a Newfoundland, but very gaunt, shaggy, with long ears and tail, eyes like balls of fire, and large, long teeth, for he opened his mouth and seemed to grin at us. In a few minutes the dog disappeared, seeming to vanish like a shadow, or to sink into the earth, and we drove on over the spot where he had lain."

¶ This is B of Theo Brown's black dog classification, and v, A, 3 of the Kristensen classification [*Spectral dogs*]. Theo Brown points out a frequent connection between black dogs and gallows.

This black dog is an aftermath of the notorious witch-ducking case, in which two old people were so maltreated that they died.

THE GUARDIAN BLACK DOG

Augustus Hare, *In My Solitary Life*, p. 188.

Mr. Wharton. . . said, "When I was at the little inn at Ayscliffe, I met a Mr. Bond, who told me a story about my friend Johnnie Greenwood, of Swancliffe. Johnnie had to ride one night through a wood a mile long to the place he was going to.

"At the entrance of the wood a large black dog joined him, and pattered along by his side. He could not make out where it came from, but it never left him, and when the wood grew so dark that he could not see it, he still heard it pattering beside him. When he emerged from the wood, the dog had disappeared, and he could not tell where it had gone to. Well, Johnnie paid his visit, and set out to return the same way. At the entrance of the wood, the dog joined him, and pattered along beside him as before; but it never touched him, and he never spoke to it, and again, as he emerged from the wood, it ceased to be there.

"Years after, two condemned prisoners in York Gaol told the chaplain that they had intended to rob and murder Johnnie that night in the wood, but that he had a large dog with him, and when they saw that, they felt that Johnnie and the dog together would be too much for them.

"Now that is what I call a useful ghostly apparition," said Mr. Wharton.

¶ This story was fairly widespread during the early 1900s, when Augustus Hare heard it. I was told it as a child in 1910, by an old clergyman, called Hosey, in London. A similar story was told in Yorkshire, about a well-known Nonconformist minister who had been making a charitable collection in a lonely part of the country.

See "A Good Black Dog".

LYME REGIS BLACK DOG LEGEND

J. S. Udal, *Dorsetshire Folk-Lore*, p. 167.

Near the town of Lyme stands a farm-house which once formed part of an old mansion that was demolished in the Parliamentary wars, except the small part still existing. The sitting-room now used by the farmer, and also by his predecessors for a century or two, retains the large old-fashioned fireplace with a fixed seat on each side under the capacious chimney. Many years ago, when the then master of the house, as his custom was after the daily toils were over, used to settle himself on one of these snug seats in the chimney corner, a large black dog as regularly took possession of the opposite one.

This dog, for many nights, weeks and months sitting *vis-à-vis* to the farmer, cast a gloom over his evening's enjoyment. At length, as he received no harm from the appearance, he began to look upon him as quite one of the family circle.

His neighbours, however, often advised him to get rid of the fiend-like intruder, but the farmer, not relishing a contest with him, jestingly replied: "Why should I? He costs me nothing; he is the quietest creature in the house; besides, he eats nothing." One night, however, the farmer having been drinking too freely with a neighbour and excited with his taunts about the black dog, determined his courage should be no more called in question. Returning home in a rage, he no sooner saw the dog in his usual seat than, seizing a poker, he rushed with it toward his mysterious companion. The dog fled into an attic, and just as the farmer entered it, he saw it spring from the floor and disappear through the ceiling. Enraged at being thus foiled, he struck with the poker the part where the dog had passed through and down fell a small old-fashioned box, which on being opened, was found to contain a large sum in gold and silver coins of Charles I's reign.

The dog was never more seen indoors, but to the present day continues to haunt at midnight a lane which leads to this house, and which has long borne the name of "Dog Lane". A small inn by the roadside still invites the passing stranger by the ominous sign of "The Black Dog" portrayed in all his spectral frightfulness.

The dog has been seen as recently as 1856, and may be seen at the present time by anyone curious enough to watch at midnight for its appearance.

Dogs should on no account be allowed to stray late at night in this neighbourhood, as there have been many cases of their disappearance in a mysterious manner, most likely frightened to death by the spectre!

¶ There seems at first sight no doubt that this dog was the ghost of a person, walking for the very common reason of having hidden treasure and died without telling of it. A strange feature, however, is that the ghost, though banished from the house by the finding of the treasure, continued to haunt the lane outside it, and to frighten mortal dogs to death, like a Barguest or Padfoot. One solution might be that the Barguest was harnessed by magic, and set to guard the treasure. If this were so, one might say that the spell was broken when the farmer struck him with cold iron.

PART 7
BOGIES

It is sometimes difficult to decide whether a tale is told about a bogie, a black dog, a devil or a fairy. In Somerset, *Bogie* is one name for the devil, but in general bogies, bogles, bug-a-boos and so on are frightening and mischievous spirits—minor devils, if they are devils at all. They sometimes appear as black dogs, but they have the power of shape-shifting, which the black dogs have not. The mildest of them are boggarts, which are brownies gone to the bad. The typical tale told of boggarts is "The Boggart" (ML7020). A tale told of a boggart, a bogie or the devil is Type 1090, of which there are several versions scattered through the country, a typical one being "The Farmer and the Boggart" from Lincolnshire. Two versions of Type 1676, A (Big 'Fraid and Little 'Fraid), come from places as distant as Lancashire and Cornwall. Nuckelavee is one of the most evil and diabolical of the bogies, and it may be doubted whether Vinegar Tom is a bogie or a minor devil. It is pleasant to find a story of the Buttery Spirit, one form taken by the Abbey Lubbers, which were supposed to haunt the abbeys inhabited by gluttonous monks. There are many descriptions of other bogies, such as Bloody-bones, Thrumpin, and Tom Dockin, but no real stories about them. Yet this small section ranges from the harmless, if irritating, merriment of the boggart to the hideous malignity of Nuckelavee.

THE BOGGART

Keightley, *The Fairy Mythology*, p. 307.

In the house of an honest farmer in Yorkshire, named George Gilbertson, a Boggart had taken up his abode. He here caused a good deal of annoyance, especially by tormenting the children in various ways. Sometimes their bread-and-butter would be snatched away, or their porringers of bread-and-milk be capsized by an invisible hand; for the Boggart never let himself be seen; at other times, the curtains of their beds would be shaken backwards and forwards, or a heavy weight would press on and nearly suffocate them. The parents had often, on hearing their cries, to fly to their aid. There was a kind of closet, formed by a wooden partition on the kitchen-stairs, and a large knot having been driven out of one of the deal-boards of which it was made, there remained a hole.* Into this one day the farmer's youngest boy stuck the shoe-horn, with which he was amusing himself, when immediately it was thrown out again, and struck the boy on the head. The agent was, of course, the Boggart, and it soon became their sport (which they called *laking†* *with Boggart*) to put the shoe-horn into the hole and have it shot back at them.

The Boggart at length proved such a torment that the farmer and his wife resolved to quit the house and let him have it all to himself. This was put into execution, and the farmer and his family were following the last loads of furniture when a neighbour named John Marshall came up. "Well, Georgey," said he, "and soa you're leaving t'ould house at last?" "Heigh, Johnny, my lad, I'm forced tull it; for that damned Boggart torments us soa, we can neither rest neet nor day for't. It seems loike to have such a malice again t'poor bairns, it onmost kills my poor dame here at thoughts on't, and soa, ye see, we're forced to flit loike." He scarce had uttered the works when a voice from a deep upright churn cried out, "Aye, aye, Georgey, we're flitting ye see." "Od damn thee," cried the poor farmer, "if I'd known thou'd been there, I wadn't ha' stirred a peg. Nay, nay, it's no use, Mally," turning to his wife, "we may as weel turn back again to t'ould hoose as be tormented in another that's not so convenient."

* The *Elfbore* of Scotland, where it is likewise ascribed to the fairies, Jamieson, *s.v.* The same opinion prevails in Denmark, where it is said that anyone who looks through it will see things he would not otherwise have known; see Thiele, ii, 18.

† The Anglo-Saxon *laean, laecan,* to play.

Abridged from the *Literary Gazette*, No. 430, 1825.

¶ This is a common tale in the British Isles. There is an Irish version given in *The Folk-Lore Journal*, I, p. 167, and Welsh one in Sikes, *Goblins*, p. 117, and Jones, *Folktales of Wales*, p. 50. There are Yorkshire, Lancashire, Lincolnshire and Shropshire versions. Tennyson versified the story in "The Northern Farmer: Old Style".

See "The Saut-Box", "The Farndale Hob", "Yes, We're Flutting" (B, V).

THE BUTTERY SPIRIT

Scott, *Minstrelsy of the Scottish Border*, II, p. 406.

An ancient and virtuous monk came to visit his nephew, an innkeeper, and, after other discourse, inquired into his circumstances. Mine host confessed, that, although he practised all the unconscionable tricks of his trade, he was still miserably poor.

The monk shook his head, and asked to see his buttery or larder. As they looked into it, he rendered visible to the astonished host an immense goblin, whose paunch, and whole appearance, bespoke his being gorged with food, and who, nevertheless, was gormandizing at the innkeeper's expense, emptying whole shelves of food, and washing it down with entire hogsheads of liquor. "To the depredation of this visitor will thy viands be exposed," quoth the uncle, "until thou shalt abandon fraud, and false reckonings." The monk returned in a year. The host having turned over a new leaf, and given Christian measure to his customers, was now a thriving man. When they again inspected the larder, they saw the same spirit, but woefully reduced in size, and in vain attempting to reach at the full plates and bottles, which stood around him; starving, in short, like Tantalus, in the midst of plenty.

¶ This tale may be found versified in Heywood's *Hierarchie of the Blessed Angels*, 1635, pp. 577–80.

In Sikes' *British Goblins*, pp. 180–1, there is a tale of a poltergeist which ate and destroyed food, but nothing so explicit as this Buttery Spirit, which is akin to the Abbey Lubbers, which haunted abbeys where the monks were given to gluttony.

See "Friar Rush" (A, II).

THE FARMER AND THE BOGGART

Norton Collection, III, p. 54.

T'boggart, a squat hairy man, strong as a six-year old horse, and with arms almost as long as tackle-poles, comes to a farmer who has just taken a bit of land, and declares that he is the proper owner, and the farmer must quit. The farmer proposes an appeal to the law, but boggart will have naught to do wi' law, which has never yet done him justice, and suggests that they should share the produce equally. "Very well," says the farmer, "wilt thou tek what grows above ground, or what grows beneath ground? Only, moind, thou mun stick to what thou sattles; oi doant want no back-reckunings after." He arranges to take what grows above ground, and the farmer promptly sets potatoes. Of course, when the boggart comes at harvest-time to claim his share, he gets nothing but the haulms and twitch, and is in a sore taking. At least, however, he agrees to take all that grows beneath ground for next season, whereupon the farmer sows wheat, and when boggart comes round at t'backend, the farmer gets corn and straw, and nought is left for boggart but the stubble.

Boggart then insists that next year wheat should be sown again, and that they should mow together, each taking what he mows. The farmer consults the local wise man, and studs boggart's "falls" with thin iron rods, which wear down boggart's strength in cutting, and take all the edge of his scythe. So boggart stops to whet, and boggart stops to rest, but the farmer mows steadily on, till at last the boggart throws down his scythe in despair, and says, "Ye may tek t'mucky old land, an' all 'at's on it; I wean't hev no more to do wi' it." And off he goes, and nivver comes back no more, leastways, not after no land, but awms about t'delves, an' skears loane foaks o' noights; an' if thou leaves thy dinner or thy tools about it, ofttimes he meks off wi' 'em.

Originally printed in Mabel Peacock's *Tales and Rhymes in the Lindsey Folk-Speech*, 1886; then in *The Saga-Book of the Viking Club*, III, pp. 37–8. From Mumby, near Alford.

⁋ See "The Bogie's Field", "Jack o' Kent and the Devil" (B, III).

NUCKELAVEE

Douglas, *Scottish Fairy and Folk-Tales*, p. 160.

Nuckelavee was a monster of unmixed malignity, never willingly resting from doing evil to mankind. He was a spirit in flesh. His home was the sea; and whatever his means of transit were in that element, when he moved on land he rode a horse as terrible in aspect as himself. Some thought that rider and horse were really one, and that this was the shape of the monster. Nuckelavee's head was like a man's, only ten times larger, and his mouth projected like that of a pig, and was enormously wide. There was not a hair on the monster's body, for the very good reason that he had no skin.

If crops were blighted by sea-gust or mildew, if live stock fell over high rocks that skirt the shores, or if an epidemic raged among men, or among the lower animals, Nuckelavee was the cause of all. His breath was venom, falling like blight on vegetable and with deadly disease on animal life. He was also blamed for long-continued droughts; for some unknown reason he had serious objections to fresh water, and was never known to visit the land during rain.

I knew an old man who was credited with having once encountered Nuckelavee, and with having made a narrow escape from the monster's clutches. This man was very reticent on the subject. However, after much higgling and persuasion, the following narrative was extracted:

Tammas, like his namesake, Tam o'Shanter, was out late one night. It was, though moonless, a fine starlit night. Tammas's road lay close by the seashore, and as he entered a part of the road that was hemmed in on one side by the sea, and on the other by a deep fresh-water loch, he saw some huge object in front of, and moving towards him.

What was he to do? He was sure it was no earthly thing that was steadily coming towards him. He could not go to either side, and to turn his back to an evil thing he had heard was the most dangerous position of all; so Tammie said to himself, "The Lord be aboot me, an' tak' care o' me, as I am oot on no evil intent this night!"

Tammie was always regarded as rough and foolhardy. Anyway, he determined, as the best of two evils, to face the foe, and so walked resolutely yet slowly forward. He soon discovered to his horror that the gruesome creature approaching him was no other than the dreaded Nuckelavee. The lower part of this terrible monster, as seen by Tammie, was like a great horse, with flappers like fins about his legs, with a mouth as wide as a whale's, from whence came breath like steam from a brewing-kettle. He had but one eye, and that as red as fire. On him sat, or rather seemed to grow from his back, a huge man, with no legs, and arms that reached nearly to the ground. His head was as big as a clue of simmons (a clue of straw ropes, generally about three feet in diameter), and this huge head kept rolling from one shoulder to the other, as if it meant to tumble off. But what to Tammie appeared most horrible of all, was that the monster was skinless; this utter want of skin adding much to the terrific appearance of the creature's naked body—the whole surface of it showing only red raw flesh, in which Tammie saw blood, black as tar, running through yellow veins, and great white sinews, thick as horse tethers, twisting, stretching, and contracting as the monster moved. Tammie went slowly on in mortal terror, his hair on end, a cold sensation like a film of ice between his scalp and his skull, and a cold sweat bursting from every pore. But he knew it was useless to flee, and he said, if he had to die, he would rather see who killed him than die with his back to the foe. In all his terror Tammie remembered what he had heard of Nuckelavee's dislike to fresh water, and, therefore, took that side of the road nearest to the loch.

The awful moment came when the lower part of the head of the monster got abreast of Tammie. The mouth of the monster yawned like a bottom-less pit. Tammie found its hot breath like fire on his face: the long arms were stretched out to seize the unhappy man.

To avoid, if possible, the monster's clutch, Tammie swerved as near as he could to the loch; in doing so one of his feet went into the loch, splashing up some water on the foreleg of the monster, whereat the horse gave a snort like thunder and shied over to the other side of the road, and Tammie felt the wind of Nuckelavee's clutches as he narrowly escaped the monster's grip. Tammie saw his opportunity, and ran with all his might; and sore need had he to run, for Nuckelavee had turned and was galloping after him, and bellowing with a sound like the roaring of the sea. In front of Tammie lay a rivulet, through which the surplus water of the loch found its way to the sea, and Tammie knew, if he could only cross the running water, he was safe; so he strained every nerve. As he reached the near bank another clutch was made at him by the long arms.

Tammie made a desperate spring and reached the other side, leaving his bonnet in the monster's clutches. Nuckelavee give a wild unearthly yell of disappointed rage as Tammie fell senseless on the safe side of the water.

¶ For escape from a hideous monster see "The Creech Hill Bull-beggar".

THE WHITE BUCCA AND THE BLACK

W. Bottrell, *Traditions and Hearthside Stories*, 1st series, p. 143.

There is a story told of an old lady who lived long ago at Raftra, in St. Levan.

The old dame, when more than fourscore, was so fond of card playing, that she would walk, almost every winter's night, in spite of wind or weather, to the village of Trebear, distant a mile or more, that she might enjoy her favourite pastime with a family of congenial tastes, who resided there. The old lady's stepdaughter wished to put a stop to what she regarded as rather scandalous vagaries, as the old dame seldom arrived home before the small hours of the morning; with this intention the young mistress persuaded the serving-man to array himself in a white sheet, etc., so as to personate a ghost that was supposed to wander about a lonely spot over which old madam would have to pass. The winter's night was dark and rainy, when, about midnight, the ghost seated himself on the side of Goonproynter stile, where he had to wait two or three hours.

The dear old lady was in no hurry to leave pleasant company, as it was Christmas-time. At last she passed Padz-Jiggs, mounted the stile, and seated herself opposite the ghost. Over a while she said, "Hullo! Bucca-gwidden [white spirit], what cheer? and what in the world dost thee do here, with Bucca-dhu so close behind thee?" This cool address so frightened Bucca-gwidden that he ran off as fast as he could lay feet to the ground, the old lady scampering after, clapping her hands and calling, "Good boy, Bucca-dhu. Now thee best catch Bucca-gwidden, and take'n away with thee!" The ghost was so frightened that he fell in a fit, and was never right in the head after. The strong-minded old lady enjoyed many more years of her favourite pastime with her friends in Trebear.

¶ See "Black Devil and White Devil".

PART 8
DEVILS

The Devil has played an enormous part in the folk-traditions of these islands, and his role has been rather variable. He shares some stories with the gullible giants of the folk-tales. He is always being tricked, given impossible tasks, sent on fools' errands, and generally being mocked and deluded by mankind. He shares with giants, too, the habit of lifting and hurling stones about and of moving shovelfuls of earth to bury towns. Sometimes he goes further than the giants, and lifts whole towns from one place to another. In a more formidable aspect he has taken over from Odin and other pagan gods the spectral ride which hunts lost souls. Sometimes he shares this habit with human ghosts, so that it is sometimes the Devil who hunts with the pack of Dandy Dogs, and sometimes the lost soul of Dando the Priest.

Another aspect is the relation between the Devil and the magician, in which the Devil is coerced or compelled by the superior power of magic, and occasionally by the power of holiness, as in the story of "The Devil to the Rescue", or the better-known legend of "The Devil and St Dunstan". Sir John Schorn, who conjured the Devil into his boot, was another ecclesiastic who could control the Devil. Indeed, a dauntless heart and a determination to have the last word will often worst him.

In the fairy tales the Devil is always foiled, but in the legends the issue is more tragic and the Devil more formidable. This is not only so in the tales from Puritan times; in tales from the medieval chronicles, such as "The Witch of Berkeley" from William of Malmesbury (see Part 17), he is no less irresistible, and the soul and body of the wretched woman are carried off together in spite of all precautions. When the witchcraft scare added to his prestige, he was to be found round every corner, presenting temptations, changing shape like a bogie beast, or disguising himself as a parson, a monk, or a beautiful woman. A large section of Chapter G in the *Motif-Index* is devoted to the attributes and activities of the Devil, but only a few stories could be included in this Sampler.

THE BLACK RIDER

Ruth L. Tongue, *Somerset Folklore*, p. 125.

Sam Thatcher was taking a bit of pudding and some teddies [potatoes] to Granny Thatcher down Combwich Track. His missus had just heard that the old lady was but poorly and a hotted-up pudding might cheer her up, and what was two-three teddies for a strong feller like Sam to carry to his mother. It was too late to send the children, so after his mug of tea, and bacon and cabbage, Sam set out again to walk back to Combwich. He slouched along the dark way wishing he had a match for his baccy, or a bit of company on the road. Then glancing up he saw a rider beside him. The track was pitch dark but he *saw* the huge black horse and its shrouded headless rider. He heard no sound as they passed and vanished. Sam looked at the dark way and took a firm grip on the sack of teddies. 'Twould make a club of sorts and Granny Thatcher must have her pudding.

When he got to her cottage she met him briskly. "Sammy," she cried joyfully, "I be so happy as a mouse in cheese. I bant over-looked [bewitched] no more. The old black witch down to Stert—have felled in rhine and drowned. The Black Man have took she, and I'll do justice to Susie's puddin'."

¶ There are many and widespread legends of the Devil as a huntsman, carrying off souls. In the Scandinavian stories it is often wood-wives whom he hunts, in England generally witches, though sometimes children, as in "The Demon Huntsman". See also "The Hunted Soul".

DANDO AND HIS DOGS [abridged]

Hunt, *Popular Romances*, p. 220.

In the neighbourhood of...St. Germans formerly lived a priest connected with the old priory church of this parish...He lived the life of the traditional "jolly friar". He ate and drank of the best the land could give him, or money buy; and it is said that his indulgences extended far beyond the ordinary limits of good living. The priest, Dando, was, notwithstanding all his vices, a man liked by the people. He was good-natured, and therefore blind to many of their sins.

As a man increases in years, he becomes more deeply dyed with the polluted waters through which he may have waded...So was it with Dando.

The sinful priest was a capital huntsman, and scoured the country far and near in pursuit of game, which was in those days abundant and varied over this well-wooded district. Dando, in the eagerness of the chase, paid no regard to any kind of property. Many a cornfield has been trampled down, and many a cottage garden destroyed by the horses and dogs which this impetuous huntsman would lead unthinkingly over them. Curses deep though not loud, would follow the old man, as even those who suffered by his excesses were still in fear of his priestly power...

Dando worshipped the sensual gods which he had created, and his external worship of the God of truth became every year more and more a hypocritical lie. The Devil looked carefully after his prize...and Dando was...lured towards the undoing of his soul. Health and wealth were secured to him, and by and by the measure of his sins was full, and he was left the victim to self-indulgences—a doomed man. With increasing years, and the immunities he enjoyed, Dando became more reckless... His days were devoted to the pursuits of the field; and to maintain the required excitement ardent drinks were supplied him by his wicked companions...Even on the Sabbath, horses and hounds were ordered out, and the priest would be seen in full cry.

One Sabbath morning, Dando and his riotous rout were hunting over the Earth estate; game was plenty, and sport first-rate. Exhausted with a long and eager run, Dando called for drink...

"Whence can we get it?" cried one of the gang.

"Go to Hell for it, if you can't get it on earth," said the priest, with a bitter laugh at his own joke on the Earth estate.

At the moment, a dashing hunter, who had mingled with the throng unobserved, came forward, and presented a richly-mounted flask to Dando, saying:

"Here is some choice liquor, distilled in the establishment you speak of. It will warm and revive you, I'll warrant. Drink deep, friend, drink."

Dando drank deep...and removed the flask, exclaiming, "By Hell, that was a drink indeed. Do the gods drink such nectar?"

"Devils do," was the reply.

"An they do, I wish I were one," said Dando..."Methinks the drink is very like——" The impious expression died upon his lips.

Looking round...Dando saw that his new friend had appropriated several head of game. Notwithstanding his stupid intoxication, his selfishness asserted its power, and he seized the game, exclaiming..."None of these are thine."

"What I catch, I keep," said the hunter.

"By all the devils, they're mine," stammered Dando.

The hunter quietly bowed.

Dando's wrath burst at once into a burning flame, uncontrolled by reason. He rolled himself off his horse, and rushed, staggering as he went, at the steed of his unknown friend, uttering most frightful oaths and curses.

The strange hunter's horse was a splendid creature, black as night, and its eyes gleamed...with unnatural lustre. The horse was turned adroitly aside, and Dando fell to the earth with much force...Aided by his attendants, he was speedily on his legs, and again at the side of the hunter, who shook with laughter, shaking the game in derision, and quietly uttering "They're mine."

"I'll go to Hell after them, but I'll get them from thee," shouted Dando.

"So thou shalt," said the hunter, and, seizing Dando by the collar, he lifted him from the ground, and placed him, as though he were a child, before him on the horse.

With a dash, the horse passed down the hill...and the dogs, barking furiously, followed impetuously. These strange riders reached the banks of the Lynher, and with a terrific leap, the horse and its riders, followed by the hounds, went out far in its waters, disappearing at length in a blaze of fire, which caused the stream to boil for a moment, and then the waters flowed on as tranquilly as ever over the doomed priest...

Dando never more was seen, and his fearful death was received as a warning by many, who gave gifts to the Church. One amongst them carved a chair for the bishop, and on it he represented Dando and his dogs, that the memory of his wickedness might be always renewed.

Cf. 'The Devil and his Dandy Dogs", T. Q. Couch, *Folk-Lore of a Cornish Village*.

¶ "The Devil's Dandy Dogs", one form which the Wild Hunt takes in the West Country, is supposed to be the ride of Dando and his hounds.

See "The Devil and His Dandy Dogs".

THE DEVIL AT THE CARD PARTY

Burne and Jackson, *Shropshire Folk-Lore*, p. 116.

A party of clergy were assembled one Sunday night at Plaish playing cards. All the doors were locked, when suddenly they burst open without any apparent cause. The men locked them again, but presently they burst open a second time, and again a third. Then the Old Gentleman appeared in the midst of the company, and they all rose up and fled, excepting the host, whom the others basely left face to face with the Enemy. None ever saw that wretched man again, either alive or dead.

Only a great stain of blood, shaped like a human form, was found on the floor of the room and, despite all efforts, the mark could never be washed out. Ever since then a ghostly troop of horse rides through the house at midnight, with such a noise that none can sleep.

¶ A story very like this is told of Glamis Castle to account for the secret room.

As a rule, the issue is less fatal, but in this version there is the extra aggravation of the Sabbath. An Irishman working at the Admiralty Stores in Perthshire during World War II told a more usual version of the story, in which the Devil joined the card-party incognito, and was recognized by his cloven hoof. The policeman and the minister were sent for to dismiss him without success, and he was finally exorcised by the Catholic priest. Informant, Elspeth Briggs.

See also "The Card-player and the Devil".

THE DEVIL AT LITTLE DUNKELD MANSE

Collected by K. M. Briggs from Mary Crerer, Dunkeld, 1926.

A long time ago there was a servant lassie, who worked for the Minister at Little Dunkeld. She was a quiet lass, who had no mind for dances and such follies, and she liked fine to go for long walks on Birnam Hill.

After a time she told the Minister that she had met a grand gentleman there, who used to walk and talk with her, and he was courting her. The Minister thought that a fine gentleman would be dangerous company for the lass, and he told her to bring him to the Manse, and let him see what kind of a man he was.

The lassie was pleased enough, and next Saturday she brought in her jo.

He was a grand-looking gentleman, sure enough, and pleasant spoken, but when the Minister looked down at his feet, the blood ran cold in his veins, for he saw that he had cloven hoofs, and he knew that there was just one person that had that. So, when the stranger had gone, he said to the lassie: "That's a braw man, yon, but did you see the feet of him?"

"Aye, did I," said the lass, "and bonnie feet he has, with braw shining boots."

"Take another look on them, when you see him again," said the Minister.

But nothing he could say made any difference. She was still terribly taken up with him. At last it came to this, that the braw gentleman asked her to marry him. When the Minister heard that, he was sorely put about, but at length he said: "Well, you may be married on one condition, that none shall wed you but me, and that the wedding shall be in the Manse."

The lassie was well enough pleased at that, for it would be a grand wedding for her, and when the day came, half the parish came to see it. All the guests were waiting, and the bride in her bonnie new gown, and there was no sign of the bridegroom. But at length they heard a great rumbling, and a chariot drove up to the door, with six black horses. In comes my fine gentleman, bowing and smiling around him. The guests were terribly taken up with him, but the Minister saw the cloven hoofs of him as plain as ever.

So the Minister took a candle, and he lighted it at both ends, as they do for the bidding at a roup [auction], and he said: "Now, when this candle is burnt out I'll marry you, and not a minute before."

The stranger looked black at this; but the Minister held the candle steadily bet ween his two fingers, while the bride cried, and the bridegroom scowled, and the guests shuffled their feet and whispered. The wax dripped and dripped, and the candle burnt and burnt, till the one flame was about two inches from the other. Then, whilst it was still burning, the Minister put it into his mouth and swallowed it.

"Now," he said, "the candle will never burn out, and you will never be married."

With that the stranger gave a most awesome shriek, and leaped out of the window, and vanished into the earth, and his coach and six with him. And outside Little Dunkeld Manse there is a black spot of earth where they say no grass will grow to this day.

¶ Mary Crerer is of an old Dunkeld family and had this tale from an old woman, a neighbour. The same tale was collected by Grace Underwood from an inhabitant of Birnam, and published in *Folk-Lore*, XXII, 1911, pp. 330–1.

See also "Betty's Candle", "The Candle", "The Devil's Wooing".

A MINISTER MOLESTED

W. Henderson, *Folk-Lore of the Northern Counties*, p. 278.

A country minister, after attending a meeting of his presbytery, had to return home alone, and very late, on a dark evening. While riding in a gloomy part of the road, his horse stumbled, and the good man was flung to the ground. A loud laugh followed, so scornful and so weird, that the minister felt no doubt of the quarter whence it proceeded. However, with a stout heart, he remounted without delay, and continued his journey, crying out, "Ay, Satan, *ye* may laugh; but when I fall, I can get up again; when *ye* fell, *ye* never rose"—on which a deep groan was heard. This was firmly believed to have been an encounter with the Evil Spirit, and a great triumph for the dauntless minister.

THE PRIZE WRESTLER AND THE DEMON
[shortened]

W. Bottrell, *Hearthside Stories and Legends of the West of Cornwall*, 3rd series, p. 3.

There was a famous wrestler of Ladock, called John Trevail, more generally known as "Cousin Jackey", from the common practice of thus styling favourites who may be no relation. One Midsummer's Day Jackey went into a neighbouring parish and threw their champion wrestler. In his pride, as he swaggered round the ring, he said, "I am open to a challenge from any man, and wouldn't mind having a hitch with the Devil himself."

After the wrestling he passed a few hours with his comrades in the public house. On his way home alone, about the "turn of the night", he came to a common called Le Pens Plat, two miles or more from Ladock Churchtown. As he was going on slowly, from being somewhat tired, and not very steady in the head, he was overtaken by a gentleman dressed like a clergyman, who addressed him in gentle tones, saying:

"I was at the wrestling today, and I think you are the prize wrestler. Am I right?"

"Yes, sir. I won the prize that I now carry," replied Trevail, who felt very uneasy at meeting there such a strange black-coated gentleman at that time of night, though a full moon and clear sky made it almost as light as day.

"I am very fond of wrestling myself," resumed the stranger; "and as I want to learn more science in my play, I should much like to try a bout with you; say, for your gold-lace hat and five guineas, which I will stake."

"Not now, sir, for I'm tired," Jackey replied, "but I'll play you after dinner-time, if you please, when I've had a few hours' rest—say two or three o'clock, if it will please you."

"Oh, no; it must be at midnight, or soon after, now the nights are short," said the stranger; "it would never do for one in my position to be seen wrestling with you by day."

Trevail hesitated, and thought of the wild words he had uttered in the ring. He·had then challenged the Devil, and he felt persuaded that he was now face to face with his enemy, in this lonely spot. However, he agreed to the stranger's proposal to meet him there at midnight, or soon after; they shook hands on the bargain, and the gentleman gave him a purse with five guineas in it for his stake, saying:

"You are well known to be an honest fellow. I've no fear of your not bringing the money and the prize won today; and if, by any mischance, I shouldn't come, the money is yours; but there's little doubt of my being here sharp at midnight."

He wished Jackey good-morrow, and went away over the common by another path leading northward. The poor fellow felt as good as gone; in looking down as he said "Good-morrow" (he couldn't bear the stranger's eye) he had seen what he believed to be a cloven hoof. But he could devise no plan to avoid his fate.

Dragging himself along, he got to his dwelling about three o'clock in the morning. His wife, seeing Jackey's haggard looks, refrained from "jawing" him as usual, and the want of her rough tongue made him feel worse than ever. Throwing the bag of guineas into the tool-chest, he said, "Molly, my dear, doesn't thee touch that shammy-leather bag for the world! 'Tes the Devil's money that's in am!" Little by little he told her what had happened, and concluded by moaning out:

"Molly, my dear, thee hast often wished that Old Nick would come and take me away bodily, and now et do seem es ef thy prayers are to be answered."

"No, no, Jackey, my son, never think of et," sobbed she; "whatever I said was only from the lips outward, and that's of no effect, my darlin'. Bad as thee art, it might be wes [worse] without thee. Go thee ways up to bed; I'll this minute put on my cloak and away to the passen. No good for thee nor all the world to say no, for he only can save thee."

On her way to beg Mr Wood's assistance, she called up a croney with whom she was on pretty fair terms just then, and said, "Come along to the passen's. I'm so flambustered I can hardly speak. Something dreadful have happened to our Jackey; and you mustn't drop a word to anybody, for your life, of what I'll tell 'e on the road."

The reverend gentleman was standing at his door, looking out in the grey of the morning, when he saw the two women, in much agitation, coming towards him. Jackey's wife with her apron to her eyes, sobbed out her case, and when he had an inkling of it he said:

"Make haste home, my good woman, and tell Jackey, from me, to cheer up; I'll see him presently, and tell him how to act."

Shortly after sunrise Mr Wood entered the wrestler's dwelling, and found him stretched out on the chimney-stool, fast asleep. Mr Wood roused him, and said:

"Jackey, is there any truth in what your wife has told me, or did you fall asleep on the common, and have an ugly dream? Tell me what happened, from first to last, and let's see the bag."

"'Tes all like an ugly dream, sure enow, your Reverence," he replied, "but the Old 'Un's money es there in my tool-chest, and I remember every word that passed; besides, such fiery eyes I never beheld in any other head"; then Jackey brought the bag, holding it at arm's length with a pincers, as he might a toad. He opened it, and the parson said: "The sight of these spade guineas, with what you have told me, leave no doubt that you bargained to wrestle with the Devil. But take courage; you must be as good as your word. Don't fail to be at the appointed place by midnight and take with you the stakes as agreed on."

Jackey looked very dejected and answered that he had hoped to have Mr Wood's company.

"No. I shall not go with you" he answered. "Yet depend on it, I'll be near at hand to protect you against foul play."

Whilst saying this, Mr Woods took from his pocket-book a slip of parchment, on which certain mystic signs and words were traced or written.

"Secure this in the left-hand side of your waistcoat," said he, "don't change your waistcoat, and be sure to wear it in the encounter; above all, show no fear; behave with him precisely as you would with any ordinary wrestler, and don't spare him, or be fooled by his devices."

He cautioned him to keep the matter private.

"That I will," replied Jackey. "I haven't told a living soul but my wife, and she can keep a secret first-rate—for a woman."

At the appointed time he went boldly to Le Pens Plat Common, and at midnight the stranger in black appeared by the same path he took in the morning. They looked hard at each other for some minutes without speaking, till Trevail said, "I've come in good time, you see, and there are the prizes on the rock. You know the rules of the game, I suppose, that one must lay hold above the waist; whichever makes three falls in five bouts wins the prize; it belongs to you, as the challenger, to take the first hitch."

Still the stranger made no reply, and kept his gleaming eyes fixed on the wrestler, who, feeling uncomfortable under his persistent stare, said; "Then, if you won't wrestle, take your money, and no harm done."

That instant he felt himself seized, all unawares, by his waistband, and lifted clear of the ground. It seemed as if the Old One rose with him many yards above the earth, but during a desperate struggle in the air, the man got his right arm over his opponent's shoulder, and grabbing him on the back with a good holdfast, took a crook with his legs. As he did so, his waistcoat touched the Evil One, who on the instant, lost his hold, fell flat on his back, as if knocked down, and writhed on the ground like a wounded snake. The wrestler pitched to his feet, never the worse, as the other rose to his feet in fury, and exclaimed, "You have some concealed weapon about ye that has wounded me; cast off that waistcoat."

"No, by golls," replied Jackey, "feel my jacket, ef you like; there's no weapon in am, not even a pin's head; but 'tes you that show the queer tricks; catch me off my guard again if you can."

He clenched the Old One like a vice; for five minutes they struggled together at arm's length; the Old One seemed afraid to close in. Jackey feared the blasting gleams of his evil eyes, and couldn't get a crook with his legs, but at length making a desperate plunge, he freed himself from the Devil's grasp, took him with the "flying mare", and threw him on his back with such a "qualk" as made him belch brimstone fumes.

He quickly sprang up, looking furious, and said, "I'm deceived in you, for your play is very rough. Request Parson Wood to go home. I am confused and powerless while he is looking on."

"I don't see Mr Wood," returned Jackey.

"I can see his eyes glaring at me from between the bushes," replied the other; "and I hear him mumbling something too. If I am foiled again, it will be all owing to your confounding parson."

"Never mind our passon; he can wrestle very well himself," said Jackey, "and do like to see good play; so come on, at it again." He grasped his opponent in a "Cornish hug," with more vigour than ever, laid him on his back, and said; "There, you have had three fair falls, but if they don't satisfy ye, I've more science to teach ye yet." But during the half-minute or so that he watched the prostrate demon crawling on the ground like a serpent, the sky became overcast, and the moon obscured with gathering clouds which seemed bursting with thunder. In the dim light Jackey saw that in a twinkling the black gentleman's feet and legs had become like those of a huge bird; his skirts changed to a pair of wings; and his form was still changing to that of a dragon, when he flew away, skimming the ground at first, and leaving a wake of lurid flame; then soared to the clouds, which on the instant became ablaze with lightning, and the thunder roared from hill to hill. The black cloud, as it rose, seemed like a huge wheel, revolving in the air, flashing lightning, and shooting thunderbolts from all around its border.

As Jackey gazed stupefied at the clearing sky, Parson Wood touched him on the shoulder, saying, "Well done, my boy; I was proud to see thy courage and good play. Take up thy prizes and let's be off home." As Jackey hesitated to touch the bag of guineas, he added: "Take the money; it's fairly won." Trevail took the bag, and as he pocketed it a flash of light drew their attention to the fiend's retreat, now a mere dot in the clear sky. They saw a streak of fire leave it, and fall, like a shooting star, in a neighbouring parish.

"Mark that, Jackey," exclaimed Mr Wood. "It strikes me we haven't seen the last of your wrestling devil yet. He's down among the St Endor witches."

On their way home, Mr Wood told Jackey that it was only his fright that had made him think the devil had carried him high in the air; but this Jackey could never quite believe, and to his dying day, asserted that on his first hitch he was taken up "towers high". Then Mr Wood told him that, long before midnight he had been at the spot, and summoned many powerful spirits to watch the wrestling, for such matches between men and demons, once common, had become rare of late. The fiend, too, had been attended by a host of lower devils, as well as by vagrant spirits of the night, visible to the parson, though not to Jackey. Bets were exchanged among the watchers, and many of the demon's backers were now bound, in consequence, to serve the winners for many ages, which at least would somewhat alleviate their eternal restlessness and boredom.

Mr Wood's only regret was, that, in climbing a hedge, he had lost in the brambles the ebony stick with which he had hoped to thrash the beaten devil, in revenge for his assuming the dress of the sacred office. In the moment before he could recover his stick, the demons had effected their master's escape.

The devil's money did little good to its winner; for the woman to whom Trevail's wife had confided her trouble had not kept it to herself; and the rumour spread that the Trevails' new clothes, and grand appearance in church, were the result of Jackey's having sold himself to the Devil. But Jackey continued for many years as the champion wrestler of the neighbourhood.

¶ See "Parson Woods and the Devilish Bird", "The Devil and the Blacksmith".

PART 9
DRAGONS

In Fairy Tales the dragons are occasionally like the heraldic dragon, with bats' wings, a scaly body and tail, four legs ending in claws, and a fiery breath. It is such a winged dragon that St George fights; but in the legends the dragon is more like the Scandinavian worms. "The Gurt Vurm of Shervage Wood" is a common type. This worm shares with the snake, in popular belief, the power of joining its parts together if it is cut in pieces. The Dragon of Wantley had wings, the Dragon of Kingston had a fiery breath, but these are exceptions; the rule is for snake-like dragons of great cunning and a poisonous rather than a fiery breath, who wind themselves round their victims like boa constrictors. Often these creatures come out of the sea like the worm in the story of "King Arthur and the Dragon", though this worm was completely dominated by the holiness of St Carantacus.

In "The Linton Worm" we see the development of the great snake into the winged, poison-breathing dragon, tentatively beginning in tales about the worm which were told to Somerville of Lariston.

THE DRAGON OF WANTLEY [summary]

Harland and Wilkinson, *Legends and Traditions of Lancashire*, p. 265.

This dragon was the terror of all the countryside. He had forty-four iron teeth, and a long sting in his tail, besides his strong rough hide and fearful wings.

He ate trees and cattle, and once he ate three young children at one meal. Fire breathed from his nostrils, and for long no man dared come near him.

Near to the dragon's den lived a strange knight named More of More Hall, of whom it was said that so great was his strength that he had once seized a horse by its mane and tail, and swung it round and round till it was dead, because it had angered him.

Then, said the tale, he had eaten the horse, all except its head. At last the people of the place came to More Hall in a body, and with tears implored the knight to free them from the fearful monster, which was devouring all their food, and making them go in terror of their lives. They offered him all their remaining goods if he would do them this service. But the knight said he wanted nothing except one black-haired maid of sixteen, to anoint him for the battle at night, and array him in his armour in the morning. When this was promised, he went to Sheffield, and found a smith who made him a suit of armour set all over with iron spikes, each five or six inches in length.

Then he hid in a well, where the dragon used to drink, and as it stooped to the water, the knight put up his head with a shout and struck it a great blow full in the face. But the dragon was upon him, hardly checked by the blow, and for two days and a night they fought without either inflicting a wound upon the other. At last, as the dragon flung himself at More with the intention of tossing him high into the air, More succeeded in planting a kick in the middle of its back. This was the vital spot: the iron spike drove into the monster's flesh so far, that it spun round and round in agony groaning and roaring fearfully, but in a few minutes all was over, it collapsed into a helpless heap, and died.

¶ A point worth noting in this legend is the preparatory anointing of the hero by a black-haired maiden.

For the armour covered with spikes, see "The Lambton Worm" (A, II). "The Dragon of Loschy Hill."

THE GURT VURM OF SHERVAGE WOOD

Ruth L. Tongue, *Somerset Folklore*, pp. 130–1.

"Now, look see, I wad'n there then so I couldn' swear 'twas the truth, could I now? But 'twas like this, see.——

"There was a tremenjus gurt vurm up-over in Shervage Wood. Ah—all a-lyin' in and out the trees an' round about the Camp, so big and fat round as two-three girt oaks. When her felt hungry her just u'n swallow down 'bout six or sebm ponies or sheep and went to sleep comfortable.

"Well then, by'n by, farmers do notice sheep idn' upalong an' there wadn' more'n a capful of skinny old ponies for Bridgewater Fair that year.

"Where was t'others gone to, then?

"Arter a shepherd an' a couple of Stowey broom-squires went upalong to look-see and didn' come back neither there wadn' nobody at all ready to go pickin' worts on the hill when Triscombe Revel time come around next year.

"The vurm he were gettin' a bit short on his meals like. The deer an' the rabbits they was all over to Hurley Beacon t'other side of the hills, and there wadn' a sheep left, and the ponies, I reckon, had run down over valley to Forty Acre.

"Now, I did hear there were a poor old soul who sold the worts for Triscombe Revel. Her made they tarts beautivull and filled'n up with a thick dap o' cream that made 'ee come back for more so fast as a dog'll eat whitpot. Well, look see, there wadn' likely to be no tarts for her to sell on account of no one going up over to see how worts was ripenin', 'n if her didn' sell no tarts to Triscombe Revel her'd get no money for the rent. Poor ould soul! Her was in a shrammle!

"Well then, there come a stranger to Crowcombe, all the way from Stogumber I expect, and he were a woodman looking for work. So her up'n tells'n, 'Why don't 'ee try cuttin' in Shervage Wood upover, and look-see if worts is getting ripe?' Poor old soul were desperate, see. So her give'n a cider firkin and bread'n cheese, and watches'n go off up combe.

"Being a Stogumber stranger he wadn' used to Quantock hills and by the time he'd a-walked into Shervage Wood and seed a wonderful fine lot of worts on the way he were feeling 'twere quite time for his cider.

"So he looks round like and he seed a bit of a girt log in the fern. So down he quots an' takes a swig from the firkin an' gets out his bread an' cheese. He'd just got nicely started on his nummet when the log begins to squirmy about under'n.

"'Hold a bit!' says he, picking up his axe. 'Thee do movey, do thee? Take that, then.'

"And the axe came down so hard on the log he cutt'n in two—mind, I'm only telling 'ee what 'tis said—and both the ends of the log begun to bleed!

"Then the one end it up and run as hard as it could go to Bilbrook, and t'other end it runned to Kingston St Mary, and since they two halves went the wrong way to meet, the gurt vurm couldn' nowise grow together again—so her died.

"Folks down to Bilbrook they call their place Dragon Cross, and folk to Kingston St Mary they boasts about the same old tale of a fiery dragon —might be as they got the head end of our gurt vurm—but he were all Quantock to start with!

"Well then, the woodman he just sat and finished his nummet, and cut his faggot, and took the poor old soul a girt hatful of worts.

"'There were a dragon there fust go off,' he tells her very thoughtful.

"But all her says, is, 'Didn' 'ee know? Didn' someone tell 'ee?'

"Her were a Crowcombe woman."

I have written this from early recollections of a jovial Nether Stowey teller of the tale in my childhood and the recitals of local epics and libels by a thatcher of my acquaintance.

¶ Baughman cites Whistler, *Folk-Lore*, 1908, for a version of this story, which is halfway between a jocular tale and a dragon-legend.

KING ARTHUR AND THE DRAGON

Ruth L. Tongue.

Once long ago, when the high tide used to come right over Carr Marshes to the foot of Dunster Castle, a great serpent lived in the wet marshes, and used to come out to kill men and cattle all over the countryside. At length the people sent to King Arthur in Camelot, and asked him to rid the country of it. He came himself, and rode down to Carhampton to the marshes, but the creature hid itself away, and search as he might, he could not find any trace of it. As he was riding along by Carhampton (or, some say, Cleeve), he saw a strange, table-like thing of coloured marble floating on the water. He drew it to land, and found engraved on it "The altar of St Carantacus". He remembered then how the story went that St Carantacus had flung his massy altar into the Severn, and meant to build a church where it came to land. So King Arthur covered it carefully, and rode on. After a while a stranger met him, and asked if he had seen the altar of Carantacus. "Who are you?" said the King, for he did not wish the holy altar to fall into the hands of some sorcerer.

"I am Carantacus," replied the stranger. Arthur still mistrusted him. "If you are indeed the saint," he said, "call up the dragon I am hunting from his hiding-place, and I will show you the altar." The stranger turned to the marsh, and said a word, and at once the whole bog heaved, and a wave of mud came up with a great stench, at their feet. Out of it came the dragon, and crawled up to the saint, who tied his stole round its neck.

King Arthur led the way to the altar, St Carantacus followed, with the dragon crawling meekly behind. Where the altar lay, the king gave twelve portions of land for a church, but the altar itself he took back to Camelot, and made it into his round table. But what came to the dragon is more than anyone remembers.

From local traditions of Carhampton and Billhook.

THE LINTON WORM

James Fleming Leishman, *Linton Leaves*, p. 10.

During the twelfth century the people of Linton were in great distress by reason of a voracious monster or worm, whom a writer of the seventeenth century describes as being "in lenth three Scots yards, and somewhat bigger than ane ordinary man's leg...in form and callour to our common muir edders". This monster had its lair in a hollow in the northeast side of Linton Hill, a spot which is known to this day as the Worm's Den. From thence it used to creep out "and wander the feildes over to catch somewhat", which it easily did, so that "the whole countrymen thereabouts were forced to remove their bestiall, and transport themselves three or four miles from the place, leaving the country desolate; neither durst any passenger go to the church or mercet upon that rod for fear of this beast".

Somerville of Lariston, who was at this time in the south, became curious to see the monster about which he had heard so many strange tales, and he travelled north to Jedburgh with this intent. Here he found many panic-stricken country folk who had fled to the town for refuge. Some said the monster was beginning to grow wings, and others that it shot fire out of its mouth at will, and yet others that its very breath was so venomous that it could kill cattle at a distance. But these exaggerated rumours only made Somerville the more curious to view the beast, and so he rode one day at dawn to the mouth of its den. When it crawled forth and observed the horseman so near its den, "it lifted up its head and half of its body and long time stared him in the face with open mouth", after which it apparently returned to its lair and did him no harm. After this, young Somerville, who was now quite determined to kill the monster, began to watch its habits and movements with the greatest care. Noticing that it invariably stared an observer in the face with open mouth, he hit upon an ingenious plan. He had a long lance made, of great strength, with a slender iron wheel half a foot from the point, which turned upon the slightest touch. Upon the point he placed a lighted peat, bedaubed with pitch and brimstone, and then for several days he rehearsed his proposed attack till his horse grew accustomed to the smoke and fire blowing in his face. When everything was in readiness, he "gave advertisement to the gentlemen and commons in that country that he would undertake to kill the monster or die in the attempt". His older neighbours, some of whom had already tried in vain to kill the worm with arrows and darts, scoffed at his announcement as the madness or bravado of youth. But Somerville took little heed of their scepticism, and, accompanied by a trusty servant, he rode to the worm's den at sunrise on the appointed day.

The moment the beast's head and part of its body appeared the servant set fire to the peats. Then Somerville, spurring his practised horse, advanced at full gallop and thrust the blazing lance into the beast's open mouth and down its throat. As the horse rebounded the lance broke, but the fatal blow had been given, and the monster, writhing "in the pangs of death (some part of its body being within the den) raised up the whole ground that was above her, and overturned the same to the furthering of her ruin".

For his heroic deed Somerville won universal applause and gratitude, and besides being appointed Royal Falconer was honoured with knighthood, and made first Barrone of Lintoune.

The ancient tympanum over the church door is traditionally reputed to have been placed there to commemorate his prowess. Despite 800 years' exposure to the elements, the rude sculpture on flaky sandstone is still quite traceable. It depicts a man in full armour bearing a falcon on his arm, in the act of charging a four-footed animal which—unfortunately for the verity of the legend—more resembles a wolf or bear than a serpent. One of the supposed versions of the inscription, which is now effaced, runs:

The Wode Laird of Laristoune

Slew the Worm of Worme's Glen
And wan all Linton Parochine.

Though some affirm that it was the monument that gave rise to the legend, rather than the legend to the monument, the Somerville Stone is of unique interest, not only on account of its great age and connection with local history, but as the only complete example of a tympanum with figure carving left in Scotland.

¶ For this method of killing a dragon see "The Mester Stoorworm" (A, II).

THE LONGWITTON DRAGON

F. Grice, *Folk-Tales of the North Country*, p. 95.

In a wood not far from the village of Longwitton are three wells which have been famous for many years. Long ago people used to travel from far and near to drink the water from the wells, for it was as sweet as wine and had great healing powers. Many a shepherd whose bones ached after the long, wet winter on the hills came to drink and ease his pains, and many a sickly child found new health there. The people of Longwitton were justly proud of their wells, for there seemed to be magic in them.

One day, however, a ploughman, going to quench his thirst, was alarmed to find a huge dragon there. It had coiled its tail round one of the trees, and pushed its long black tongue into the well, and was lapping the water like a dog. When it heard him approach it vanished; but the ploughman knew that it had only made itself invisible, for he heard its claws in the dead leaves, and felt its hot breath on his face. He fled from it in terror, and only escaped by zigzagging through the trees.

From that day no pilgrim dared visit the magic wells, for the dragon haunted them. It was a fearsome monster, with a skin as warty as a toad's and a long tail like a big lizard's. It tore up the ground with its claws, and scraped the bark from the trees as it brushed past them. But few people caught sight of it, for when anyone drew near it made itself invisible, and nothing could be seen except the leaves trembling before its breath and the flowers being crushed beneath its feet. It did little harm, and seemed content to live alone in the wood and drink from the wells; but whenever the men of Longwitton set out to attack it, it was infuriated, and the trees shook round about it as if a whirlwind had suddenly struck the wood. It seemed to have claimed the wells and would not give them up to anyone. The wells grew overgrown and untidy, while the shepherds had to nurse their aches as best they could. But one day there came riding by Longwitton a knight in search of adventure.

"We have here a jealous dragon, sir," said the people of Longwitton to him, "which we would gladly be rid of, but it has the power of making itself invisible, and no man can get near enough to strike a blow at it."

"I will overcome that difficulty," said the knight. "I will stay here tonight, and give battle to the dragon tomorrow."

So the next morning he anointed his eyes with a magic ointment which he had been given on his travels, and rode to the wood. The dragon was lying sleeping near one of the wells, but when it heard the sound of the horse's hoofs in the dry leaves its ears pricked up, and the spines on its back rose. Then, trusting to its invisibility, it charged. The knight was ready. The dragon, over-careless, struck wildly with its claws, and the knight plunged his sword into its side. The dragon roared with pain, for the wound was severe, but it backed quickly, until it stood defending the well, and prepared to attack again. But no matter how dreadful a wound the knight inflicted, the dragon seemed to keep its strength, and the wounds healed as quickly as they were received. For hours they fought, the dragon with its clumsy movements being no match for the nimbler man; but at last the knight, worn out and arm-weary, rode away.

He was almost ashamed to confess his failure to the villagers, but he was not easily dismayed.

"I will fight the dragon again tomorrow," he said.

But the next day, although he delivered enough blows to kill a thousand dragons, the beast was as strong at the end of the day as at the beginning, and the knight was forced to retire again.

"I will try a third time," he said. "This dragon must possess some other magical power which I have not noticed. Tomorrow I will use my eyes more and my arm less."

So he went out the third day, and for the third time attacked the dragon. But this time, as he laid about him, he kept his eyes wide open, and at last he noticed that, no matter how fiercely he drove against the dragon, it would not stir from the well; and then looking more clearly he observed that it always lay so that the tip of its tail dipped into the water.

"Ah! That is the secret," he said. And he dismounted from his horse, and led it a little into the wood. Then he approached the dragon on foot, and pierced it lightly here and there till, enraged, it roared wildly and leapt at him. Then he retreated, fighting faintly and deluding the monster into thinking that he was exhausted and beaten. Step by step he fell back until he had lured it from the well. Then, suddenly leaping on to his horse, he rode round the dragon, and placed himself between it and the well. The dragon perceiving how it had been tricked roared like a mad bull, and fought desperately to get back to the well. But this knight, knowing now that he had mastered it, dealt it blow on blow, and this time every wound weakened it more and more. The blood dripped from its side and burned the grass beneath it; it grew feebler and feebler until it fell heavily and lay still.

The next day the people of Longwitton buried it. Then they tidied the wells, and sent out news that the monster was dead, and there was rejoicing that night in every cottage for twenty miles round.

PART 10
FAIRIES

There are a few creatures among the fairies of the English-speaking people which have no real stories attached to them. Their attributes and habits were known, but no memorable anecdotes were told of them. Such were Kit Canstick, Lob-lie-by-the-Fire, urchines, kilmoulis and others. The names and some of the attributes of these creatures may be found in *The Fairies in Tradition and Literature*; all those of whom I have succeeded in finding any stories are grouped together in the Fairy section of *The Dictionary of British Folk-tales*. It will be seen that they are of very different kinds and powers, ranging from the small, helpless people, like Colman Grey and Skillywidden, to the formidable fairy of "The Fairy Follower", who haunted and engrossed the man who had raised her. Some are always small, some are of human size, some can change size and shape at will. Some are solitary, some social, some, like the brownies, devote themselves to the service of man. Some are beautiful, some hideous.

Their reputed origins are as various as their characteristics. Some are supposed to be the dead, or certain of the dead, some fallen angels, some nature spirits, and some "spiritual animals".

The commonest types of fairy anecdote are those of changelings, of human midwives, and of mortals carried off into fairyland. Almost equally common are tales of fairy thefts, often of the goodness, or "foison", taken out of the milk, cattle, or grain of the fairies' human neighbours, and there are tales of mischief and misleading. On the other hand, there are examples of fairy gratitude and of helpful hobgoblins of the brownie type, who labour in farms or houses without hire or reward.

The story which gives the most explicit account of the origin and social history of the fairies is Bottrell's tale of "The Fairy Dwelling on Selena Moor". It contains so many elements of fairy belief as to be most instructive. The danger of eating food in fairyland, the fairies as ghosts of prehistoric people, the fairy desire to reinforce their stock by the theft of humans, the power of taking the form of birds or animals, and the fairies' dwindling size, are all exemplified in this tale, which is so lengthy that it has had to be summarized. In some ways the story is reminiscent of the medieval version of Orpheus and Eurydice, in which Queen Meroudys is carried away by the King of Fairy because she has slept under a grafted apple tree.

ANNE JEFFERIES AND THE FAIRIES [summary]

Hunt, *Popular Romances of the West of England,* pp. 127–9.

Anne Jefferies was the daughter of a poor labourer in the parish of St Teath. It is said that she lived from 1626 to 1698.

At nineteen she became a servant in the family of Mr Moses Pitt. She was a brave, bold girl, and her great wish was to make friends with the fairies. So often after sunset she would look for them under the fronds of ferns, and in the bells of the foxgloves, singing:

> "Fairy fair and fairy bright,
> Come and be my chosen sprite."

Or on a moonlight night, walking in the valley against the stream, she would sing:

> "Moon shines bright, waters run clear,
> I am here, but where's my fairy dear?"

For a long time the fairies tested her. They never lost sight of her, but would run from frond to frond of the ferns, so that she should never see them.

But at last, when Anne was sitting in her master's garden after her morning's work, she heard the branches moving, and thought her sweetheart had come to look for her. So she sat still, saying nothing, attending to her knitting, and soon she heard a soft laugh. Still no one appeared, and she said half-aloud, "You may stay there till the kueney [moss or mildew] grows on the gate ere I'll come to 'ee."

A strange, ringing and musical laugh, which she knew was not her lover's, startled her. But she was a favourite in the parish, and told herself that no one would harm her. She heard the garden gate open and close again very softly, and soon she saw at the entrance to the arbour where she was sitting six little men handsomely dressed in green. They had charming faces and bright eyes, and the grandest of them wore a red feather in his cap. He came forward, bowed to her, and when she held out her hand, jumped on to it, climbed into her lap, and up to her neck and face, and began kissing her. Presently he called the others, and they all came and kissed her. She was altogether charmed, until one of them pricked her eyes, and blinded her for a time. They carried her away to some distant place, flying through the air, and then one of them said, "Tear away!"—or so it sounded to Anne. Her sight was restored, and she found herself in a most beautiful place. The temples and palaces were of gold and silver; the lakes full of gold and silver fish, and the trees laden with fruit and flowers. Now the little people seemed no smaller than herself, and Anne joined in their play and dancing, dressed as splendidly as the rest. Her six friends constantly attended her, but the one who had spoken to her first aroused the jealousy of the rest because he remained always her favourite. At last they separated themselves, and went into a most lovely garden, where Anne would have wished to stay for ever. But the other five found the place, and came at the head of a fierce mob of the little people to attack her lover, who soon lay wounded at her feet. Then the fairy who had blinded her before laid his hands on Anne's eyes, and amid darkness and strange noises she felt herself whirled through space, as if a thousand flies were buzzing round her. When she opened her eyes, she was lying on the ground in the arbour with an anxious crowd of faces watching her. All thought she had suffered some kind of convulsion, from which she was now recovered.

¶ According to Anne Jefferies, this incident was only the beginning of her fairy experiences. After that the fairies were constantly with her, though invisible to other mortals. They fed her with fairy food, so that between harvest-time and Christmas she ate nothing else. They gave her the gift of prophecy and a healing touch. Her cures became famous, and her prophecies were all in favour of the Royalists. This, and her ardent Episcopalianism, got her into trouble with the Parliament, and in 1646 she was imprisoned and prosecuted as a witch by the famous John Tregeagle (see B, VI).

A contemporary account of her was written by Moses Pitt, to whose parents she had been apprenticed, and is quoted by Hunt (Appendix K, p. 470). The best and fullest account of Anne Jefferies is given by Barbara C. Spooner in *John Tregeagle of Trevorder, Man and Ghost*, pp. 14–17.

See "Cherry of Zennor".

THE BROKEN BILK

Hartland, *English Fairy and Folk-Tales*, p. 90.

As a countryman was one day working in a field in Upton Snodbury, he all of a sudden heard a great outcry in a neighbouring piece of ground, which was followed by a low, mournful voice, saying, "I have broke my bilk, I have broke my bilk"; and thereupon the man picked up the hammer and nails which he had with him, and ran to the spot from whence the outcry came, where he found a fairy lamenting over his broken bilk, which was a kind of cross-barred seat; this the man soon mended, and the fairy, to make him amends for his pains, danced round him till he wound him down into a cave, where he was treated with plenty of biscuits and wine; and it is said that from thenceforward that man always did well in life.

¶ See also "The Broken Ped", "The Fairy's Kirn-staff", "The Fairy's Spade".

THE BROWNIE

Keightley, *The Fairy Mythology*, p. 358.

A good woman had just made a web of linsey-woolsey, and, prompted by her good nature, had manufactured from it a snug mantle and hood for her little Brownie. Not content with laying the gift in one of his favourite spots, she indiscreetly called to tell him it was there. This was too direct, and Brownie quitted the place, crying,

> "A new mantle and a new hood:
> Poor Brownie! ye'll ne'er do mair gude!"

Another version of this legend says that the gudeman of a farm-house in the parish of Glendevon having left out some clothes one night for Brownie, he was heard to depart, saying,

> "Gie Brownie coat, gie Brownie sark,
> Ye'se get nae mair o' Brownie's wark!"

At Leithin-hall, in Dumfriesshire, a Brownie had dwelt, as he himself declared, for three hundred years. He used to show himself but once to each master; to other persons he rarely discovered more than his hand. One master was greatly beloved by Brownie, who on his death bemoaned him exceedingly, even abstaining from food for many successive days. The heir returning from foreign parts to take possession of the estate, Brownie appeared to do him homage, but the Laird, offended at his mean, starved appearance, ordered him meat and drink, and new livery. Brownie departed, loudly crying,

> "Ca', cuttee, ca'!
> A' the luck o' Leithin Ha'
> Gangs wi' me to Bodsbeck Ha'."

In a few years Leithin Ha' was in ruins, and "bonnie Bodsbeck" flourishing beneath the care of Brownie.

Others say that it was the gudeman of Bodsbeck that offended the

Brownie by leaving out for him a mess of bread and milk, and that he went away, saying,

> "Ca', Brownie, ca',
> A' the luck of Bodsbeck awa to Leithenha'."

¶ Similar tales are told of other fairy creatures. See "The Fairy Threshers", "Hob Thrust", "The Kind Pixy", "The Pixy Threshers", "The Piskie Threshers", "Rewarding a Pixy".

THE CAPTURED FAIRIES

Bowker, *Goblin Tales of Lancashire*, p. 72.

In the village of Hoghton, where all industrious people were weavers, there were two idle fellows, who did no work, but spent their days at dominoes, and their nights in poaching. Each of them owned a lurcher, but the dogs grew so clever that they would often go off alone, and both of them were at last shot by keepers, who were waiting for a chance to rid the neighbourhood of them. Soon afterwards the two men themselves narrowly escaped being caught, and as a result they lost their nets, and being too poor to buy new ones, they were compelled to use sacks for their poaching instead. One night they entered a warren, put a ferret down a hole, and fixed their sacks at the mouths of the burrows. Almost at once there was a frantic struggling in the sacks, so the men seized them firmly, recovered their ferret, and made for home. What was their horror when they suddenly heard a voice from one of the sacks, "Dick, where art thou?" A voice from the other sack replied,

> "In a sack,
> On a back,
> Riding up Hoghton Brow."

The men dropped their loads in terror, and fled home, leaving their sacks full of fairies. Next morning, when they ventured back, they found the sacks neatly folded at the roadside, but no trace of their occupants. They picked up the sacks with care, crept home, and entirely gave up poaching as a means to a living. Their conversion into industrious weavers aroused suspicion in the village, and at last they were driven to confess what had happened. The tale made them the butt of the village youngsters, who would often in mischief, cry out in their hearing, "Dick, where art thou?"

¶ A Yorkshire version of the tale is in *Folk-Lore*, v, 1894, pp. 341–2.
For a similar tale from Sussex see "The Stolen Pig and the Fairy".

THE FAIRY DWELLING ON SELENA MOOR

W. Bottrell, *Traditions and Hearthside Stories of West Cornwall*, Penzance, 1870–80,
3 vols., II, pp. 95–102, as summarized in *The Fairies in Tradition and Literature*,
K. M. Briggs, pp. 15–19.

The tale is about a Mr Noy, a well-liked farmer, who lived near Selena
Moor and who went out to the neighbouring inn one night to order
drink for the Harvest Home next day. He left the inn, but never arrived
home. They searched for him for three days, and at last, passing within
half a mile of his home, they heard dogs howling, and a horse neighing.
They went over the treacherous bogland of the moor, and found a great
thicket, where Mr Noy's horse was tethered, with the dogs beside it. The
horse had fed well on the rich grass, but the dogs were very thin. The
horse led them to a ruined bowjey (or barn) and there they found Mr Noy
fast asleep. He was surprised to see that it was morning already, and was
very dazed and bewildered, but at last they got his story from him. He
had made a short-cut through the moor, but had lost his way and had
wandered, he thought, many miles over country unknown to him, until
he saw lights in the distance and heard music. He hurried towards it,
thinking that he had come at last to a farmhouse, where they were perhaps
holding a Harvest Home supper. His horse and dogs shrank back and
would not come with him, so he tied his horse to a thorn, and went on
through a most beautiful orchard towards a house, outside which he saw
hundreds of people either dancing or sitting drinking at tables. They were
all richly dressed, but they looked to him very small, and their benches
and tables and cups were small too. Quite close to him stood a girl in
white, taller than the rest, and playing a kind of tambourine. The tunes
were lively, and the dancers were the nimblest he had ever seen. Soon the
girl gave the tambourine to an old fellow near, and went into the house
to fetch out a black-jack of ale for the company. Mr Noy, who loved
dancing and would have been glad of a drink, drew near to the corner
of the house, but the girl met his eyes, and signed to him to keep back.
She spoke a few words to the old fellow with the tambourine, and then
came towards him.

"Follow me into the orchard," she said.

She went before him to a sheltered place, and there in the quiet starlight,
away from the dazzle of the candles, he recognized her as Grace Hutchens,
who had been his sweetheart for a long time, but had died, or was thought
to have died, three or four years before.

"Thank the stars, dear William," she said, "that I was on the look-out to stop ye, or ye would this minute be changed into the small people's state, like I am, woe is me!"

He would have kissed her, but she warned him anxiously against touching her, and against eating a fruit or plucking a flower if he wished ever to reach his home again.

"For eating a tempting plum in this enchanted orchard was my undoing," she said. "You may think it strange, but it was all through my love for you that I am come to this. People believed, and so it seemed, that I was found on the moor dead; what was buried for me, however, was only a changeling or a sham body, never mine, I should think, for it seems to me that I feel much the same still as when I lived to be your sweetheart."

As she said this several little voices squeaked, "Grace, Grace, bring us more beer and cider, be quick, be quick!"

"Follow me into the garden, and remain there behind the house; be sure you keep out of sight, and don't for your life touch fruit or flower."

Mr Noy begged her to bring him a drink of cider too, but she said she would not on his life; and she soon returned, and led him into a bowery walk, where all kinds of flowers were blooming, and told him how she came there. One evening about dusk she was out on Selena Moor looking for a stray sheep, when she heard Mr Noy hallooing to his dogs, so she took a short-cut towards him, and got lost in a place where the ferns were above her head, and so wandered on for hours until she came to an orchard where music was sounding, but though the music was sometimes quite near she could not get out of the orchard, but wandered round as if she was pixy-led. At length, worn out with hunger and thirst, she plucked a beautiful golden plum from one of the trees, and began to eat it. It dissolved into bitter water in her mouth, and she fell to the ground in a faint. When she revived she found herself surrounded by a crowd of little people, who laughed and rejoiced at getting a neat girl to bake and brew for them and to look after their mortal babies, who were not so strong, they said, as they used to be in the old days.

She said their lives seemed unnatural and a sham. "They have little sense or feeling; what serves them in a way as such, is merely the remembrance of whatever pleased them when they lived as mortals—maybe thousands of years ago. What appear like ruddy apples and other delicious fruit are only sloes, hoggins [haws] and blackberries."

Mr Noy asked her if any fairy babies were born, and she answered that just occasionally a fairy child was born, and then there was great rejoicing

—every little fairy man, however old and wizened, was proud to be thought its father. "For you must remember that they are not of our religion," she said in answer to his surprised look, "but star-worshippers. They don't always live together like Christians and turtle-doves; considering their long existence, such constancy would be tiresome for them; anyhow, the small tribe seem to think so."

She told him also that she was now more content with her condition, since she was able to take the form of a small bird and fly about near him.

When she was called away again Mr Noy thought he might find a way to rescue them both; so he took his hedging gloves out of his pocket, turned them inside out and threw them among the fairies. Immediately all vanished, Grace and all, and he found himself standing alone in the ruined bowjey. Something seemed to hit him on the head, and he fell to the ground.

Like many other visitors to Fairyland, Mr Noy pined and lost all interest in life after this adventure.

¶ This tale exhibits a remarkable collection of fairy beliefs, particularly those held by Cornishmen. Bottrell gives a summary of another similar tale, about a farmer named Richard Virgoe, who was pisky-led in Treville Cliffs. This Fairyland, a pleasant, underground country, was reached by a cavern. The fairies were hurling with a silver ball, which recalls Elidor's Golden Ball.

See "True Thomas" (A, II).

THE GREEN CHILDREN

Hartland, *English Fairy and Folk-Tales*, p. 132.

"Another wonderful thing," says Ralph of Coggeshall, "happened in Suffolk, at St Mary's of the Wolf-pits. A boy and his sister were found by the inhabitants of that place near the mouth of a pit which is there, who had the form of all their limbs like to those of other men, but they differed in the colour of their skin from all the people of our habitable world; for the whole surface of their skin was tinged of a green colour. No one could understand their speech. When they were brought as curiosities to the house of a certain knight, Sir Richard de Caine, at Wikes, they wept bitterly. Bread and other victuals were set before them, but they would touch none of them, though they were tormented by great hunger, as the girl afterwards acknowledged. At length, when some beans, just cut, with their stalks were brought into the house, they made signs, with great avidity, that they should be given to them. When they were brought, they opened the stalks instead of the pods, thinking the beans were in the hollow of them; but, not finding them there, they began to weep anew. When those who were present saw this, they opened the pods, and showed them the naked beans. They fed on these with great delight, and for a long time tasted no other food. The boy however was always languid and depressed, and he died within a short time. The girl enjoyed continual good health, and, becoming accustomed to various kinds of food, lost completely that green colour, and gradually recovered the sanguine habit of her entire body. She was afterwards regenerated by the laver of holy baptism, and lived for many years in the service of that knight (as I have frequently heard from him and his family), and was rather loose and wanton in her conduct. Being frequently asked about the people of her country, she asserted that the inhabitants, and all that they had in that country, were of a green colour; and that they saw no sun, but enjoyed a degree of light like what is after sunset. Being asked how she came into this country with the aforesaid boy, she replied, that as they were following their flocks they came to a certain cavern, on entering which they heard a delightful sound of bells; ravished by whose sweetness, they went for a long time wandering on through the cavern, until they came to its mouth. When they came out of it, they were struck senseless by the excessive light of the sun, and the unusual temperature of the air; and they thus lay for a long time. Being terrified by the noise of those who came on them, they wished to fly, but they could not find the entrance of the cavern before they were caught."

From Keightley, *The Fairy Mythology*, p. 281 quoting *Ralph of Coggeshall*.

¶ This story is also told by William of Newbridge, who places it in the reign of King Stephen. He says he long hesitated to believe it, but he was at length overcome by the weight of evidence. According to him, the place where the children appeared was about four or five miles from Bury St Edmunds. They came in harvest-time out of the wolf-pits; they both lost their green hue, and were baptized, and learned English. The boy, who was the younger, died; but the girl married a man at Lenna, and lived many years. They said their country was called St Martin's Land, as that saint was chiefly worshipped there; that the people were Christians, and had churches; that the sun did not rise there, but that there was a bright country which could be seen from theirs, being divided from it by a very broad river. This is one of those curiously convincing and realistic fairy anecdotes which are occasionally to be found in the medieval chronicles.

HORSE AND HATTOCK

Scott, *Minstrelsy of the Scottish Border*, II, p. 367.

The Laird of Duffus was walking out in his fields one day, when a cloud of dust whirled past him, and from the midst of it he heard a shrill cry of "Horse and Hattock". Being a bold man, he repeated the cry, and immediately found himself whirled away in the air with a troop of fairies to the King of France's cellar. There they caroused all night so merrily that the Laird fell asleep and was left behind. The royal butler found him next day, still fast asleep, with a cup of curious workmanship in his hand. He was taken before the King, and told him all that had happened. The King pardoned him, and he returned home with the fairy cup, which was kept in his family for several generations.

Retold in *The Personnel of Fairyland*, p. 65.

¶ See "Hupp Horse and Handocks", "The Piskies in the Cellar", "The Boy and the Fairies", "The Black Laird of Dunblane", "Da Trow's Spell".

INKBERROW'S TING-TANG [summary]

Hartland, *English Fairy and Folk-Tales*, p. 90.

Long ago the church at Inkberrow was pulled down and rebuilt upon a new site, which chanced to be near a spot where the fairies lived. They took offence, and for a long time tried to obstruct the building, carrying back the stones every night to the place from which they had come.

However, the builders had their way at last, and the new site was secured. But for many years afterwards it is said that from time to time a voice was heard lamenting:

"Neither sleep, neither lie,
For Inkbro's ting-tang hangs so high."

From Jabez Allies, *On the Antiquities and Folk-Lore of Worcestershire*, p. 418.

¶ See "Departure of the Fairies", "Withypool Ding-dongs".

JEANNIE'S GRANNY SEES A FAIRY

Hamish Henderson, School of Scottish Studies.

My grannie thought that she wouldna like to go til her bed and lie down and sleep and her horse having nothing to eat. So she, jist being about sixteen or seventeen, so when she thought that everything was quiet, she went for a little shawl that they drew over their head, you know, and their shoulders, and she made to the nearest field, and she goes up a wee bittie, up through the field; they were beginning to pile the stooks up, ye know. And when she went so far, she noticed this thing getting' up—this, you know, this little image-thing. It could have been a child, ye know, because they did wear queer dresses in these days, but she thought, to her, she said, it was like a fairy, and she said that when she went up near it, it lookit to her to be like a little lady, ye know, beautifully dressed, and it seems it lookit at her and it stoppit in front of her, and when she walkit it was jumpin' frae stook to stook, frae stook to stook, ye know, and she did get feart. She says, "A well, God bless us, I cam here to steal, but now," she says, "When I see that," she says, "I'm not goin' to touch this corn. I'll turn," she says, "and I'm gaun back withoot it." And she did but she lookit at it, and it kept goin' awa from her, like—it was steeppin' frae stook to stook through the field. But she did get a good look at it. And she aye swore to us eftir that it was a fairy, and naebody wad change her mind.

She was a wummin that never drank in her life, and she was very very sensible, and she says, "Well," she says to me, "it might have been a spirit or something, I dinnae ken, but," she says, "to me it lookit like a little wee wummin," she says, "lovely dressed, and it kept steppin' and jumpit up nae far frae me," she says—"When I cam right up I got a good look at it, when it jumpit on a stook, kept gaun on the stooks in front of me till it gaed right out of sight." An' she says. "I jist gied awa to bou doun to take the corn," she says, "and then when it did appear to me, I couldnae take the corn," she says. "I jist watched it gin up owre the stooks, and I turned," she says, "and went back the road." She believes it was a fairy, and she wouldnae touch it.

From Jeannie Robertson, 1959.

⁋ The special function of this little solitary fairy, leaping from stook to stook, without oversetting them, seems to have been to act as a guardian of the cornfield.

JOHNNIE IN THE CRADLE

Hamish Henderson, School of Scottish Studies.

A man and his wife were not long married, and they had a wee kiddie called Johnnie, but he was always crying and never satisfied. There was a neighbour near, a tailor, and it came to market day, and Johnnie was aye greeting, and never growing. And the wife wanted to get a day at the market, so the tailor said he'd stay and watch wee Johnnie. So he was sitting sewing by the fire, and a voice said: "Is ma mother and ma faither awa'?" He couldn't think it was the baby speaking, so he went and looked out of the window, but there was nothing, and he heard it again. "Is ma mother and ma faither awa'?" And there it was, sitting up, with its wee hands gripping the sides of the cradle. "There's a bottle of whisky in the press," it says. "Gie's a drink." Sure enough, there was one, and they had a drink together. Then wee Johnnie wanted a blow on the pipes, but there was not a set in the house, so he told the tailor to go and fetch a round strae from the byre, and he played the loveliest tune on the pipes through the strae. They had a good talk together, and the wee thing said, "Is ma mother and ma faither coming home?" And when they came, there he was "Nya, nya, nya", in the cradle. By this time the tailor knew it was a fairy they had there, so he followed the farmer into the byre, and told him all that had happened. The farmer just couldn't bring himself to believe it; so between them they hit on a contrivance. They let on that a lot of things had not been sold at the market, and there was to be a second day of it, and the tailor promised to come over again to sit by the bairn. They made a great stir about packing up, and then they went through to the barn, and listened through the keek hole in the wall. "Is ma mother and ma faither gone?" said the wee thing, and the mother could just hardly believe her ears. But when they heard the piping through the cornstrae, they kent it was a fairy right enough, and the farmer went in to the room, and he set the gridle on the fire and heated it red hot, and he fetched in a half bagful of horse manure, and set it on the gridle, and the wee thing looked at him with wild eyes. When he went to it to grip it, and put it on the gridle, it flew straight up the lum, and as it went it cried out, "I wish I had a been longer with my mother. I'd a kent her better."

Told by Andrew Stewart.

¶ See "The Changeling, II", "The Fairy Changeling, II".

THE LAIRD OF BALMACHIE'S WIFE

Gibbings, *Folk-Lore and Legends, Scotland*, p. 52.

In the olden times, when it was the fashion for gentlemen to wear swords, the Laird of Balmachie went one day to Dundee, leaving his wife at home ill in bed. Riding home in the twilight, he had occasion to leave the high road, and when crossing between some little romantic knolls, called the

Cur-hills, in the neighbourhood of Carlungy, he encountered a troop of fairies supporting a kind of litter, upon which some person seemed to be borne. Being a man of dauntless courage, and, as he said, impelled by some internal impulse, he pushed his horse close to the litter, drew his sword, laid it across the vehicle, and in a firm tone exclaimed:

"In the name of God, release your captive."

The tiny troop immediately disappeared, dropping the litter on the ground. The Laird dismounted, and found that it contained his own wife, dressed in her bedclothes. Wrapping his coat around her, he placed her on the horse before him, and, having only a short distance to ride, arrived safely at home.

Placing her in another room, under the care of an attentive friend, he immediately went to the chamber where he had left his wife in the morning, and there to all appearance she still lay, very sick of a fever. She was fretful, discontented, and complained much of having been neglected in his absence, at all of which the laird affected great concern, and, pretending much sympathy, insisted upon her rising to have her bed made. She said that she was unable to rise, but her husband was peremptory and having ordered a large wood fire to warm the room, he lifted the impostor from the bed, and bearing her across the floor as if to a chair, which had been previously prepared, he threw her on the fire, from which she bounced like a sky-rocket, and went through the ceiling, and out at the roof of the house, leaving a hole among the slates. He then brought in his own wife, a little recovered from her alarm, who said that some time after sunset, the nurse having left her for the purpose of preparing a little caudle, a multitude of elves came in at the window, thronging like bees from a hive. They filled the room, and having lifted her from the bed, carried her through the window, after which she recollected nothing further, till she saw her husband standing over her on the Cur-hills, at the back of Carlungy. The hole in the roof, by which the female fairy made her escape, was mended, but could never be kept in repair, as a tempest of wind happened always once a year, which uncovered that particular spot, without injuring any other part of the roof.

¶ See "Katherine Fordyce", "Mary Nelson", "Mind the Crooked Finger", "Sandy Hairg's Wife", "The Stolen Wife".

THE MIDWIFE

Hamish Henderson, School of Scottish Studies.

There was once an old midwife fetched by two little men. They took her to a house she did not know, and as they were coming in at the door, they both dipped their hands in a bowl of water, so she did the same. After that she did her work, and a baby boy was born. Then one of the men said, "Just bake us some bannocks before you go. There'll be just enough to do us in the jar there, but mind and put the scrapings of oatmeal from the board back into the jar." Then they went out, and the old wife started baking the bannocks, putting the spare meal back into the jar. But the jar was never emptied. She went on baking and baking, but it was half full, just as it was at the start. Then the woman on the bed said to her:

"You'll never be done if you put the spare meal back. Fling it on the fire."

She did that, and she came to the end of the oatmeal at once. The woman said:

"They'd have had you baking for ever, if you hadn't heeded me." So the men came back, and took her home. Some while later she saw one of the little men, and asked him how the baby was. "Do you see me?" he said. "With which eye?"

"With the both." "Did you wash your eyes with our water?" "I just did as you did," said the old wife. "Well, we'll soon cure that," he said, and he blew on her eyes, and she never saw the fairies again.

From C. Stewart.

¶ The advice which enables a mortal to escape from Fairyland is generally that of a fellow mortal imprisoned there. The fairy mother in this tale was probably a stolen mortal. The fairies here were milder than usual, for they only took away the magic sight, without blinding the midwife.

See "Marie Kirstan, the Midwife", "How Joan lost the Sight of One Eye", etc.

SIR GODFREY MACCULLOCH

Douglas; *Scottish Fairy & Folk-Tales*, p. 106.

The Scottish fairies...sometimes reside in subterranean abodes, in the vicinity of human habitations, or, according to the popular phrase, under the "doorstane", or threshold; in which situation they sometimes establish an intercourse with men, by borrowing and lending, and other kindly offices. In this capacity they are termed "the good neighbours", from supplying privately the wants of their friends, and assisting them in all their transactions, while their favours are concealed. Of this the traditionary story of Sir Godfrey Macculloch forms a curious example.

As this Gallovidian gentleman was taking the air on horseback, near his own house, he was suddenly accosted by a little old man arrayed in green, and mounted upon a white palfrey. After mutual salutation, the old man gave Sir Godfrey to understand that he resided under his habitation, and that he had great reason to complain of the direction of a drain, or common sewer, which emptied itself directly into his chamber of dais.* Sir Godrey Macculloch was a good deal startled at this extraordinary complaint; but, guessing the nature of this being he had to deal with, he assured the old man, with great courtesy, that the direction of the drain should be altered; and caused it to be done accordingly. Many years afterwards Sir Godfrey had the misfortune to kill, in a fray, a gentleman of the neighbourhood. He was apprehended, tried, and condemned. The scaffold upon which his head was to be struck off was erected on the Castle Hill of Edinburgh; but hardly had he reached the fatal spot, when the old man, upon his white palfrey, pressed through the crowd with the rapidity of lightning. Sir Godfrey, at his command, sprung on behind him; the "good neighbour" spurred his horse down the steep bank, and neither he nor the criminal was ever seen again.

Denham Tracts, II, pp. 61–2 (summarized version).
¶ See "The Laird o' Co".

THE WHITE POWDER

Gutch, *County Folk-Lore*, VI, *East Riding of Yorkshire*, p. 55.

It happened in my time, and I was both eye and ear witness of the trial of the person accused. And first take a hint of it from the pen of *Durant Hotham*, in his learned epistle to the *Mysterium Magnum* of *Jacob Behemen* upon *Genesis* in these words:

"There was (he saith) as I have heard the story credibly reported in this Country a man apprehended for suspicion for Witchcraft; he was of that sort we call white Witches, which are such as do cures beyond the ordinary reasons and deductions of our usual practitioners, and are supposed (and most part of them truly) to do the same by ministration of spirits (from whence under their noble favours most Sciences first grew) and therefore are by good reason provided against by our Civil Laws, as being ways full of danger and deceit, and scarce ever otherwise obtained than by a devilish compact of the exchange of ones Soul to that assistant spirit, for the honour of its Mountebankery. What this man did was with a white powder which, he said, he received from the Fairies, and that going to a Hill he knocked three times, and the Hill opened, and he had access to, and converse with a visible people; and offered, that if any Gentleman present would either go himself in person, or send his servant, he would conduct them thither, and show them the place and persons from whom he had his skill." To this I shall only add thus much, that the man was accused for invoking and calling upon evil spirits, and was a very simple and illiterate person to any man's judgment, and had been formerly very poor, but had gotten some pretty little meanes to maintain himself, his Wife, and diverse small children, by his cures done with this white powder, of which there were sufficient proofs; and the Judge asking him how he came by the powder, he told a story to this effect. "That one night before the day was gone, as he was going home from his labour, being very sad and full of heavy thoughts, not knowing how to get meat and drink for his Wife and Children, he met a fair Woman in fine cloaths, who asked him why he was so sad, and he told her it was by reason of his poverty, to which she said, that if he would follow her counsel she would help him to that which would serve to get him a good living; to which he said he would consent with all his heart, so it were not by unlawful ways; she told him that it should not be by any such ways, but by doing of good and curing of sick people; and so warning him strictly to meet her there the next night at the same time, she departed from him and he went home. And the next night at the time appointed, he duly waited, and she (according to promise) came and told him that it was well he came so duly, otherwise he had missed of that benefit, that she intended to do unto him, and so bade him follow her and not be afraid. Thereupon she led him to a little Hill, and she knocked three times, and the Hill opened, and they went in, and came to a fair hall, wherein was a Queen sitting in great state, and many people about her, and the Gentlewoman that brought him, presented him to the Queen, and she said he was welcom, and bid the Gentlewoman give him some of the white powder, and teach him how to use it; which she did, and gave him a little wood box full of the white powder, and bid him give 2 or 3 grains of it to any that were sick, and it would heal them, and so she brought him forth of the Hill, and so they parted." And being asked by the Judge whether the place within the Hill, which he called a Hall, were light or dark, he said indifferent, as it is with us in the twilight; and being asked how he got more powder, he said when he wanted he went to that Hill, and knocked three times, and said every time, "I am coming, I am coming," whereupon it opened, and he going in was conducted by the aforesaid Woman to the Queen, and so had more powder given to him. This was the plain and simple story (however it may be judged of) that he told before the Judge, the whole Court and the Jury, and there being no proof, but what cures he had done to very many, the Jury did acquit him; and I remember the Judge said, when all the evidence was heard, that if he were to assign his punishment, he should be whipped thence to Fairy-Hall, and did seem to judge it to be a delusion or an Imposture.

Webster, *Displaying of Supposed Witchcraft*, pp. 300–2.

PART II
GHOSTS

Almost every village in England has several ghost stories attached to it, but these are often accounts or rumours of apparitions, with no beginning or end. A satisfactory ghost story ought to be something more than a mere account of an apparition. Ideally, it should have a beginning and an end as well as a middle. We should learn how the ghost came to haunt the place and how it was laid. A good example is "A Lay Ghost-Layer". This has several points of interest—the ghost in animal form, the method of laying and the widely distributed tale-type 930 A (The Murdered Son) which appears in it. Other tales are of special interest as exhibiting the technique of ghost-laying or illustrating some aspect of folk-belief. Anything hidden before death, especially money, is said to cause haunting, and country people are still careful not to hide even a tool in case it makes them uneasy after death. A friend told me once that she was walking out one evening when an old neighbour passed her, and said, "Tell my girl it's on the top shelf." "Very well", she said, and only when she had walked on did she remember that the old man had died the week before. However, she went to the daughter and told her, and the daughter said, "Oh, that's where it is, is it?" She was too polite to ask what "it" was, so heard no more of the matter.

From the earliest times it has been thought that an unburied corpse will walk, demanding proper burial rites. Such a tale was told by Pliny Secundus in his *Letters*, and the belief is exemplified in "The Death 'Bree'", though the courage of the desecrator of the tomb and the reasonableness of the ghost brought the woman off more safely than might have been expected.

Vampire ghosts, another form of the reanimated corpse, are rare in this country. "Croglin Grange", like other stories collected by Augustus Hare, may owe something to literary reminiscence. It is as horrific as one of James's *Ghost Stories of an Antiquary*.

Some ghost stories are not to be found among the legends, as they are obviously exercises in folk fiction. Examples of the kind of thing are two terse ghost stories which are fairly widely known: one of a nervous guest in a haunted room who locked the door, closed the shutters, looked under the bed and into the cupboards before getting into bed, and, just as he blew out the candle, heard a tiny voice coming from the curtains at the head of his bed, "Now we're shut in for the night." The other, which is supposed to be the shortest ghost story in the world, runs: "He woke up frightened and reached for the matches, and the matches were put into his hand."

Hauntings can generally be divided into those who have done wrong and those who suffered it. Sometimes the sufferers seeking revenge are the more malevolent of the two, but we have occasional stories of ghosts who come back to repay kindness done to them in their lifetime. A beautiful example of this is Christina Hole's story of "The Grateful Ghost".

In this section, where it is impossible to hope to reproduce all the stories, I have tried to give them in something of the numerical proportion in which they are to be found. It will be seen that the most numerous are those about the laying of ghosts and about the unquiet wanderings of people who have met a violent end or who have wronged others, either by violence or fraud. Some of the less common but most picturesque ghost stories are those in which whole scenes from the past are presented to the spectator, sometimes passing before him like a picture, sometimes only heard, and occasionally particpated in. Because of their interest, I have perhaps included an undue proportion of these.

Many other ghost stories are to be found in such books as *The Ghost World*, by Thistleton Dyer, *The Night Side of Nature*, by Catherine Crowe, and *Haunted England*, by Christina Hole.

THE BISHOPSTHORPE GHOST

County Folk-Lore, II, *North Riding of Yorkshire*, etc., pp. 93–4.

The most veritable ghost...was the one which was supposed to be the ghost of Archbishop Scrope, who for many years walked the road to conduct his own funeral procession, and perhaps the most persistent story told of his appearance was that told by a man who made his living as a slaughterman....He used to speak with confidence of what he saw....

This Robert Johnson, accompanied by a boy who was apprenticed to a Jubbergate butcher was sent one night to a farm beyond Bishopsthorpe to fetch some sheep. As they returned in the darkness, nearing the hauling lane, each suddenly saw a coffin suspended in the air, and moving slowly along in the direction of York. It tilted occasionally, as if borne on the shoulders of men who were thrown out of step by the rugged character of the roadway. The coffin was covered with a heavy black pall of velvet, fringed with white silk, and was in size and appearance the resting-place of a full-grown man. Behind it, with measured tread, walked a Bishop in lawn, bearing on his hands a large open book, over which his head bent, but from his lips no sound came. On went the procession, with the steady precision observed in bearing the dead to the grave, whilst the sheep kept pace, and would not be driven past the strange sight. Nobody could be mistaken in the apparition. The night, though dark, was too light to admit of mistake....The spectre procession moved at a leisured pace for some considerable distance till it came to the field where the Archbishop was beheaded. Then it disappeared as hastily as it had come, and returned to its rest. But not so with the man and boy....Having arrived at their destination...after very few particulars, spoken amid much fear, they were taken off to bed, where they remained for many days, wrung in mind and body by the terrible shock....When sufficiently recovered, their story was repeated with particular detail, and gained universal credence, from the fact many villagers and many citizens had experienced like sight and sensation. The boy forsook his business and took to the sea, lest he should ever again be compelled to take a similar journey, and be subject to like experience, whilst the man ever after avoided that road at nightfall, but never swerved from declaring his story true....More than once after this, men who had sat late at their cups were frightened into sobriety by the reappearance of the strange funeral procession, but the ghost has done its work, for in our day it never appears.

From Camidge, *From Ouse Bridge to Naburn Locks*, pp. 199–201.

¶ See "The Phantom Funeral" (B, XII).

THE BUSSEX RHINE, AND KING'S SEDGEMOOR

Ruth L. Tongue. *Somerset Folklore*, p. 101.

Believing that the Battlefield of Sedgemoor must be badly haunted, an elderly gentleman in the eighteenth century began to make inquiries. He was met by stolid stares, but at last a local farmer said: "I been over they parts, man and boy. Never seed nothing, never heard nothing neither but one foggy night, and then 'twas a drunken chap somewhere t'other side of the rhine, shouting, 'Come over and fight!' But there, I'd other things to mind."

It will be remembered that "Come over and fight!" was the despairing cry of Monmouth's army as they were mowed down by the King's guns.

Told to Miss Phoebe Chatworthy in Taunton, about 1890.

¶ This is one of many traditions of "Duking Days" (Somerset name for the Monmouth Rebellion) hauntings.

See "Dolly and the Duke" "The Rebel and His Dog", "The Ghost of Marlpits Hill".

CROGLIN GRANGE [shortened]

Augustus Hare, *In My Solitary Life*, p. 50.

For hundreds of years the ancient family of the Fishers has owned a curious old place in Cumberland named Croglin Grange. This house has never been more than one storey high, but it has a terrace from which large grounds sweep away towards the church in the hollow, and a fine distant view.

Even when the family outgrew the house, they did not add to its extent, but went to live in the South at Thorncombe, near Guildford, and Croglin Grange was let to tenants, two brothers and a sister.

This new family settled quickly and happily into the life of the district, and soon became very popular. One hot summer day, when the sultry atmosphere had made work of any kind almost impossible, the three dined early, and afterwards sat out on the veranda, enjoying the cooler air, and watching the moon rise in full brilliance over the lawn and gardens.

When at last they went indoors to their rooms, the sister still felt the heat too great for sleep, and sat up in her bed, still watching the moonlight through her window, for she had not closed her shutters. Gradually she became aware of two lights which flickered in and out in the belt of trees which separated the lawn from the churchyard, and as her gaze became fixed upon them she saw them emerge, fixed in a dark substance, a definite ghastly *something*, which seemed every moment to come nearer, increasing in size as it approached. Every now and then it was lost in the long shadows which stretched across the lawn, then it emerged larger than ever, and still coming on—on. She was seized with horror, and longed to get away, but the door was close to the window, and while unlocking it she must be for that instant nearer to *it*. She longed to scream, but her throat seemed paralysed.

Suddenly, she could never explain why, the terrible object seemed to turn aside, and to be going round the house, instead of straight towards her. She sprang from her bed to unlock the door, but at the instant she heard scratch, scratch, scratch at her window, and saw a hideous brown face with flaming eyes glaring in at her. She took comfort in the thought that the window was securely locked on the inside, but all of a sudden the scratching ceased, and a kind of pecking sound took its place. The creature was unpicking the lead! A diamond-shaped pane fell on to the floor, and a long bony finger came inside, and found the latch of the window, and turned it. She had fled back into her bed, but the creature came into the room, and twisted its long bony fingers into her hair, and dragged her head over the side of the bed, and bit her violently in the throat.

Now at last she did scream aloud, and her brothers rushed to her aid. But they had to break in the still-locked door, and by the time they got inside the creature had disappeared through the window, and their sister lay bleeding and unconscious. One brother tried in vain to pursue the monster, which vanished with gigantic strides, and seemed to disappear over the wall into the churchyard, so the pursuer returned to his sister's room. She was fearfully wounded, but recovered with amazing strength, and refused to let her terrible experience drive her from the house where they had been so happy. Both her doctor and her brothers, however, found it hard to believe that she could be so completely recovered as she seemed, and insisted on taking her away to Switzerland for a mental and physical change. There she threw herself into all the interests and occupations of the country, and seemed so fully restored to health that in the autumn she herself proposed that they should return to England. Her dreadful visitor, she maintained, must have been some escaped lunatic, and was not likely to return; besides, only one of the seven years for which they had leased their house had passed.

They therefore returned to Cumberland, but the sister always thereafter kept her shutters fast closed at night, and the two brothers each kept a loaded pistol in their room.

After a peaceful winter, in the following March the sister was suddenly awakened by the same dreadful scratching at her window, and saw the same hideous brown shrivelled face looking in through the one pane left uncovered at the top of the window by the shutters. (This was a common fashion in certain old houses.)

She screamed as loud as she could, and her brothers rushed with their pistols out of the house, to find the creature already scudding away over the lawn. One brother fired, and hit it in the leg, but it got away, nevertheless, and scrambled over the wall and seemed to disappear into a vault belonging to a family long extinct.

Next day, in the presence of all the tenants of Croglin Grange, this vault was opened, and a scene of horror presented itself; the coffins with which the vault was filled were all broken open save one, and their mangled contents scattered over the floor. On the last coffin the lid still lay, but it was loose, and when they raised it there lay inside, brown and withered but quite entire, the same frightful figure which had looked in at the window of the Grange, with the mark of a recent pistol-shot in one leg. They did the only thing that can lay a vampire—they burnt it.

¶ The vampire belief is strongest in eastern Europe, Greece, and China, and so complete a vampire story as this is not common in England. It may well have had a literary origin. There are, however, traces of vampire belief in England, as in the story of the lover's ghost in "The Fair Maid of Clifton". MacCulloch points out in the article "Vampires" in *Hastings' Encyclopaedia of Religion and Ethics* that the stake with which suicides were pierced may show that they were once feared as vampires, for this was the recognized treatment of vampires in eastern Europe. The alternative was burning, as in this case.

See "The Fair Maid of Clifton".

THE DEATH "BREE"

Gibbings, *Folk-Lore and Legends, Scotland*, p. 189.

There was once a woman who lived in the Camp-del-more of Strathavon whose cattle were seized with a murrain, or some such fell disease, which ravaged the neighbourhood at the time, carrying off great numbers of them daily. All the forlorn fires and hallowed waters failed of their customary effects: and she was at length told by the wise people whom she consulted on the occasion, that it was evidently the effect of some infernal agency, the power of which could not be destroyed by any other means than the never-failing specific—the juice of a dead head from the churchyard—a nostrum certainly very difficult to be procured, considering that the head must needs be abstracted from the grave at the hour of midnight. Being, however, a woman of stout heart and strong faith, native feelings of delicacy towards the sanctuary of the dead had more weight than had fear in restraining her for some time from resorting to this desperate remedy. At length, seeing that her stock would soon be annihilated by the destructive career of the disease, the wife of Camp-del-more resolved to put the experiment in practice, whatever the result might be. Accordingly, having with considerable difficulty engaged a neighbouring woman as her companion in this hazardous expedition, they set out a little before midnight for the parish churchyard, distant about a mile and a half from her residence, to execute her determination. On arriving at the churchyard, her companion, whose courage was not so notable, appalled by the gloomy prospect before her, refused to enter among the habitations of the dead. She, however, agreed to remain at the gate, till her friend's business was accomplished. This circumstance, however, did not stagger the wife's resolution.

She, with the greatest coolness and intrepidity, proceeded towards what she supposed an old grave, took down her spade, and commenced her operations. After a good deal of toil, she arrived at the object of her labour. Raising the first head, or rather skull, that came her way, she was about to make it her own property, when a hollow, wild, sepulchral voice exclaimed. "That is my head; let it alone!" Not wishing to dispute the claimant's title to this head, and supposing she could be otherwise provided, she very good-naturedly returned it, and took up another. "That is my father's head," bellowed the same voice. Wishing, if possible, to avoid disputes, the wife of Camp-del-more took up another head, when the same voice instantly started a claim to it as his grandfather's

175

head. "Well," replied the wife, nettled at her disappointments, "although it were your grandmother's head, you shan't get it till I am done with it." "What do you say, you limmer?" says the ghost, starting up in his awry habiliments. "What do you say, you limmer?" repeated he, in a great rage. "By the great oath, you had better leave my grandfather's head." Upon matters coming this length, the wily wife of Camp-del-more thought it proper to assume a more conciliatory aspect. Telling the claimant the whole particulars of the predicament in which she was placed, she promised faithfully that, if his honour would only allow her to carry off his grandfather's skull, or head, in a peaceable manner, she would restore it again when done with. Here, after some communing, they came to an understanding; and she was allowed to take the head along with her, on condition that she should restore it before cock-crowing, under the heaviest penalties.

On coming out of the churchyard, and looking for her companion, she had the mortification to find her "without a mouthful of breath in her body", for, on hearing the dispute between her friend and the guardian of the grave, and suspecting much that she was likely to share the unpleasant punishments with which he threatened her friend, at the bare recital of them she fell down in a faint, from which it was no easy matter to recover her. This proved no small inconvenience to Camp-del-more's wife, as there were not above two hours to elapse ere she had to return the head, according to the terms of her agreement. Taking her friend upon her back, she carried her up a steep acclivity to the nearest adjoining house, where she left her for the night; then repaired home with the utmost speed, made *dead bree* of the head ere the appointed time had expired, restored the skull to its guardian, and placed the grave in its former condition. It is needless to add that, as a reward for her exemplary courage, the "bree" had its desired effect.

The cattle speedily recovered, and, so long as she retained any of it, all sorts of diseases were of short duration.

❡ There are various stories on these lines, some of them dealing with practical jokes, most with fear tests. See "A Brave Boy" (A, II), "A Wager Won" (A, III).

On the subject of the dead's vengeance for theft of a part of the body, see "The Bone" (A, V), etc. For the reason of their indignation, see "Sammle's Ghost".

A DOCTOR'S STRANGE EXPERIENCE

Elliot, Notebook, School of Scottish Studies.

Away in the Highlands of Scotland some of the shepherds' houses are so isolated and far from the main road they are hard to reach. In fact, a lot of them has only a track to reach them, and in either mist or darkness is easy lost, and this accident happened many years ago.

A shepherd's wife turned ill, and it was at one of these isolated houses, far from the main road, and they had sent word for the doctor.

It was the short days of winter, and wet and misty weather prevailed; the doctor's way of travelling was on horseback, and it was mid-afternoon as he set out on his journey across the moors for the shepherd's house.

He had been there before, and he knew the track, but the mist and darkness came down, and he lost the track. He kept on trying to find it, till he was utterly lost. As he kept on wandering up and down, he saw a light through the mist and darkness, and he thought it must be a shepherd's house, and he made his way for it, as he thought they would be able to put him on the track. But before he reached the cottage the light went out, and when he reached it all was darkness. He thought they must have gone to bed, and he knocked at the door, but got no answer. So he went to the outhouse, and managed to get his horse into the byre, then he went back to the door, and, as he got no answer, he tried the door, and found it was not locked. So he went in; but to his great astonishment, the place was like as if no one had been in it for a long time, as the furniture was so dusty, and no signs of life. So he thought he would make the best of it for the night; and he managed to light a fire, and he had a bit lunch with him, he sat down at the fire and ate it. Then he had a look into what looked like the room end, where there was a bed, and a little table at the side of it. So, after sitting at the fire for some time, he rose and shut the outer door, and went ben into the room, and prepared to go to bed, as the night was so dark and misty he could not proceed any further the night.

As he undressed he laid his purse and his gold watch on the little table, then went to bed. He was just beginning to dover over to sleep when he heard voices ben in the kitchen. They were men's voices, and they seemed to be arguing over something. He creeped over the bed, and very quietly keeked ben into the kitchen, and he was very surprised to see two rough-looking men sitting at the table playing cards. There was a dispute about one of them cheating, and one had dropped a card, and as he stooped to pick it up, the other drew a long knife and stabbed him to death. The doctor got such a fright he crept back to bed, where he lay in terror. He kept well hidden under the clothes, and it was not long or the man came ben and looked round the room, and came up to the table at the bedside and lifted the doctor's watch and his purse of money. The doctor lay there sweating with fear, and lamenting the loss of his purse of money and his gold watch.

He lay for some time till he heard the man go out the door, but he lay listening in fear he would come back, till, overcome with sleep, he must have dovered away to sleep, and lay there till morning, and waked up, and his first thoughts were of the night before and the two men, and remembering his loss of his purse of money and gold watch. And it was his first thought—the two men and the murder. He thought of the murdered man lying on the floor, and he thought the sooner he was out of bed and out of this the better; so he jumped out of bed and was putting on his clothes, and, still thinking about his lost watch and purse, he happened to look down at the little table where he had laid his watch and money, when, to his great surprise, his gold watch and his purse were lying as he had left them the night before. He could hardly believe his own eyes, as he saw the murderer lift them the night before. He was not long in getting them into his pocket; and when he keeked ben into the kitchen he saw no man lying murdered on the floor, and everything was the same as when he left it the night before. He made for the byre to get his horse, as the mist had cleared away, and he now knew he could find his way. After getting his horse out, he rode off, and soon found the hill track to the shepherd's house. When he got there he told them of his experience last night.

After the shepherd thought awhile, he remembered and told the doctor he had been in the drainers' haunted cottage, where the drainers lived, and one murdered his mate and fled the country, and was never heard of again, and the cottage has been haunted ever since.

¶ A puzzling feature of this tale is the disappearance of the doctor's purse and watch, and their reappearance. In some of the re-enacted tragedies the ghosts seem unconscious of spectators; in others, the mortals enter and re-shape the play. This tale seems to come halfway between. A house at Rye that had been an inn frequented by smugglers was the nightly scene of spectral brawls and killings, but the spectators did not participate in the drama.

See "Ghosts at Edgehill", "Dolly and the Duke".

THE DRUMMER OF AIRLIE

From *Thatched with Gold: the Memoirs of Mabell, Countess of Airlie*, 1962, pp. 47, 92.

The ghostly drummer of Airlie, who was supposed to drum before the death of each head of the family of Ogilvie, was heard drumming before the death of the 8th Earl of Airlie who died in America in 1881. He was heard by Lady Dalkeith and the Countess of Latham when they were staying at Achnacany, the seat of the Earl of Airlie. Making allowance for the difference in time, he drummed one hour before the Earl's death. He was also heard drumming before the death of the 9th Earl, who was killed in action in the Boer War on June 11, 1900. The drumming was heard on the 10th, which was a Sunday. The Boer prisoners complained of the profanation of the Sabbath and were told that there was no drummer in the camp.

The story dates back to 1640, when Argyle burned down the house of Airlie. A drummer of the Cameron Clan had been posted in a watch-tower to give warning, and when the surprise attack was made the Ogilvie clansmen, thinking he had betrayed them, left him in the burning tower. He climbed up to the battlement, protesting his innocence, and continued to drum until the flames overpowered him. Since then he is supposed always to drum before the death of the head of the Ogilvies.

¶ Argyle's burning of Airlie gave rise to the Child ballad of "The Bonnie House of Airlie".

THE GHOST OF GAIRNSIDE

Hamish Henderson, School of Scottish Studies.

Tell us, John, what is this story about the Ghost of Gairnside?

Ah, well, jist about a crofter and his son at the top of Gairnside.

The crofter, he had a son, and his son was carryin' on with his sweetheart for over a year, and he'd always over a mile and a half to go down to meet her every Sunday night. He always met her about half-past ten every Sunday night, and this meetin' lastit for over a year, and he was workin' aboot the farm in [?] Auld Ringie. His father used to say to him, say to his mother, like, "I dout there's something happent to John." For he was always a cheery chap when he was workin', whistlin' aboot and aathing when he was plewin' up the ground and that, "Ach," he says, "he's jist like oorsels when we were young—perhaps he's makin' it up to get married, or something."

Oniegait, when he was away down come Sunday, he had to go down to meet his sweetheart. So he went away down and aathing, and he's always meeting' her at a certain place at the back of a bush, aboot four and a half mile frae his own place. So when he went down to where he was always meetin' his sweetheart, there was a white lady stannan up against a gate. So when he lookit up tae her, he says, "What are ye doin' staundin' there?"

She says tae him, "Where are ye goin'?"

"Oh," he says, "I'm gaun to meet my sweetheart."

She says, "I know," she says, "ye're goin' to meet your sweetheart, but I've been stannin' here," she says, "for over a year, and," she says, "I know," she says, "that you've been meetin' your sweetheart all this time," she says, "every Sunday night, at half-past ten, and," she says, "your sweetheart's not fair to you," she says, "for she's carryin' on with another chap."

"Oh," he says, "I wouldn't believe that."

"But," she says, "all right," she says, "you can go up," she says, "to meet her, but go up to the bush farther on, and you'll hear for yourself."

So when he went up to the bush farther on, he heard this sweetheart sayin' to his own sweetheart, "He's always carryin' on wi' ye."

"Ah, well, I'll need to hurry on," she says, "for that boy frae the top of the glen's comin' doon to meet me, and I dinnae want tae make a fool of him, ye know," she says, "kiddin' him on."

So he staunds, hearin' aa this. So anyway, he left her and cam' back to the gate, and here's this lady always standin' at the gate, dressed in white. So she says to him, "Now you've found out for yourself."

"Yes," he says, "I've found out for myself."

"Well," she says, "now, what are ye goin' to do now?"

"Well," he says, "I've nothing to do now but go home again."

"Well," she says, "I know you've been meetin'," she says, "this girl friend of yours for over a year," she says. "Could you meet me," she says, "for a week?"

"Well," he says, "I dinnae know, for a week—I dinnae see no harm of meetin' ye for a week," he says, "when I could come for over a year meetin' her, always at half-past ten at night. There could be no harm in meetin' ye for a week."

"Well," she says, "I want you to meet me every night for a week, at half-past ten, the same time. Could ye do that?"

"Well," he says, "I dinnae see nothing haudin' me back frae daein that, when I'm happent to meet this girl for over a year."

"Well," she says, "the bargain's made?"

"Yes," he says, "the bargain's made."

Now he's away. He left her again, and promised to meet her next Monday.

So when he was away from home now, he was wonderin', like, aboot the girl, like, false to him all the time, ye see—he went away home—never tellt his mother that she'd been false to him. But next morning he was oot in the field again, for he used to enjoy himsel, whistlin' and singin' to himsel when he was workin'. But Monday mornin', when he went oot, he never sung nor anything, he wudnae eat nothing, so he's aye thinkin' awa to himsel. So his father says, "Well," he says, "there must be something ado wi' the laddie." "Ach," she says. "There's nothing."

So he asked the foreman, "What like is the boy getting on in the field?"

"Well," he says, "there's something ado wi' the bodie. He'll no hardly do nae work nor nothing. An," he says, "he'll no whistle nor anything."

So anyway, whenever night's come, he got his supper again, and he's away down now, meetin' his sweetheart again.

So when he was away doon meetin' his sweetheart, the aul' man says. "Whaur is he awa tae?"

"Och," she says, "ye ken what like you and me was when we were young. He's been gaun that lang," she says, "that he'll—be getting' mairrit."

"Oh," he says, "there might be something in that, tae."

So he's away down, meetin' his sweetheart again, but he cam back again —he's aye gettin' worse and waur, every day and nicht, wi' meetin' her, he's aye gettin' worse. So began this twelve months.

"Well," he says, "I dinna like the look of my son, he's been gettin' waur, every day meeting' her—he's aye gettin' worse."

"Oh," he says, he says, "I'll tell the foreman to go doon eftir him aa richt."

So the next nicht again, when he got up he got his bitie of supper, and he's away doon meetin' his sweetheart again. So when he went away down now, the foreman followed him. So when he was awa aboot a mile and a hauf or two miles doon the road, here he seen the young fella throwin' his airm roon the same as that—a boy throwin' his airm roon a lassie goin' awa doon the road, and then speakin' tae hes-sel an aathing.

"Gode bliss me!" he saud, "what's adae wi' him?" he says. "Has he gone off his heid?"

So he was talkin' to him aa the time gaun doon and aathing, same as a bloke speakin' tae his sweetheart. So he seen this chap gaun in through a gate, and gaun into an auld wash-been, like aa ruins. So he was stannin' back—when he seen this thing he made hame, to tell the auld man.

So the auld man says, "I dinnae ken what to dae wi' him."

So anyway, the next nicht again he says, "The best thing ye can dae," he says, "is I think I'll go doon masel," he says, "and see whit the laddie is gettin' on."

So the aul' man next nicht followed them doon. So whenever he seen him there he seen his son throwin' his airms roòn this lassie's neck and speakin' awa and aathing, and then he listened for a while, and he heard the lassie speakin' back tae him. So when he heard that, he says, "Gode bliss me!" he says, "I hope," he says, "he didnae dae the ither lassie in."

Away he cam hame. So we leave with the aul' man goin' to the young boy and the lady—so he went doon to this old washbeen and doon tae a little room. An' here when he cam doon to the little room here was the table spread and fire burnin' and aathing, and wine and everything on the top of the table. So they dined there tae aboot twelve o'clock. So when they dined there tae twelve o'clock, she lookit at the young fellie; she says, "Ten meenits to twelve," she says, "aboot time," she says, "ye're gettin' hame. And" she says, "I'll convoy you," she says, "on to the [?] haa road, and up to the fairm."

"Aye," he says tae hessel, "well," he says, "I've been carryin' on with a girl," he says, "for over a year, an'," he says, "that's a thing that she never said to me, for to convoy me," he says, "home." He says, "It's always me, it's left to the gentleman to convoy the girl home." The two of them went away. She says, "You don't need to stand," she says, "and speak," she says, "for I'll need all my time."

So the two of them left. So she cam up to the road turnin' up to the fairm. Well, she's been aboot close on two miles away, from the auld ruins. So she says, "I'll have to be biddin' ye good-night," she says.

So he told her, "Good-night."

"Be sure and see me the morn," she says, "it's the last night."

So she was away. So he was goin' up frae the wood, and he happened to say to hissel, "Perhaps—I hope," he says, "it's not a ghost I'm speakin' to, and not makin' dates with."

"Oh no," she says, "it's not a ghost," she says. "I'm always here."

So anyway, Jeck, he went away now; well he's aye broodin' afore, but he was broodin' twenty times worse now when he went hame an—what he was doin'.

So next mornin' again, it was the last day, so he went away doon this night again, but the whole three of them went down this time—father and mother and son. So the two of them was goin' down the road after the son, when the father and mother seen his hauns goin' round the lady, and the lady speakin' back to him and asked if he had seen nothing but hesself. So the mother thocht that he was goin' off his head, and thought, like, that he'd done his sweetheart in. So she says, "The best thing I can do," she says, "is go up to the farm where the girl's workin' and see if she's always there."

So the farmer he went up to the farm, "Oh, yes," he says, "the girl's always here—how are ye askin' that?"

"Well," he says, "it's the funny things that happen. So," he says, "are ye sure," he says, "the girl's——"

"Oh yes," he says, the other farmer, "the girl's here, for she's jist newly home after milkin'."

So they cam down and aathing now. An' I'll leave off o' them again, back into John again.

So Jack he went intae the house again where the lady was. So he dined away there again. So, anyway, when—she says, "This is the last night," she says, "it's time," she says, "twelve," she says, "ye'd better be goin' home."

When she said that, he went out again and made home again, and——

"Now," she says, "it's the last night. Don't come down again here again," she says. "I'll come up there to-morrow. I'll come to you," she says, "in the mornin'."

So he was wonderin' now what kind o' a lady he feart to tell his people about—comin' up, and didnae know whit she wis, when she says——

So anyway the morn cam anyway, and Jeck he was sittin' at his breakfast, when a rap cam to the door. So when the rap cam to the door, the mother went ootside and see who was there, and here was the young lady.

So she said. "Who are ye wantin'?"

"Oh," she said, "ye've a young man stayin' here," she says.

"Yes," she says, "I've only one young man, and that's my son."

"Oh," she says, "I'm the lady," she says, "he's been walkin' out with."

So when the son went out, here was the young lady, and she cam and took him inside, and the young lady cam in, the auld man went out, and here when he lookit round here's a great big—where the wash-beens, auld ruins wis, wis a castle.

So he asked her, "What's the idea?" he says, "of stoppin' doon in that auld ruins?—in aboot the castle, all the time."

"Oh," she says, "this is a long story," she says, "a long time back," she says, "I was the young lady, jist what I'm now," she says, "and my brother was left that place, and he was a jealous brother. I was coortin' a young gentleman," she says, "and my brother was jealous, and," she says, "he got a witch that stopped at the other side of the hill, to enchant me intae a ghost," and the first man as could carry on and make love to her for a week would break her enchantment. That's the only way that they could get her enchantment broken.

(My brother told me that one. His full name, James Higgins, out at [?] Blackmyre [?] Blacknile. He is from Aberdeen originally.)

From John Higgins, 1955.

¶ This rather subtle and poetic story is unusual in describing a perfectly harmless intercourse with a hitherto unknown ghost. It differs from "The Unquiet Grave" in the fact that the young man has been cast off by his own sweetheart and finds refreshment in intercourse with this ghost, which really plays more the part of a fairy than of a ghost, except that the week's intercourse lays her.

THE GRATEFUL GHOST

A STORY OF THE GREAT NORTH ROAD

C. Hole, *Haunted England*, pp. 144–5.

A certain coachman was engaged to Nance, a farmer's daughter at Sheriff Hutton. The wedding-day was already fixed when she threw him over in favour of another man, a stranger to the village, who married her and took her away with him. A year later, as Tom, the coachman, was nearing York, he saw the girl standing by the roadside with a baby in her arms, looking very ill and exhausted. She told him that her alleged husband had turned out to be a highwayman, who was already married, and that she had left him.

Tom took her up in the coach, and left her at the York Tavern, to be looked after by the landlady. He was obliged to go on with his passengers, and shortly after he left the girl died, but not before she had promised that her ghost would return to warn him, his children, and his grandchildren, whenever danger threatened them.

Nothing happened for two years, and then Tom was sent to Durham on a special errand. He was to bring four very important passengers to York; these men urgently wished to be at their destination quickly, and promised him the then considerable sum of four guineas if he could get them there by eight o'clock at night. Seven miles outside the city the coach ran into fog, which normally would have precluded all hope of arrival at the stated time. Suddenly the ghost of Nance appeared on the box beside the coachman and laid her hands on the reins. The horses at once broke into a gallop and kept it up through the fog all the way to the Black Swan Inn in Coney Lane, which they reached at exactly five minutes to eight. We are told that the passengers were frightened, and one wonders what their feelings must have been, boxed up inside the coach as it swayed from side to side in its mad career through the mist, over unfenced roads and down the narrow streets of the city. But the ghost was a better driver than her human lover, and there was no accident either to the coach itself or to any of the other vehicles it met on the way.

This was not the only occasion on which Nance came to the coachman's aid and, when he retired, he told his son that if she ever appeared, he was to do exactly as she ordered, and to let her drive if she wished. This injunction was handed on to his grandson when he in turn became a mail-coachman. A man named Peter Jackson told Mr Blakeborough that he and his brother had once seen the ghost when they were travelling by coach in the grandson's time. They were going from Pickering to York; amongst the outside passengers was a man whom the coachman suspected of being in league with the local highwaymen. Just outside Malton the horses suddenly swerved to avoid a woman standing in the roadway. Although she was clearly visible in the moonlight, none of the passengers saw her, except the two Jacksons, and a lady who afterwards said she had seen her signalling to the driver. A moment afterwards she had disappeared. The coachman told his friends it was Nance, and she had been pointing in a warning manner to the suspicious passenger. He pretended to find something wrong with the springs, and insisted on driving back to Malton. Once there he collected a band of men, and then persuaded the passengers to spend the night at the Black Swan Inn, on the grounds that the coach was unsafe. All agreed except the outside passenger, but he was quietly overpowered and locked up in a shed, while the coach, now full of vigilant men, drove off again towards York. As they had expected, they were stopped at Barton Corner by three masked men, who were considerably astonished to find their confederate absent, and the inside filled with hefty labourers, by whom they were soon disarmed and captured. Whether Nance ever appeared again after the railways had ruined the coaches I do not know.

Her promise was to help Tom's family down to the third generation, and this promise was fulfilled, as we have seen. But a ghost's memory is long, and perhaps one day we shall hear of some descendant of his being saved from a motor accident on the Great North Road by this gentle spirit, or driven safely through the fog at ninety miles an hour on some occasion when speed is a matter of supreme importance.

From Blakeborough, *The Hand of Glory*. Told to his father by a local man.

¶ In this tale the obligation was incurred while the ghost was alive, and it does not belong strictly to the type of the "Grateful dead".

JOHN RUDALL AND THE GHOST OF DOROTHY DINGLETT

C. Hole, *English Folk-Lore*, p. 162.

In Puritan times, exorcism often took the form of lengthy prayers and long arguments between the demon and the exorcist, but there were other methods. One of the most interesting cases known to us is preserved in the *Diurnall* of the Rev. John Rudall, who was a curate of Launceston in 1665. This gentle and holy man, a scholar of great learning, seems to have combined the rites of the Church with certain ancient practices more often associated with magic. His help was sought by a Mr Bligh, of Bothaten, whose son was haunted in a curious manner. Every morning, on his way to his tutor's house, this lad used to meet the ghost of Dorothy Dinglett, a woman he once knew well, but who had died some three years before. He saw her always in the same place and at the same time; she seemed to glide over the top of the grass without walking, and kept her hand outstretched as though pointing to some distant object. She used to pass him without speaking or looking at him, but the strange haunting was affecting the boy's nerves and general health.

Accordingly, Mr Rudall went with him on the following day to the field, and both saw the apparition. The minister relates:

"The aspect of the woman was exactly that which had been related by the lad. There was the pale and stony face, the strange and misty hair, the eyes firm and fixed, yet not on us, but on something that they saw far, far away: one hand and arm stretched out, and the other grasping the girdle of her waist. She floated along the field like a sail upon a stream, and glided past the spot where we stood, pausingly. But so deep was the awe that overcame me, as I stood there in the light of day, face to face with a human soul separate from her bones and flesh, that my heart and purpose failed me. I had resolved to speak to the spectre in the appointed form of words, but I did not. I stood like one amazed and speechless until she had passed clean out of sight."

He then returned home, and sought permission from his Bishop to exorcise the ghost. Two days later, on January 12th, he again visited the scene of the haunting, wearing a brass ring traced with the *scutum Davidis* and carrying a rowan-wood stick. He tells us:

"First, I paced and measured out my circle on the grass. Then I did mark my pentacle in the very midst, and at the intersection of the five angles I did set up and fix my crutch of rowan. Lastly, I took my station south, at the true line of the meridian, and stood facing due north. I waited and watched for a long time. At last there was a kind of trouble in the air, a soft and rippling sound, and all at once the shape appeared, and came towards me gradually. I opened my parchment scroll and read aloud the command. She paused, and seemed to waver and doubt; stood still; then I rehearsed the sentence again, sounding out every syllable like a chant. She drew near my ring, but halted at first outside, on the brink. I sounded again, and now, at the third time, I gave the signal in Syriac— the speech which is used, they say, where such ones dwell and converse in thoughts that glide."

He goes on to say that the spirit finally entered the circle and stood still, while he, summoning all his courage, and remembering that the pentacle and ring would bind her safely, asked her why she was not at rest. She said it was because of a certain sin, which she confessed. "We conversed," he says, "with many more words, but it is not lawful for me to set them down. Pen and ink would degrade and defile the thoughts she uttered, and which my mind received that day. I broke the ring, and she passed, but to return once more next day."

On the following morning, at sunrise, he once more drew his circle and pentacle on the ground, and this time the ghost entered it willingly. He says:

"I went through the proper forms of dismissal and fulfilled all as it was set down and written in my memoranda, and then, with certain fixed rites, I did dismiss that troubled ghost until she peacefully withdrew, gliding towards the west. Neither did she ever afterwards appear, but was allayed until she shall come in her second flesh to the Valley of Armageddon on the last day."

¶ Presumably the secrets which John Rudall would not disclose were secrets of the Confessional, and the ghost was laid by confession and absolution. According to Hunt, Dorothy Dinglett had had a love-affair with the elder brother of the lad whom she haunted.

LADY HOWARD'S COACH

S. Baring-Gould, *A Book of Folk-Lore*, p. 67.

The wagon of the Ankou is like the death-coach that one hears of in Devon and in Wales. It is all black, with black horses drawing it, driven by a headless coachman. A black hound runs before it, and within sits a lady—in the neighbourhood of Okehampton and Tavistock she is supposed to be a certain Lady Howard, but she is assuredly an impersonification of Death, for the coach halts to pick up the spirits of the dying.

> Now pray step in! my lady saith;
> Now pray step in and ride.
> I thank thee, I had rather walk
> Than gather to thy side.
>
> The wheels go round without a sound
> Or tramp or turn of wheels.
> As cloud at night, in pale moonlight,
> Along the carriage steals.
>
> I'd rather walk a hundred miles
> And run by night and day,
> Than have that carriage halt for me,
> And hear my lady say—
>
> Now pray step in, and make no din,
> Step in with me to ride;
> There's room, I trow, by me for you,
> And all the world beside.

❡ This Lady Howard was not the notorious Frances, Lady Howard, who was implicated in Overbury's murder, but a sixteenth-century Lady Howard who survived four husbands, and was evidently popularly credited with being responsible for their deaths.

For the phantom coach as a death-warning, see "The Lift that Fell" (B, XII).

A LAY GHOST-LAYER

Myra E. Jennings, *Old Cornwall*, Summer Number, 1934.

This ghost story was told by my great-grandmother to my mother, who told it to me.

A wayside cottage had belonged to two old people, who died, leaving it in very bad repair. Their only son had gone out years before to Australia, and no word had been heard from him since. So, after some time the cottage was done up, and new tenants moved in.

They found it impossible to live there, though, because of the strange sounds they heard at night. So badly was the cottage haunted that, though the parson was called in, his efforts were all in vain, and it remained empty.

Then, one day, an old stranger woman came through the village, selling brooms, and hearing of the haunted house, she offered to lay the spirit herself. All she asked was a fire in the room, a table and chair, a Bible, and some sewing to busy her hands with.

These she was gladly given, and she settled down to keep her lonely watch.

At midnight, the door burst open, and in lurched—a monstrous pig! Laying her hand on the Holy Book, the old woman said, "Satan, depart, and let this spirit come back in its natural form!" On this, the pig went out, and a young man came in its place, and when told to "speak in God's name!" this is the story he told:

He was the missing son of the old people who had lived there. Out in Australia he had fallen on bad times, and for lack of any good news to send had not written home for years. Suddenly he struck gold, and having made his fortune, he decided to come home and give his parents a joyful surprise. He arrived at the town near his old home too late to bank his money as he had intended, and took it with him, as he walked out to his parents' cottage. When he got there and found that he had altered so much that his own parents did not recognize him, he carried on the joke, as he thought, by asking and obtaining a night's lodging; and, listening over a scanty supper to their tale of poverty and distress, he went to bed glad in his heart to think of the grand sensation he would cause when he revealed himself and his riches to them in the morning.

But the old people, poor wretches, were even more desperate than he had realized. Somehow they had caught the gleam or felt the weight of his gold, and, falling under the dreadful temptation, they killed the "stranger" in his sleep, and buried him behind the house.

"Come," said the spirit, "and see where my bones lie. Let them be gathered, and laid in consecrated ground, and I will trouble this place no more."

The old woman followed, and, as the spirit hovered over one particular spot in the garden, and then disappeared, fearing that she should not recognize the exact spot by daylight, she took off the thimble which she was still wearing, and with it marked the place. Next day, the ground was dug over, bones were found there, and duly buried in the churchyard, after which the cottage remained as quiet at night as any other.

¶ This is a dramatic and logical development of Type 939A (The Killing of the returned soldier). This type was studied by Professor Maria Kosko, and is found in Eastern Europe and America, as well as in England.

See "The Penryn Tragedy" (B, VIII).

THE LORD PROTECTOR

Received from Mrs R. Tanner

The late H. G. Lee, historian and school inspector, told of a curious experience he had while working in Northamptonshire, not long after the last war.

Finding himself with some time to spare one lunch-hour between school visits, he decided to go and look at a nearby church which he had not seen for many years, but remembered as being worth a call at least for its exterior; inside it had been too well "restored". While he was looking round the outside and making some notes a very sudden storm blew up, and having no car he thought he would take shelter inside until the weather cleared. On entering he saw with a shock of surprise and pleasure that he had been wrong about the restoration; this church was entirely unspoilt. About the most "modern" item of furniture was a fine carved Jacobean pulpit: he could not even see any sign of an organ. He sat down in one of the front pews to drink it in and make more notes. A very beautiful arched entrance into what seemed to be a small chapel specially delighted him. Soon he was a little startled to hear a man's voice close behind him, not having heard anyone approach through the noise of the rain outside; he looked round and saw a middle-aged cassocked clergyman standing in the aisle. This must be the Vicar, he thought.

"So you are interested in our fine old church," said the vicar. "Indeed I am" said Mr Lee, "and it is a rare delight in these days to find a church so unspoilt and so beautifully preserved." "We have seen troubled times," agreed the vicar, "and some churches have suffered great damage. But I trust in the Lord Protector to see that my beautiful church is safe from harm."

It seemed a strange way of referring to God's providence, but the Vicar's next words were even stranger. "You see," he smiled, "the Lord Protector is an old friend of mine. We were at college together. And now, if you have the time, let me show you some of our treasures."

Considerably puzzled—could the Vicar be a harmless lunatic?—Mr Lee followed his guide and soon forgot any alarm in his pleasure at the extraordinary wealth of interest the church contained. At last he realized that the weather had cleared and that it was time for him to go. Together they went down the aisle and out through the porch into the now sunlit churchyard. An aeroplane zoomed suddenly overhead and Mr Lee automatically glanced up at it: when he looked down again the Vicar was not there. He could not have had time to reach the gate or even turn the corner of the wall, so he must have gone back into the church. Feeling that he had not thanked him properly, Mr Lee followed and received another shock. This was the church he had expected to see when he first came in. The Jacobean pulpit was still there, but everything else was different. A rather unsightly modern organ masked the beautiful chapel arch. The Vicar was nowhere to be seen, either in the church itself or in the vestry; but on the vestry wall was a list of incumbents from the church's foundation, and he made a note of the name of the one who had held the living under the Protectorate. Going back down the aisle, he remembered that the Vicar's footsteps had made no sound on the stone tiles.

Later he did some research and found that a person of that name did matriculate from Sidney Sussex College, Cambridge, in 1616, and could have known Oliver Cromwell.

SAMMLE'S GHOST [anglicized]

M. C. Balfour, "Legends of the Cars", *Folk-Lore*, II, p. 415.

Anyways, they told me there was a lad—granfer called him Sammle—as were burnt to death, all gone to ashes, and maybe cinders. But in a while he got up (the inside of him, I mean) and gave himself a shake, and thought what he mun do next—for naturally he weren't used to things, and were a bit strange like. And 'twould be sort of queer, I reckon, lots of bogles and things all about him. Maybe he were a bit feared like, at first. Well, by and by something said to him:

"Thou must go in the graveyard and tell the Big Worm thou's dead, and ask him to have thou eaten up, or else thou'll never rest in the mould."

"Must I?" said the lad. "Well, I'm willing."

Well, he went on, asking his way, and rubbing shoulders with all the horrid things that glowered about him.

And by and by he came to a great place where it was dark, with glimmering lights crossing it, and full of an earthy smell, like the mools in spring, and whiffs of an awful stink, that would turn one sick and feared; and underfoot were creeping things, and all round were crawling, fluttering things, and the air were hot and mucky, and at the end of the place were a horrid great worm, coiled up on a flat stone, with his slimy head moving and swinging from side to side, as if it were smelling for its dinner.

I reckon Sam were main feared when he heard his name called, and the worm shot out its horrid head right in his face.

"Thou, Sammle? So thou're dead and buried, and food for the worms, art thou? Well, where's thy body?"

"Please, your worship"—Sammle didn't want to anger it, naturally—"I'm all here."

"No," said the worm. "Dost thou think we can eat thee? Thou must fetch thy corpse if thou wants to rest in the mould."

"But where is it? Ma corpse?" said Sammle, scratching his head.

"Where is it buried?" said the worm.

"'Tain't buried, that's just it," said Sammle. "'Tis ashes. I were burnt up."

"Hi!" said the worm. "That's bad. Thou'lt not taste so good. Never fret: go fetch the ashes, and bring 'em here, and we'll do all we can."

Well, Sammle went back, and he looked and looked, and by and by he got all th' ashes together that he could see, and took them off in a sack to the great worm.

And he opened the sack, and the worm crawled down and smelt them, and turned them over and over.

"Sammle," he says by and by, "something's missing," says he. "Thou'rt not all here, Sammle. Where's the rest of thee? Thou'll have to seek it."

"I've brought all I could find," said Sammle.

"Nay!" said the worm. "There's an arm missing."

"Ah! That's so!" said Sammle, nodding. "I'd lost an arm, I had. Cut off it were."

"Thou mun find it, Sammle."

"Well, I've no idea where the doctor put her, but I'll go and see."

So off he went again, and looked here and looked there, and by and by he got it.

Back he went to the worm.

"Here's the arm," said he.

And the worm turned it over.

"No, there's summat still, Sammle," says he. "Had thou lost anything else?"

"Let's see," said Sammle, thinking. "I'd lost a nail, and it never growed again."

"That's it, I reckon," says the worm. "Thou's got to find it, Sammle."

"I reckon I'll never find that, then, master," says Sammle, "but I'm willing to try."

And off he went.

But a nail's an easy matter to lose, see'st thou, and a hard thing to find, and though he sought and sought, he couldn't find nothing, so at last he went back to the worm.

"I've sought and I've sought, and I've found nought," says he. "Thou must take me without my nail—it's no great loss, I'm thinking. Can't 'ee make shift without it?"

"No," said the worm. "I can't; and if thou can't find it—are thou certain sure thou can't, Sammle?"

"Certain, worse luck!"

"Then thou must walk all the time! I'm main sorry for thee, Sammle, but thou'll have lots of company!"

And all the creeping things and the crawling things took and turned Sammle out; and ever since, if he's not found his nail, he's walking about seeking for it.

That's all. Granfer told me one day when I were asking where all the bogles come from. 'Tis not much of a tale, but I can't mind another now, and it's sort of funny, isn't it?

❡ This gruesome tale explains the belief behind MOTIF E.235.4 [*Return from dead to punish theft of part of corpse*], of which there are so many examples in English tradition, as "The Bone" (A, V).

THE SILKEN SHAWL

From G. Hodge, *Remembered Wraiths and Tokens*, *Old Cornwall*, Vol. 3, 1937–42, p. 416.

After several bad fishing seasons, the desperate Newlyn men turned to cold-blooded piracy, and made their blindfolded victims walk the plank into the sea to drown.

On one of the unlucky passing ships that were attacked by the Newlyn pirates the Captain happened to have a wife aboard. She was wearing a very beautiful silken shawl as she too walked the plank to her death, and this one of the pirates snatched from her shoulders before she fell, and then took home as a present for his wife, saying nothing of how he came by it. On the following Sunday, while dressing to go to church, she put it on, and was admiring its lovely pattern and colours as it fell in graceful folds around her, swaying in front of a mirror, when suddenly she saw reflected in the glass the pale, tragic face of the drowned woman looking at her over her shoulder, and a hand that pointed to the shawl. The pirate's wife, we were told, was so horrified that she went raving mad, and died shortly afterwards. What became of that haunted shawl we never heard, but it may be guessed that no one was found so bold as knowingly to put it on again. Let us hope it was burnt!

¶ The motif of a ghost seen in a mirror, though otherwise invisible, is fairly widely distributed. W. Henry Jewitt cites one in *Folk-Lore*, XIV, pp. 183–5.

A house in St Leonard's School, St Andrews, was haunted by a ghost who could only be seen in a mirror. Informant, the late Miss Katharine McCutcheon.

THE SIX DEAD MEN

G. F. Black, *County Folk-Lore*, III, p. 31.

[After a wreck] some people saw the six men who had been in the boat at the south end of the island, near a well-known Trow haunt. They looked just as they had been in life, only for the kind of something in their faces that was no' just earthly altogether. And often after that they were seen—always the six of them—walking with their faces aye turned to the sea. Sometimes they appeared in the daytime and sometimes at night, but no one had the courage to speak to them until a sensible woman did so. They were passing near her house and she exclaimed, "Oh! what is this?" Then she called the skipper by his name, and he spoke, but his voice was like a clap of thunder, and she could not understand him. She said, "Moderate your speech, for I'm no' fit to stand it." Then the man spoke quite naturally, and the first thing he said was, "What is it that goes before the face of the Almighty?" and she replied:

> "Justice and judgment of Thy throne
> Are made the dwelling place;
> Mercy, accompanied with truth,
> Shall go before Thy face."

After that the man conversed just as if he had been alive and he told her that when their boat came off the mouth of the fiord, Madge Coutts (a witch who disliked them) came into the boat and seated herself on the thwart, and they knew by her look that she had "designed for their lives". They hoped to get rid of her by striking her with their Luggie-staff [large fish-clip] and actually succeeded in turning her over the gunwale, but in a moment she dived under the boat and got in on the other side in the form of a large black ox. Putting down her horns, she struck them into the boat and drew out the *hassen* [board adjoining the keel to which the binders of a boat are attached], and then of course, the boat went to pieces. The skipper said he could not rest because of some transaction that was not quite honest between himself and a brother, and he begged the woman to set it right that the brother might have his own. She did so, and the six men were seen no more. It was remembered that upon the day of the accident Madge Coutts was seen going in at her own chimney in the form of a grey cat, and that immediately afterwards a sulphur-tainted smoke was seen ascending.

Edmonston and Saxby, p. 219.

¶ This tale illustrates many beliefs, both about ghosts and about witches, in a compact form.

THE TREASURE OF DOWNHOUSE

J. R. W. Coxhead, *Devon Traditions and Fairy Tales*, pp. 39–41.

About half a mile to the west of the market town of Tavistock, in Devon, there stands a large farmstead called Downhouse. Although the house was rebuilt about the year 1822, the original building was considered to have been an extremely ancient place, and to have possessed a reputation for being haunted by the ghost of a very tall man.

The family who resided at Downhouse before the building was rebuilt knew by long experience the exact hour of the night at which the ghost made its appearance, and they always took great care to be in bed before the dreaded hour arrived.

Now it happened that one of the children living in the house fell desperately ill, and while the worried mother was watching anxiously by the bedside, the child asked for water. The woman quickly fetched a jug of water which was standing on a table near the bed, but the child refused to drink any of the contents of the jug, and demanded fresh water straight from the pump in the yard.

The little boy's request caused the poor woman great distress, as it was just about the time of night the ghost was in the habit of walking.

While the distracted mother was considering what course to take, the sick child again asked fretfully for fresh water from the pump, and, bravely suppressing her fear for the sake of her darling son, the woman exclaimed, "In the name of God, I will go down," and she walked swiftly from the room.

As she went down the stairs she fancied she saw a shadow following her, and then she clearly heard footsteps, and just as she reached the pump, she felt a hand on her shoulder. With a start of terror she turned round, and saw the shadowy figure of a tall man standing close behind her. Summoning up all her courage, she said to the spectre, "In the name of God, why troublest thou me?" The ghost replied, "It is well for thee that thou hast spoken to me in the name of God, this being the last time allotted to me to trouble this world, or else I should have injured thee. Now do as I tell thee, and be not afraid. Come with me and I shall direct thee to a something which shall remove this pump: under it is concealed treasure."

Whatever the "something" happened to be, when used it enabled the pump to be removed without any great difficulty, and in a cavity thus revealed a great heap of gold and silver coins!

The spectre instructed the woman to take the treasure and use it to improve the farm, and if anyone were foolish enough to molest her, or steal the money, the person concerned would suffer great misfortune.

The ghost then ordered the woman to take fresh water to her sick child, who, as a reward for the mother's great courage and firm trust in God, would soon recover from his serious illness.

Suddenly a cock crowed loudly in the farmyard, and, as though the sound were a signal that the time had come for departure, the apparition became less distinct, rose slowly into the air, and, after assuming the shape of a small bright cloud, gradually disappeared.

From *The Borders of the Tamar and the Tavy*. Date 8 January 1833. Mrs Bray.

¶ See "The Old Lady of Littledean", "The Tin Box", "The Haunted Castle" (A, II).

PART 12
GIANTS

It is a matter of some difficulty to distinguish the fairy tale giant from the giant of legend. The legendary giants are often those responsible for some topographical detail of the landscape, some hill, mound, or rock. Sometimes rocks or land formations are supposed to be petrified giants, or objects dropped by giants. It is on those grounds that "The Origin of the Wrekin" has slipped into this section, though it might be considered to have plot enough to qualify as a fairy tale. It is difficult to believe that these tales were ever told as more than playful guesses at the origin of certain natural features, or of place-names, as in the story of the giant Bel.

This is a small section because the giant myths fail to qualify in two ways, either as being so slight as to have no narrative content at all, such as the description of Stonehenge as "The Giant's Dance", or so obviously a flight of fancy as to slip across the borderline into the fairy tales. Such a tale is "Tom the Giant and Jack the Tinkeard", which is full of local references and local scenery, but is yet one of the fantasticated tales told by the droll-tellers.

The remaining giants vary greatly in size and type, from the Giant Goemagog, who was a mere ten feet high, to the giant Bolster, who had a stride of six miles. A few were gentle and well-disposed to men, like Holiburn of Carn Galva, the greater part were rapacious and destructive, treasure-hoarders and stone-throwers. The men of large stature and tremendous powers, like Tom Hickathrift and William of Lindholm, are not included in this section.

The giant figures of Cerne Abbas and Long Wilmington have contributed something to the traditions of the giants.

BRUTUS AND CORINEUS

Hunt, *Popular Romances of the West of England*, p. 44.

... "Brutus, finding now his powers much lessn'd, and this not yet the place foretold him, leaves Aquitain, and with an easy course arriving at Totness in *Dev'nshire*, quickly perceivs heer to be the promis'd end of his labours....

"The Iland, not yet *Britain*, but *Albion*, was in a manner desert and inhospitable, kept only by a remnant of *Giants*, whose excessive Force and Tyrannie had consumed the rest. Them Brutus destroies, and to his people divides the land, which with some reference to his own name, he thenceforth calls *Britain*. To Corineus, *Cornwall*, as we now call it, fell by lot; the rather by him lik't, for that the hugest giants in Rocks and Caves were said to lurk still there; which kind of Monsters to deal with was his old exercise.

"And heer, with leave bespok'n to recite a grand fable, though dignify'd by our best Poets: While *Brutus*, on a certain Festival day, solemnly kept on that shoar where he first landed (Totness), was with the people in great jollity and mirth, a crew of these savages, breaking in upon them, began on a sudden another sort of Game than at such a meeting was expected. But at length by many hands overcome, *Goëmagog*, the hugest, in hight twelve cubits, is reserved alive; that with him Corineus, who desired nothing more, might try his strength, whom in a Wrestle the Giant catching aloft, with a terrible hugg broke three of his Ribs: Nevertheless Corineus, enraged, heaving him up by main force, and on his shoulders bearing him to the next high rock, threw him hedlong all shatter'd into the sea, and left his name on the cliff, called ever since *Langoëmagog*, which is to say, the Giant's Leap."

Quoted from Milton, *History of Britain, that part now especially called England.*

THE GIANT BOLSTER [summary]

Hunt, *Popular Romances of the West of England*, p. 73.

This giant held special possession of the hill formerly known as Carne-Bury-anacht, "the sparstone grave", sometimes known as "St Agnes' Ball", and "St Agnes' Pestis", and now as "St Agnes' Beacon". An ancient earthwork at the foot of the hill, once extending from Trevaunance Porth to Chapel Porth and enclosing the most important tin district in St Agnes, is constantly called "The Bolster".

Bolster must have been of enormous size. He could stand with one foot on St Agnes' Beacon and the other on Carn Brea, a distance of six miles; and in the valley running upwards from Chapel Porth the impression of his huge fingers may still be seen on a certain stone, by which he once rested to drink from the well at Chapel Porth.

He was tyrannous to his wife, who was made to labour hard at piling up on the top of St Agnes' Beacon masses of small stones, gathered from an estate at the foot of the hill. This estate is still remarkable for its freedom from stones, though most lands reclaimed from the moors of this district have stones in abundance mixed with the soil.

The giant is supposed to have fallen desperately in love with St Agnes, who was extremely beautiful, and when she rejected all his advances he persecuted her incessantly, until in despair she pretended to have been convinced of his love, and only required one more proof. There is at Chapel Porth a hole in a cliff at the end of the valley. She required the giant to fill this with his blood, to which he gladly assented, believing that it would be easy for him to fill many such holes. But since the hole opened at the bottom into the sea the blood flowed away as fast as it poured in; and eventually the giant, for all his great strength, bled to death, and the countryside was rid of its oppressor.

¶ Many of the Cornish saints were rather unscrupulous characters. See "The Crowza Stones" (B, XI) and "The Hack and Cast".

See also "Robin Hood" (A, IV).

THE GIANT OF CARN GALVA [slightly shortened]

W. Bottrell, *Stories and Legends of West Cornwall*, p. 122.

The giant of Carn Galva was more playful than warlike. Though the old works of this giant now stand desolate, we may still see, or get up and rock ourselves upon, the logan-stone which this dear old giant placed on the most westerly carn of the range, that he might log himself to sleep when he saw the sun dip himself into the waves, and sea-birds fly to their homes in the cleeves. Near the giant's rocking-seat one may still see a pile of cubical rocks, which are almost as regular and shapely now as when the giant used to amuse himself in building them up and kicking them down again for exercise or play, when alone and when he had nothing else to do. People of the northern hills have always had a loving regard for the memory of this giant, because he appears to have passed all his life at the carn in single blessedness, merely to protect his loving people of Morvah and Zennor from the depredations of the less honest Titans who then dwelt on Lelant Hills. Carn Galva giant never killed but one of the Morvah people in his life, and that happened all through loving play.

The giant was very fond of a young fellow of Choone, who used to take a turn over to the carn, every now and then, just to see how the old giant was getting on, to cheer him up a bit, play a game of bob, or anything else to help him pass his lonely time away.

One afternoon the giant was so pleased with the good play they had had together that when the young fellow of Choone threw down his quoit to go away home, the giant, in a good-natured way, tapped his playfellow on the head with the tips of his fingers. At the same time he said, "Be sure to come again tomorrow, my son, and we will have a capital game of bob." Before the word "bob" was well out of the giant's mouth, the young man dropped at his feet. The giant's fingers had gone right through his playmate's skull. When at last the giant became sensible of the damage he had done to the young man's brain-pan, he did his best to put the inside workings of his mate's head to rights, and plugged up his finger-holes, but all to no purpose; for the young man was stone dead and cold long before he ceased doctoring his head.

When the poor giant found it was all over with his playmate, he took the body in his arms, and sitting down on a large square rock at the foot of the carn, he rocked himself to and fro; pressing the lifeless body to his bosom, he wailed and moaned over him, bellowing and crying louder than the booming billows breaking on the rocks in Permoina.

"Oh, my son, my son, why didn't they make the shell of thy noddle stronger? A es as plum [soft] as a pie-crust, doughbaked, and made too thin by the half! How shall I ever pass my time without thee to play bob and mop-and-heede? [hide and seek]."

The giant of Carn Galva never rejoiced any more, but in seven years or so he pined away and died of a broken heart.

So Zennor people say, and that one may judge of the size of their giant very well, as he placed his logan rock at such a height that, when seated on it, to rock himself, he could rest his feet comfortably on the green turf below.

Some say that he gathered together the heap of square blocks, near his favourite resting-place that he might have them at hand to defend his people against the giants of Trecrobben and Trink, with whom he fought many a hard battle. Yet when they were all on good terms they would pass weeks on a stretch in playing together, and the quoits which served them to play bob, as well as the rocks they hurled at each other when vexed, may still be seen scattered all over this hilly region.

THE GIANTS OF STOWEY

Ruth L. Tongue, *Somerset Folklore*, pp. 128–9.

There was a time, long, long ago, when giants came to live close to Nether Stowey. They flung up a huge mound for their Castle, and lived under it.

Some of the people fled to Stogursey, others ran uphill for safety on Dowsboro' Camp, and others, poor things, just stayed where they were.

No one liked going past the Castle even if they had to, and most of those who *did* come back were pale and terrified. The giants had a horrible way of putting their hands out of the hill and grabbing a sheep, or a cow, or a man.

Once the monsters had tasted men's flesh they grew ravenous. They made a raid on Stogursey Castle, and beat it down flat, and chased the Stogursey people till they caught them in handfuls. When this supply ran out, they began again on the folk of Nether Stowey.

Most of them were very old (and tough) or very young (and tender), for all the able-bodied folk had run up the hills and were quite safe in Dowsboro' Camp and having a fine time. They didn't know what was going on, so a poor old gaffer tried to tiptoe past the Castle and tell them, but an arm came out and got him.

Then a little lad got on one of his father's hill ponies along with a "drift" of them, and went away past the Castle at a stretch gallop. A hand did come out, but it got such a kick it went in again mighty fast and there was a dreadful yell.

The folk on Dowsboro' heard that, and got ready to fight—but when the little lad on his pony got to them they didn't wait to give battle up there. No. "The men from Dowsboro' beat down Stowey Castle" and after that anyone could pass the hill again—they still don't like doing it at night.

THE ORIGIN OF THE WREKIN: II

Burne and Jackson, *Shropshire Folk-Lore*, pp. 2–3.

Once upon a time there was a wicked old giant in Wales, who, for some reason or other, had a very great spite against the Mayor of Shrewsbury and all his people, and he made up his mind to dam up the Severn, and by that means cause such a flood that the town would be drowned. So off he set, carrying a spadeful of earth, and tramped along mile after mile, trying to find the way to Shrewsbury. And how he missed it I cannot tell, but he must have gone wrong somewhere, for at last he got close to Wellington, and by that time he was puffing and blowing under his heavy load, and wishing he was at the end of his journey. By and by there came a cobbler along the road with a sack of old boots and shoes on his back, for he lived at Wellington, and went once a fortnight to Shrewsbury to collect his customers' old boots and shoes, and take them home with him to mend. And the giant called out to him. "I say," he said, "how far is it to Shrewsbury?" "Shrewsbury?" said the cobbler. "What do you want at Shrewsbury?" "Why," said the giant, "to fill up the Severn with this lump of earth I've got here. I've an old grudge against the Mayor and the folks at Shrewsbury, and now I mean to drown them out and get rid of them all at once." "My word!" thought the cobbler. "This will never do! I can't afford to lose my customers!" and he spoke up again. "Eh!" he said. "You'll never get to Shrewsbury, not today, *nor* tomorrow. Why, look at me! *I'm* just come from Shrewsbury, and I've had time to wear out all these old boots and shoes on the road since I started." And he showed him his sack. "Oh!" said the giant with a great groan. "Then it's no use! I'm fairly tired out already, and I can't carry this load of mine any farther. I shall just drop it here and go back home." So he dropped the earth on the ground just where he stood, and scraped his boots on the spade, and off he went home again to Wales, and nobody ever heard anything of him in Shropshire after. But where he put down his load there stands the Wrekin to this day, and even the earth he scraped off his boots was such a pile that it made the little Ercall by the Wrekin's side.

¶ In this version the villain is a giant, not the Devil, and his object is to dam the Severn and flood Shrewsbury, but the plot is the same.

See "The Devil's Spittleful" (B, III).

WADE AND HIS WIFE

Gutch, *County Folk-Lore*, II, *North Riding of Yorkshire*, p. 9.

Wade [is] an imaginary being, connected with some monstrous fables long current in this neighbourhood [Whitby]. This Wade and his wife and son, possessed the powers of the ancient Cyclops, or rather of the Titans, whose mighty grasp could lift the hills and toss the ponderous rocks. To their gigantic operations are ascribed the castles of Mulgrave and Pickering, the Roman road supposed to communicate between them, several Druidical stones in the vicinity, with other works equally stupendous. In the building of Mulgrave and Pickering castles, Wade and his wife, whose name was Bell, divided their labours, a single giant being sufficient for rearing each castle; but, having only one hammer between them, it was necessary to toss it backward and forward, giving a shout every time it was thrown, that when the one threw it to Mulgrave or to Pickering the other might be ready to catch it! The Roman road which is called *Wade's causey*, or *Wade's wife's causey*, was formed by them in a trice, Wade paving, and Bell bringing him stones; once or twice her apron strings gave way, leaving a large heap of stones on the spot!...

Young Wade, even when an infant, could throw a rock several tons weight to a vast distance; for one day, when his mother was milking her cow near Swarthouse, the child, whom she had left on Sleights Moor, became impatient for the breast, and, seizing a stone of vast size, heaved it across the valley in wrath, and hit his mother with such violence that, though she was not materially hurt, her body made an impression on the stone which remained indelible, till the stone itself was broken up, a few years ago, to mend the highways! According to one edition of these fables, *Wade's wife's causey* was laid to accommodate her in crossing the moors to milk her cow. The cow, it seems, partook of the gigantic stature of her owners; and, above 100 years ago, some wag contrived to make the jawbone of a young whale pass for a rib of Bell Wade's cow. The precious relic was long shown under this name at old Mulgrave Castle; it now lies neglected in the joiner's shop beside the present Mulgrave Castle. It is 4 ft. long and 3 or 4 inches in diameter, and is carved all over with initials, representing the names of numerous pilgrims who formerly repaired to Mulgrave, to present their offerings at the shrine of credulity.

Young, *A History of Whitby and Stoneshall Abbey*, II, pp. 724, 925.
¶ See "The Giants of the Mount".

PART 13
HISTORICAL TRADITIONS

Historical traditions are of various types, and so numerous that only representative specimens of them can be given.

I. The Migratory Legend, Type ML.8000 (Legends of Wars and Warriors), is one great sub-division of historical traditions. In the English-speaking part of these islands the wars that are most constantly remembered are, the Roman Conquest, the Danish invasions, the Norman Conquest, the wars between England and Scotland and the Border affrays that followed them, the great Civil War, the Monmouth Rebellion, and the 'Forty-five. The Monmouth Rebellion, because of the horrors that followed it, made a deep and lasting impression in the West Country, as the 'Forty-five did in Scotland. All over the country, as is natural, the great Civil War was most lastingly remembered. The Wars of the Roses, which was a nobles' war, made less impression, but some popular memories of it remain, as of the Peasants' Rising and the Chartist times. In the North, particularly, the suppression of the monasteries made a deep impression.

II. Legends of famous people are allied to these memories of wars, some of them apparently rather erratically chosen. King Alfred is rightly dear to Englishmen, but William Rufus is more remembered than one would expect, and Richard Coeur de Lion, Bonnie Prince Charlie, and Cromwell are especially conspicuous. There are some outstanding men to whom a legend of wizardry was attached, some of them men of learning, such as Roger Bacon, but others, men of outstanding brilliance, such as Sir Francis Drake.

III. Allied to the local traditions are those memories of comparatively obscure happenings which illustrate social history and show how actual events are reshaped in popular thought. These often have supernatural beliefs attached to them. With these, too, we have links with the past—long-lived individuals who have bridged generations, and fascinating instances of folk-memory, such as the tradition of Chaucer at Ewelme.

IV. A fourth type of historical tradition is that tale—often an international tale-type—which is told, circumstantially and with full belief, as having happened at various places and to various people. It is often difficult to decide whether the event has ever actually occurred, and, if so, to whom. Sometimes it is possible to find some circumstance which has given rise to the tale, sometimes again, it seems probable that it is in the main true, though details may have been attached to it to bring it in line with the archetypal tale. Examples of this kind are tale-type 990 (The Apparently Dead Revives), and "The Oxford Student," often loosely connected with the Robber Bridegroom tales, some of which are to be found among the Novelle.

The line dividing Local Legends from Historical Traditions is a narrow one, and the distinction between them is not easy to make. If a particular tale is not to be found in one division it may well turn up in another. Many favourites may, however, be searched for in vain.

BURKE AND HARE

School of Scottish Studies, John Elliott, *Notebooks*.

In the old days [in] which doctors and students needed dead bodies for science, in their medical research, doctor Knox in the Cannongate of Edinburgh, offered ten pound, and sometimes more, for a corpse, at that time in Scotland. A lot of Irish harvesters came over from Ireland to harvest, and two of these harvesters settled down in Tanners' Close, in the Grass Market of Edinburgh. Their names were Burke, and the other Hare. They were men of no human feeling, and would do anything for money. Burke was married, and his wife stopped with them in their two dark and dirty hovels.

I

A young country woman, who had a bairn to a young farmer in the country, was driven from home by her parents, sought refuge in Edinburgh, and was stopping with some people not far from Tanners' Close. Her name was Mary Paterson, and she got into bad company, and soon learned to drink. Of course her heart was fair broken, and she drank to drown her sorrows.

As Burke and Hare had learnt that Dr Knox would buy dead bodies, they went to him, and made inquiries, and was told he would give ten pound, so they met in with Mary Paterson in a pub, and Mrs Burke invited Mary to Tanners' Close for a drink.

They got her in, and sent out for drink, and kept Mary drinking till she was drunk, then they threw her into bed, and put another tyke on top of her, and smothered her.

They took her down to Dr Knox, and got the ten pound. Not long after, a little woman from the country, who had comed in to do some shopping, but was very fond of drink, was invited into Tanners' Close. She was a little bright and high-spirited woman, and sang them songs, and drank along with them. They carried her on till they got her stupid with the drink, and was not long before they were doing a roaring trade in the body-snatching.

About that time, a boy called [him] daft Jimmy roamed about the streets in search of a crust of bread, or anything he could get to make a scanty living. He was well kenned in the town, and was always ready to help anyone he thought he could get a penny from. Burke and Hare had been away lifting a dead body that had been buried the day before. They had hired a cuddy and cart, and was bringing the body up a street in the middle of the night, when the old cuddy dropped down dead. They were so feared they would be caught, that they unyoked the dead cuddy out of the cart, and got into the trams themselves, and pulled it home.

Not long after they had disposed of the body, they began to look around for another victim, and they thought of trying daft Jamie. The boy was hungry, and they told him to come in and have some tea. Jimmy sat down at the so-called table to get his tea. They slipped whiskey into his tea, but Jimmy told them he did not like the whiskey, but said, "I will take as much tea as ye like." But he did not want the whiskey, but they tried him just to take a wee drop, but he would not. Burke was not for taking Jimmy, as he kenned he would be missed off the streets, but Hare threw Jimmy into a bed, and put another tyke on him, but Jimmy was strong, and Hare could not hold him down, and he called to Burke, if he did not come and help him, he would kill him too. Burke had to go to his assistance, and poor daft Jimmy was murdered too, but Jimmy was soon missed off the streets, and he was traced to Tanners' Close. [and] They were both apprehended, and tried in Edinburgh, but Hare turned King's evidence, and was set free, but the police had to give him protection, or he got out of Edinburgh, as the crowds would have torn him to pieces. He made for Ireland, and he was not long in Ireland till one night a young student went into his house and murdered him. It was said after that the young man that murdered Hare was his own son, and did not know him. At that time kirk yards had to be watched for some time after a burial, and in a little house a man watched at night, as body-snatchers were always on the look-out for fresh dead bodies.

II

One dark night, at a wayside inn, a pony and trap drove up, and stopped. There was two men and a woman. The woman was sitting between the two men, with a hood on her head, and her face was covered with a veil. The men jumped out, and left the woman setting. They went into the pub for a drink. The ostler was busy in the stable, and one looked out, and when he saw the woman settin [by] herself, he went up to the trap, and said to the woman, "It's a cauld night the night!" But he got no answer. He spoke again, but still no answer. He had a close look at her, and he saw it was a corpse. He got up and got hold of her, and carried her into the stable, and took off her disguise, and put it on himself. Then he got into the trap in the woman's place, and was setting bolt upright and just like the woman when the men came out, and jumped in, one at either side. They just thought it was the dead woman.

After travelling some distance along the road, one of the men said to the other, "D'ye ken that body's getting warm?" The other said, "I was just thinking the same." Then the ostler spoke up and said, "If ye had been as lang in Hell as me, ye'd be warm too!" That was enough. The men jumped out and ran for their life. The ostler saw no more of them; he just turned the pony and trap, and took it back to the inn.

It was now his property, as he knew they dare not come back to claim it.

III

A school in a mining village...the schoolmaster was busy with the classes...a big boy was getting punished. Not long after the children got out for dinner, the boy who had got punished went home, and told his mother he would not go to school in the afternoon. His mother told him he would catch it from his father when he came home for not going to school. But the mother told him to go down to the grocer for half a stone of self-raising flour, as she had to bake. Away went the boy, and got the flour. By this time the school was in again, and the boy had to pass not far off the school door. He was carrying the flour. He heard the schoolmaster laying the law off inside. He noticed the door was not right shut, and he stepped up and keeked in. The schoolmaster's back was to him; he gently eased the door open, and hurled the flour at him, and nearly blinded the schoolmaster with the flour, and then he dare not go home, as he knew what he would get. So he hid in the kirk-yard under a flat headstone. He lay there till nearly midnight, when a grand trap drove into the kirk yard. Two men got out to lift a body, but they had some trouble with the horse as it would not stand.

At last the boy crawled out from below the flat tombstone, and said, "I'll haud the horse." The men bolted, and the boy kept holding the horse till daylight. The minister eyed the trap from his window, and went to see what the horse and trap were doing there. The boy told the minister that the two men ran away, and left him holding the horse.

"Well," said the minister, "the men will not come back for their horse and trap, so it is now yours. So you can drive it home to your father." So that put things right with his father and mother.

¶ This account of the fifteen murders committed by Burke and Hare is, on the whole, correct, though the discovery of the crimes was finally due to an old woman, Margaret Docherty, wife of Silly Jimmy, who had been killed earlier. Burke was executed in 1829. The crimes made an immense impression on the popular imagination, and a whole series of tales about the "Burkers" has been collected from the travelling people of Scotland.

A black coach driven by a gang of medical students in "lum hats" features in many of them, and is a kind of successor of the death-coach (see *Lady Howard's Coach*).

In England there are tales of the "Resurrection Men", "The Corpse in the Cab", one of the tales told here, is to be found among the Jocular Tales (A, III).

It will be remembered that Jerry Cruncher, in *The Tale of Two Cities*, was a Resurrection Man. The Burke and Hare story is dramatized by James Bridie in *The Anatomist*.

CROMWELL IN GLASGOW

Scott, *Minstrelsy of the Scottish Border*, II, pp. 232–3.

The following tradition, concerning Cromwell, is preserved by an uncommonly direct line of traditional evidence; being narrated (as I am informed) by the grandson of an eyewitness. When Cromwell, in 1650, entered Glasgow, he attended divine service in the High Church; but the Presbyterian divine who officiated, poured forth, with more zeal than prudence, his indignation against the person, principles, and cause, of the Independent General. One of Cromwell's officers rose, and whispered his commander; who seemed to give him a short and stern answer, and the sermon was concluded without interruption. Among the crowd, assembled to gaze at the General, as he came out of the Church, was a shoemaker, the son of one of James the Sixth's Scottish footmen. This man had been born and bred in England, but, after his father's death, had settled in Glasgow. Cromwell eyed him among the crowd, and immediately called him by his name—the man fled, but, at Cromwell's command, one of his retinue followed him, and brought him to the General's lodgings. A number of the inhabitants remained at the door, waiting the end of this extraordinary scene. The shoemaker soon came out in high spirits, and showing some gold, declared he was going to drink Cromwell's health. Many attended him, to hear the particulars of his interview; among others, the grandfather of the narrator. The shoemaker said that he had been a playfellow of Cromwell, when they were both boys, their parents residing in the same street; that he had fled, when the General had first called to him, thinking he might owe him some ill-will, on account of his father being in the service of the Royal Family. He added that Cromwell had been so very kind and familiar with him, that he ventured to ask him what the officer had said to him in the church. "He proposed," said Cromwell, "to pull forth the minister by the ears; and I answered, that the preacher was one fool, and he was another." In the course of the day, Cromwell held an interview with the minister, and contrived to satisfy his scruples so effectually, that the evening discourse, by the same man, was tuned to the praise and glory of the victor of Naseby.

TYPE ML.8000. MOTIF: J.215.1.2 [*King refuses to banish gossipers*].

¶ This anecdote has probably a good deal of truth in it, for it shows the characteristic tolerance of Cromwell, and also his concern to ingratiate himself with people who disliked him. Among the Cromwell anecdotes, see " Cromwell in Yorkshire", "The Burly Stranger", *The Grey Goose Feathers.*

DRAKE AS A WIZARD

Mrs Bray, *A Description of the Parts of Devonshire Bordering on the Tamar and Tavy* (1836), 3 vols, II, pp. 170–3.

I. DRAKE AND THE ARMADA

The day as Sir Francis Drake was playing at kales on Plymouth Hoe he had news that a foreign fleet was sailing into the harbour. He finished his game and then took a hatchet and ordered a large block of wood to be brought to him. He chopped this up into small pieces and threw them into the sea with magic words. As they touched the water each one became a fire-ship and sailed against the foreign fleet so that it was utterly destroyed.

II. DRAKE AND HIS LADY

When Drake sailed away to circumnavigate the world, and "shot the gulf", he was away so long that his lady despaired of ever seeing him again. After seven years she decided to re-marry; the bridal day came, and the bridal party were in the church.

At that moment one of the spirits who served Sir Francis brought him news, as he sailed in the Antipodes, of what was happening in England. At once he took a cannon and fired right down into the sea. So powerful was the shot and so true was his aim that the ball sped straight through the earth and landed with a loud explosion between the bride and bridegroom just as they reached the altar.

"That is Drake's shot," said his lady. "I am still a wife." And she went home and waited patiently for his return.

III. DRAKE AND THE RIVER

In Drake's days there was no fresh water at Plymouth, so that the housewives had to go all the way to Plympton to wash their clothes. Sir Francis

Drake resolved to cure this, so one day he called for his horse and rode off to Dartmoor, where he hunted about until he found a fine spring that suited his notions. He pronounced a magic word and turned his horse's head for home. Off he went as fast as he could gallop, and the spring followed his horse's heels all the way back. So the good wives of Plymouth were never without fresh water again.

IV. DRAKE'S CANNON BALL

Ruth L. Tongue, *Folktales of England*, p. 94.

There were one o' the Sydenham maids, and 'er got 'erself betrothed to Sir Francis Drake. But afore they could be married, 'e 'ad to go away on a voyage, and 'ow long it'd be afore 'e could come back, no one knew, and 'e didn't trust 'er father. So they took their troth-plight, the two of 'en, afore Drake sailed away. Well, 'e sailed away, for three long years, and Sir George Sydenham, 'e found another suitor for 'is daughter, a much richer one. Well, no matter what the maid do say, marriage were announced, and she were half afraid o' Sir Francis Drake, but she were more afraid of 'er father. So she gave in.

Well now, Sir Francis Drake, 'e did do some very strange things—'e did sit on Plymouth 'oe, a-whittling of a stick, and all the chips that fell into the sea, they did turn into ships, to go fight the Spanish Armada. Now, although 'e'd been gone three years, 'e knew what was 'appening, so at the very door o' the church, 'e dropped a red-'ot cannon ball in front o' the bridal party. Oh! give 'en a fright, did—and when 'e come 'ome at last, 'twas to find 'is bride and 'er dear father a-waiting for 'en with smiles. As for t'other bridegroom, 'e'd a-taken 'isself across the length and breadth of England. But I expect Sir Francis Drake knew where 'e was tew!

From a member of Watchet W.I., 1950. Also heard at Chipstable in 1960.

¶ Sir Francis Drake was believed to be a wizard by the Spaniards, and even in his own country he shared with other outstanding men, such as Roger Bacon, Cardinal Wolsey, Sir Walter Raleigh, Owen Glendower and Oliver Cromwell, a reputation for wizardry. The people round Combe Sydenham still believe that Drake's cannon ball rolls up and down in time of national danger, and his drum was said to sound during the Second World War. Newbolt's "Drake's Drum" is written on a variation of these traditions, by which it is said that if the drum is beaten, Drake will return. In the modern version of Drake and his Lady, Drake was merely betrothed to the Sydenham girl, as he was in Noyes' long poem on Drake, which, however, does not introduce the supernatural element.

See "Sir Francis Drake and the Devil" (B, III).

DREAM PORTENDING THE DEATH OF WILLIAM RUFUS

Roger of Wendover, *Chronicle*, I, p. 443.

A.D. 1100, King William Rufus held his court at Christmas with much magnificence in Gloucester, at Easter in Winchester and at Whitsuntide in London. On the morrow of St Peter's ad vincula* he went to shoot in the New Forest, where Walter Tyrrel, shooting at a stag, unintentionally struck the king, who fell pierced to the heart, without uttering a word, and thus by a miserable death ended his cruel life. Many signs presignified his departure; for the day before his death, he dreamed that he was bled by a physician, and that the stream of his blood reached to heaven, and obscured the sky. Upon this, he sprang up from sleep, invoking the name of St Mary, and calling for a light, kept his chamberlains with him for the remainder of the night. In the morning, a foreign monk, who was at court on some business connected with his church, related to Robert Fitz-Hamon, a powerful nobleman, intimate with the king, a wonderful dream which he had seen the preceding night; he saw the king enter a church, and cast his usual haughty look on the congregation round him, after which he took the crucifix between his teeth, and almost bit off its arms and legs; the crucifix was at first passive, but afterwards kicked the king with its right foot, so that he fell upon the pavement, and emitted such a large flame from its mouth that the smoke of it rose in a cloud even to the stars. Robert told this dream to the king, who said with a laugh, "He is a monk, and, like all monks, dreamed this to get something by it; give him a hundred shillings, that he may not say he has dreamed in vain." The king's wretched death was also foretold...by the blood which oozed out from the ground, though there was no want of other tokens, presignifying the same event. For Anselm, archbishop of Canterbury, when he was in exile for three years, through his tyranny, went from Rome to Marcenniac, about the first of August, to enjoy the conversation of Hugh, abbat of Cluny; there a conversation arose between them, concerning King William, and the abbat affirmed with the most solemn protestation of truth, that in the past night he had seen the king summoned before the throne of God, accused of his crimes, and sentenced by the just Judge to damnation; but he did not explain how he was informed of it, neither did the archbishop or any other of those who were present, ask him, out of respect to his great holiness. The following day also, the

* August 2nd.

archbishop went to Lyons, and the same night, when the monks who had accompanied him had chanted the matin-service, behold, a young man, simply dressed, and of a mild countenance, stood by one of the clerks of the archbishop, who had his eyes shut; and calling him by name, "Adam," said he, "are you asleep?" The clerk answered, "No," and the young man continued, "Do you wish to hear some news?" "Most willingly," said Adam. "Then," said the young man, "be informed for certain that the quarrel between the archbishop and king William is now put an end to." The clerk, roused by these words, looked up, and opened his eyes, but saw no one. The next night also, one of the monks of the same archbishop was standing at his post, and chanting matins, when someone held out to him a small paper to read, on which the monk read the words, "King William is dead." He immediately opened his eyes, but saw no one except his companions. A short time after, two of his monks came to him, and telling him of the king's death, earnestly advised him immediately to return to his see.

¶ The number of prophetic dreams and visions heralding the death of Rufus, the way in which the rumours spread beforehand among the common people, and the weeping crowd which followed his body, have been utilized by Dr Margaret Murray as a proof that William Rufus was a sacred king who submitted himself as a pre-arranged sacrifice. In her book on the Divine King Charles II is cited as the last example of a sacrificed king, and à Becket, Joan of Arc, and Gilles de Rais are supposed to have been willing substitutes for the monarch.

The bias of the Church against William Rufus is clear in the form these dreams took. See "The Death Fetch of William Rufus" (B, XII).

FLOOD LAW IN THE FENS [extract]

W. H. Barrett, *Tales from the Fens*, pp. 114–5.

[During a great flood]...in a few days' time the fen looked the same as it was before it was drained; all the wild water-fowl came back, and so did some of the people living on the edge of it. They came at night, trying to loot the houses, but they didn't have any luck because we were out in boats, keeping guard. They ran a big risk because, as soon as the waters came, the old fen flood law began to work. This law said that anything found floating about had to be brought to Stack's Hill at Southery, and if it wasn't claimed after a time, then the finder could have it. If anybody was found robbing a house, then he had his boat smashed in and he himself was left in the house. And he had to stay there starving for a week if he couldn't swim his way out, till a boat went to pick him up—if he was still alive, that is. This law was kept so well that a man could leave his watch on the mantelshelf and know it would still be there when he went back for it. Old Lawyer Archer of Feltwell was a very old man when he told me that this law, though it wasn't in any of his books, had been kept since long before Ely Cathedral was built.

There was another one, too, and this was that no man should go out in his boat alone. This one goes back a couple of hundred years to the time when a chap, after being flooded out, rowed back to his house to fetch some things. When he got there he found two gypsies robbing the place; they'd rowed out from Hockwold in a stolen boat. Well, the man's boat was found next day tied to the door-latch, while he was sitting on his bedroom floor with an axe stuck in his skull. Those gypsies had loaded their boat with his stuff, but they weren't looking where they were going as they made off for higher ground, because they rammed a gate-post, and ripped the bottom out of the boat. They couldn't swim, but they stood on the boat, as it lay under five foot of water, and by clinging to the gate-post they managed to keep their heads above water.

Next day a chap rowed past, towing the dead man's body in another boat, and he heard the gypsies shrieking for help. He guessed who they were, so he rowed over, staked the boat with the body in it to the post, saying they could have company, as they looked a bit lonely. Then he rowed off and left them. He came back next day, just to see how they were getting on, and the next day, but by then they'd gone, so the dead man was taken home and buried.

That's a cruel tale, I know, but everything was cruel when the waters poured in.

Told by Chafer Legge.

¶ This was the flood of 1861 between Brandon Creek and Southery. The whole chapter is worth reading for the account it gives of the precautions taken to prevent the river walls being broken by people who wanted to save the upper fens from flooding. This they often did without warning, so that the fen-dwellers were exposed to terrible risks.

Jean Ingelow's *High Tide on the Coast of Lincolnshire* tells of a similar catastrophe.

FOLK-MEMORY OF CHAUCER

H. Bett, *English Myths and Traditions*, p. 106.

An old gardener in Oxfordshire said to Mr Cecil Roberts in reference to a local road: "I've 'eard my granddad say as 'is granddad said that Mr Chaucer, the king's poet, used to walk this way."

"I suppose," said Mr Roberts, "Mr Chaucer was on his way to Oxford when he went past here?" "Not at all, sir. He was going to visit his son at Ewelme.... It's about ten miles from here, sir, just off the Oxford road. Mr Chaucer's son's buried there, where old Henry the Eighth 'ad 'is 'oneymoon—one of 'em. My granddad said the poet was very fond of the country. He wrote a lot about it."* Now Thomas Chaucer, the son of the poet, married Matilda, the daughter of Sir John Burgersh, who brought him large estates, amongst them the Manor of Ewelme, in Oxfordshire, where he is buried. There is an altar-tomb, with brasses, of Thomas Chaucer and his lady in the church, and also another magnificent altar-tomb, one of the finest in England, of the Duchess of Suffolk, the widow of William de la Pole, and the granddaughter of the poet. She founded the ancient almshouse in the village. The manor-house, or palace, of Ewelme was a splendid building, where Margaret of Anjou was confined for several years. It is a fact, by the way, that Henry VIII did spend a honeymoon there with Jane Seymour.

¶ See "A Link with the Past", "Old Parr".

THE GHOST'S "EVIDENCE"

T. F. Thistleton Dyer, *The Ghost World*, p. 83.

In "Ackerman's Repository" for November 1820, there is an account of a person being tried on the pretended evidence of a ghost. A farmer on his return from market at Southam, co. Warwick, was murdered. The next morning a man called upon the farmer's wife, and related how on the previous night her husband's ghost had appeared to him, and after showing him several stabs on his body, had told him that he was murdered by a certain person, and his corpse thrown into a marl-pit. A search was instituted, the body found in the pit, and the wounds on the body were exactly in the parts described by the pretended dreamer; the person who was mentioned was committed for trial on the charge of murder, and the trial came on at Warwick before Lord Chief Justice Raymond. The jury would have convicted the prisoner as rashly as the magistrate had committed him, but for the interposition of the judge, who told them he did not put any credence in the pretended ghost story, since the prisoner was a man of unblemished reputation, and no ill-feeling had ever existed between himself and the deceased. He added that he knew of no law

* Cecil Roberts, *Gone Rustic*, pp. 166–8.

which admitted of the evidence of a ghost, and, if any did, the ghost had not appeared.

The crier was then ordered to summon the ghost, which he did three times, and the judge then acquitted the prisoner, and caused the accuser to be detained, and his house searched, when such strong proofs of guilt were discovered that the man confessed the crime, and was executed for murder at the following Assizes.

THE GREY GOOSE FEATHERS

The Folktales of England, pp. 84–6.

Thousands and thousands of years ago, the Fenmen, living in their desolate wastes, bonded themselves into a secret society. This society was called "The Brotherhood of the Grey Goose Feathers", and anyone who was initiated into that brotherhood, and possessed a grey goose feather, was sure that whenever they were in trouble or distress, help would immediately be given by the whole Fenmen. When King Charles the First escaped from Oxford, he made his way into the uplands of Norfolk and stayed at a place called Snow Hall, just outside of Downham Market. And in passing, I may remark that I saw the chamber where, in case Cromwell's men came to look for him, he did hide. This chamber was aside of a great big chimney; it was hidden by old panelling.

Well, after Charles had consulted with his advisers, he decided to rejoin his troops just outside Oxford. The safest route in those days, for a fugitive, was through the desolate, trackless Fens. There was one man, named Porter, who kept an inn at Southery. He used to guide travellers across the trackless waste. So he was sent for, and asked if he would take a very important personage to Huntingdon, and he said, "Yes. I will." So they brought the important personage to see what sort of a man the old Fenman was, and some of the king's advisers didn't think it was safe for him to go that long journey with only one man. But Porter said if that was worrying them, he would initiate the important personage into the Brotherhood of the Grey Goose Feathers. So they brought a feather, and Porter severed it down the centre, and gave half to the important personage, and retained half himself. As he did so, he said, "Whilst fishes have scales, and birds have feathers, I will do all I can for you, and so will every other man who belongs to the Brotherhood of the Grey Goose Feathers."

Well, the King's advisers seemed quite satisfied to let Porter take him across the Fens alone. When they arrived at St Ives, they had to cross the river by a ford. Guarding this ford were two of Cromwell's soldiers. But when Porter produced the grey feather, they said, "Pass, all is well." They were Fenmen. So eventually King Charles arrived at the "Bell" Tavern, in Huntingdon, and he gave a reward to Porter for taking of him over, but he retained the grey goose feather. Some time afterwards, the King was taken prisoner, but before that happened, one of the officers in charge of the troops in Cromwell's army, heard about how the sentry let them through, and he brought them along to Cromwell. But Cromwell was a Fenman too; so he said to the officer, "It is better for a king to escape than for the Fenman to go back on a man who carries the split goose feather."

So he let the men go, and not long after that King Charles was caught, and they brought him up to London and tried him, and he was sentenced to death. But the night before the execution, when Cromwell was sitting down to supper with his staff, a messenger came from the King, and Cromwell told his servant to let him in.

The messenger said: "His Majesty does not beg for mercy, but he demands as a right the help you must give to every man who carries this token."

And he flung down a grey goose quill on the table in front of Cromwell. Cromwell told everyone to go out, and he sat looking at the grey goose feather. And in the morning when the servants came in he was still looking at it.

Well, the King was beheaded, but Cromwell was never the same man again. He brooded and brooded, and what made things worse, all the Fenmen, who had served him well up to that time, sent back their goose feathers, all broken and bent, and they said they were going back to the Fens, where there were still men who kept their word. And as he'd been false to the old custom of the feathers, none of the promises that went with it would ever be made to him or any of his family again.

Recorded from W. H. Barrett, 11 October 1963. Mr Barrett heard this tradition from Chafer Legge in 1900. His written version is in *Tales from the Fens*, pp. 148–9.

¶ Snow Hall, Snore, or Snowre Hall is in the parish of Fordham, Norfolk, three miles south of Downham Market. Charles I was received here on 30 April 1646 by Mr Skipworth, who was aiding his escape from Oxford before his surrender at Newark on 5 May 1646.

Tales of the Fens gives further particulars of the goose-feather customs. See "French Prisoners in the Fens".

KING RICHARD AND THE
PENITENT KNIGHT [abbreviated]

Roger of Wendover, *Chronicle*, II, p. 547.

(A.D. 1232.) A certain English knight, living in the New Forest, who had long made a practice of clandestinely hunting the king's deer, was on one occasion caught with some stolen venison, and by a decree of the court of the king was condemned to exile. This merciful king had mitigated the law in reference to stolen venison...he...considered it quite a sufficient punishment for any, who was caught committing that offence, either to be banished from England, or to undergo imprisonment saving his life and limbs. The above-mentioned knight then was sent into exile, and he, who had formerly enjoyed all the dainties of life, was, with his wife and children, obliged to beg his bread among foreigners. The knight, after some reflection, at length determined to implore the king for mercy, and for his estate to be restored to him, and he accordingly went to the king in Normandy, where he found him early in the morning in a church, about to hear Mass. The knight tremblingly entered the church, and did not dare to raise his eyes to the king, for although he was the most handsome of men to look upon, there was still something dreadful in his look; he therefore went to an image of Christ on the Cross, and, weeping incessantly, he humbly on his knees besought the Crucified One through his unspeakable grace, compassionately to make his peace with the king, by which means he might recover his lost inheritance. The king, seeing the knight thus earnestly and with unfeigned devotion praying and weeping, witnessed an occurrence wonderful and worthy of narration; for whenever the knight, who he knew was not of his retinue, bent his knees to worship the image, the image, in all humility, bowed its head and shoulders as it were in answer to the knight, and the king was struck with wonder and astonishment to see this repeated frequently. As soon as the service of Mass was ended, he sent for the knight to speak with him, and inquired of him who he was and whence he came. The knight replied with fear said, "My lord, I am your liege subject, as my ancestors also have been"; and then, beginning his history, he told the king how he had been deprived of his inheritance and banished together with his family, having been caught with some stolen venison. The king then said to the knight, "Have you ever in your life done any good act in respect, and to the honour, of the holy Cross?" The knight then, after carefully thinking over the events of his past life, related to the king the following deed, which he had done in his reverence for Christ:

"My father," said he, "and another knight divided between them a town which belonged to them by hereditary right; and whilst my father abounded in all kinds of wealth, the other knight, on the contrary, was always poor and needy, and, becoming envious of my father, he treacherously murdered him. I was then a boy, but when I arrived at manhood, and was installed in my paternal inheritance, I made a resolute determination to slay that knight in revenge for my father's death; he was, however, forewarned of my purpose, and for several years by his cunning escaped the snares I had laid for him. At length...as I was going to church, to hear Mass, I saw my enemy before me, also on his way to church. I hastened on behind him, and drew my sword to kill him, when by some chance he looked round, and, seeing me rushing upon him, fled to a cross which stood near the road, being worn down by age, and unable to defend himself. And when I endeavoured with upraised sword to slay him and dash out his brains, he encircled the cross with his arms, and adjured me in the name of that Christ, who on that day was suspended on the Cross for the salvation of the whole world, not to slay him, but faithfully promised and vowed, that he would appoint a chaplain to perform a Mass every day from that time for the soul of my father whom he had killed. When I saw the old man weeping I was moved to pity, and thus in my love and reverence for Him who, for my salvation and that of all, ascended the Cross, and consecrated it by His most holy blood, I forgave the knight for my father's murder." The king then said to the knight, "You acted wisely, for now that Crucified One has repaid one good turn by another." He then summoned the bishops and barons who were there with him, and, in the hearing of all, related the vision he had seen, how at each genuflection made by the knight, the image of Christ had humbly bowed its head and shoulders. He then summoned his chancellor to him, and commanded him by his letters patent, to order the sheriff whom the knight should name to him, at sight of the warrant, to restore to the knight the whole of his property in the same condition as he received it at the time of his banishment.

¶ Later historians have been unfavourable to Richard I, but he was revered in his own age, as various traditions show. Among them is his pardon of the young archer from whose arrow-shot he died, and the well-known, though rather late, story of Blondel. This tale of Roger of Wendover is less known, but particularly charming.

MARSHALL'S ELM

Briggs and Tongue, *The Folktales of England*, p. 96.

There were a varmer o' Walton near Street. 'E 'ad a only son, and 'e were tremenjus proud of 'e. Well, the lad, like so many more lads, 'e went to fight for Duke o' Monmouth down to Sedgemoor battle, and 'e were taken a prisoner. Well, 'is vather 'e were frantic, and 'e try and 'e try to get the lad's life saved. 'E spent all 'is savings, and 'e sold 'is 'arvest, and 'e took 'en to Judge Jefferies. And then, 'aving took all 'e 'ad to offer, the Bloody Judge gave orders the lad should be 'anged right afore 'is 'ome. Well, they did so, and the vather 'e stood by, and when 'twas all over, 'e turned round wi'out a word, and 'e go down to stables, and 'e kill 'is best bullock. And then 'e pull out the girt 'ot bleeding 'eart o' 'im, and 'e drove nail arter nail through 'en, till it looked like a red urchin. Then not saying a word, 'e go back to kitchen, and 'e carry the 'eart there, and 'e nail it up in chimney, where 'twas smoked and scorched for years.

And arter that day, the Bloody Judge, 'e were taken wi' choking coughs, and scorching burning pains all round 'is 'eart, which pierced 'en right through. And whenever 'e got an attack like that, there come a sight afore 'is eyes, no matter whether 'e closed 'em or no—the sight of a 'anging lad.

Recorded from Ruth L. Tongue, 28 September 1963, as she heard the account in 1940, while on a riding-tour in Somerset, from a Glastonbury farmer. She had heard previous mentions in the 1930s from Street.

¶ "Marshall's Elm" is the name of the tree on which the boy was hanged. It was still standing in 1946.

THE OXFORD STUDENT [shortened]

Halliwell, *Nursery Rhymes and Tales*, p. 166. Oxford.

There was once an Oxford student, who made love to the daughter of a brewer in the town, and got her with child. She pressed him to marry her, and he always put her off, but at last he said that if she would meet him at Divinity Walk the next moonlight night, he would arrange it. So early on the night of the next full moon, she set out for the open orchard land that bordered Divinity Walk in those days. She was very early, so for safety she climbed one of the apple trees and hid there. Presently she heard a heavy step, and saw her lover plodding up the hill with a spade across his shoulders. He came up to the very tree where she was hiding, and began to dig—a long, narrow, deep hole, a grave. Then he stood and waited with his dagger in his hand. But the girl, lying along the branch above him, never stirred, and at length he went away, and she ran, as fast as her feet could carry her, back to her father's house. Next day, as she was going down Brewer's Lane, the student saw her, and greeted her lovingly.

But the girl said:

> "One moonshiny night, as I sat high,
> Waiting for one to come by,
> The boughs did bend; my heart did break,
> To see what hole the fox did make."

As she spoke, the student whipped out his dagger, and stabbed her to the heart. Then there was the greatest fight between Town and Gown that ever was known, and Brewer's Lane ran with blood. The cruel student was killed, but nothing would bring the poor girl back to life, and they say she was buried in the very grave that was dug for her by her false lover.

❡ This tale is an offshoot of "The Robber Bridegroom" (Type 955) which is more exactly represented in England by *Mr Fox* and "The Cellar of Blood" (A, IV). In more or less its present form, as a *cante fable*, it is common in England, and is represented in the United States. This version was collected in Oxford by J. O. Halliwell. On p. 2 of his *Nursery Rhymes and Nursery Tales of England*, he refers to Matthew Paris as giving an account of the matter. Nothing is given in Matthew Paris's successor's account of the genesis of the 1259 riot of the Town against the Gown, except the statement that the students had possibly released one of their number convicted of murder, which looks as if it might relate to this tale, as Halliwell suggested.

Baughman cites several examples from the United States, as well as a number from all parts of England.

See "The Lonton Lass", "Mr Fox's Courtship", "The Open Grave", "The Girl who got up a Tree" (A, IV).

PUDSAY THE COINER

From Mildred E. Bosanquet, Wrotham, Kent. (Bolton Hall, Bolton-by-Rowland, Clitheroe.)

The Pudsay family were at Bolton Hall from the reign of Edward the Third. One of them, whose tomb is in the church, sheltered Henry VI after the Battle of Wrexham. His descendant in Elizabeth's reign was William Pudsay, and this is the legend about him.

At Rimington on his land lead-mines were discovered. Pudsay started making coins and the Queen's officers came to take him. His life was in danger.

Now Pudsay had the power of seeing fairies, and some time back the local elves, Lob and Michil, were outside Aithura Hoile, and he came upon them, and by his art he made them stay. They gave him a magical bit, which they said he was to keep carefully against the day when he would be in danger, for it would nourish a drooping horse from evening red to morning grey.

When the word came to Pudsay, by what faithful messenger we do not know, he went to the stable, saddled his horse, Wanton Grey, with that fairy bit, and away he went, up over Rainsbut Scaur, for his pursuers were hot on his trail. There was no other way. He looked over the river. It is ninety foot high (known as Pudsay's Leap to this day). And the brave man took his courage and his life in his hands. "I would rather die here than lose my life as a prisoner," and he leaped. And the horse bore him safely to land. And they rode on through the night, and when morning came, the horse was still fresh, and he rode into London. And when he arrived at the Queen's house he went up and asked for her. And they said she was away on her barge on the Thames. Then he set off again, and the good Wanton Grey swam out to the barge, and we hear no more of Wanton Grey. But the mudstained Pudsay clambered on to the barge, and the courtiers stared at this plain, unselfconscious Yorkshireman. But he thrust himself into the presence of her Majesty, and fell on his knees, and reminded her that she had held him at the Font, and was his kinsman, and craved her mercy.

And the royal lady said, "Whatever ails you, Cousin Pudsay?" And she asked him if he had committed murder, for, said she, she would pardon no one who had shed any of her subjects' blood. And Pudsay said, "No, not murder, it was nothing but coining." And he told his story.

And they that stood round spoke for him, saying that he had fought right well at the battle of Zutphen, and had been the Earl of Leicester's Master of the Horse, and no one had been braver than he that day.

And so Queen Elizabeth gave him her pardon, but, said she, there must be no more of the Pudsay shillings. And there wasn't!

¶ The journey to the King to ask directly for pardon occurs in several ballads, such as *Adam Bell, Clym of the Clough and William of Cloudesley.*

Yorkshire Version of End of Story

"An a fell upov his knees, an a sed, 'Pardon! Pardon!'
An shu sed, 'Wat ivver hast bin abeouet, Poodsa?'
An a sed, 'Pardon! Pardon!'
An thir wir a deal spak for him, an sed a wir a reet gentlemon, an it didn't look laike at a sud do eouet wrang.
An shu sed, 'Weel, then, eouet, coozn Poodsa, but moordir.'
An a sed it wir nobbut coinin.
So shu sed, 'Waugh.'
But shu teld him at a moodn't mak ony moar o' thir Poodsa Shillings.
An a dudn't."

William Pudsay, Esq., Lord of Bolton from 1577 to 1629, who is the hero of this legend, was Queen Elizabeth's godson, and Master of the Horse to the Earl of Leicester. The Pudsay Shillings, handed down in the family and still existing, are the shillings of Elizabeth 1562, having a mullet of six points for a mint mark; Pudsay's arms being *vert*, a chevron between three mullets pierced *or*. This is too early for William Pudsay, but his father, Thomas, Vice-President of the Council of the North, may have introduced the new Elizabethan currency into the country, so that they became Pudsay Shillings. William Pudsay got into trouble for working the "Mine Royal", which may have given rise to the legend, which was current forty years after William Pudsay's death. Webster (Johannes Hyphantes), 1671, mentions it. Michil and Lob are the two local fairies. It is still the custom to bring all the carts and gates that can be obtained on the night of 30 April to Bolton Cross, where they are piled up in a heap for a bonfire. This is locally stated to be the work of Lob and Michil; who now, however, fortunately confine their labours to erecting the pile, without setting fire to it.

Skelhorne, a limestone hill in which are the remains of lead works, is in Rimington, a township near Bolton, then belonging to William Pudsay. The lead was said by Johnson to contain silver at the rate of 25 lb. a ton.

Rainsbee Scaur, down which Pudsay is said to have leaped, is a rock overhanging the Ribble, about 90 feet high, and a few hundred yards from Bolton Hall.

These notes are from *Pudsay's Leap*, by H. A. Littledale, privately printed in 1856, and lent me by his granddaughter, Mildred Bosanquet, Wrotham, Sevenoaks, Kent (a descendant of William Pudsay).

Aithera Hoile, or Arthur's Hole, is a cavern in the woods at Bolton.

See "West Molland House".

THE SONS OF THE CONQUEROR

E. S. Hartland, *English Fairy and Folk Tales*, p. 57.

I

One day, it being observed that William was absorbed in deep thought, his courtiers ventured to inquire the cause of such profound abstraction. "I am speculating," said the monarch, "on what may be the fate of my sons after my death." "Your majesty," replied the wise men of the court, "the fate of your sons will depend upon their conduct, and their conduct will depend upon their characters; permit us to make a few inquiries, and we shall soon be able to tell you that which you wish to know." The king signifying his approbation, the wise men consulted together, and agreed to put questions separately to the three princes, who were then young. The first who entered the room was Robert, afterwards known by the surname of Courthose. "Fair sir," said one of the wise men, "answer me a question. If God had made you a bird, what bird would you wish to have been?" Robert answered: "A hawk, because it resembles most a courteous and gallant knight." William Rufus next entered, and his answer to the same question was: "I would be an eagle, because it is a strong and powerful bird, and feared by all other birds, and therefore it is king over them all." Lastly came the younger brother, Henry, who had received a learned education, and was on that account known by the surname of Beauclerc. His choice was a starling, "Because it is a debonnaire and simple bird, and gains its living without injury to anyone, and never seeks to rob or grieve its neighbour." The wise men returned immediately to the king. Robert, they said, would be bold and valiant, and would gain renown and honour, but he would finally be overcome by violence, and die in prison. William would be powerful and strong as the eagle, but feared and hated for his cruelty and violence, until he ended a wicked life by a bad death. But Henry would be wise, prudent, and peaceful, unless when actually compelled to engage in war, and would die in peace after gaining wide possessions. So when King William lay on his death-bed he remembered the saying of his wise men, and bequeathed Normandy to Robert, England to William, and his own treasures, without land, to his younger son Henry, who eventually became king of both countries and reigned long and prosperously.

Chambers, *Book of Days*, p. 328.

¶ This story, which most probably is of Eastern origin, is frequently told under various circumstances by medieval writers. A Latin manuscript of the thirteenth century relates it in the following form:

A wealthy English baron, whose broad lands extended over a large extent of England and Wales, had three sons: when lying on his death-bed he called them to him, and said: "If you were compelled to become birds, tell me what bird each of you would choose to resemble?" The eldest said: "I would be a hawk, because it is a noble bird, and lives by rapine." The second said: "I would be a starling, because it is a social bird, and flies in convoys." The youngest said: "I would be a swan, because it has a long neck, so that if I had anything in my heart to say, I should have plenty of time for reflection before it came to my mouth." When the father had heard them, he said to the first: "Thou, my son, as I perceive, desirest to live by rapine; I will therefore bequeath thee my possessions in England, because it is a land of peace and justice, and thou canst not rob in it with impunity." To the second he said: "Because thou lovest society, I will bequeath thee my lands in Wales, which is a land of discord and war, in order that thy courtesy may soften down the malice of the natives." And then, turning to the youngest, he said: "To thee I bequeath no land at all, because thou art wise, and wilt gain enough by thy wisdom." And as he foretold, the youngest son profited by his wisdom, and became Lord Chief Justice of England, which in those times was the next dignity to that of king.

¶ In both the son most commended is not the one to be chiefly endowed, though he came to the highest honours in the end.

Tale II is to be found in a little book, *Short Stories*, published by Chambers in 1878, but the book is not of much use, since it gives no sources. This tale was probably retold from Hone. Professor Archer Taylor is making an exhaustive study of this type.

THE WARDEN OF THE MARCHES [shortened]

The Book of Scottish Story, pp. 88–95.

In the reign of King James V the duty of guarding the Marches against English raiders was entrusted to Sir John Charteris of Amisfield, near Dumfries, a brave but arrogant man, whose public duties were apt to be sacrificed to his private interests.

A young farmer of Annandale, George Maxwell, was particularly active against the English, who, in reprisal, raided and plundered his house, and drove off all his livestock. In hot pursuit Maxwell overtook the raiders, but in the battle which ensued, he was killed, and his widow, Marion, was left with the charge of their nine-year-old son, Wallace.

Generous neighbours replaced her in a small farm, but in successive raids she lost so much that by the time her son reached the age of twenty, she was reduced to the occupation of a small cottage, and possessed only one cow. But the lad was brave and industrious, and a kindly farmer gave her cow pasturage, so they lived in reasonable comfort and contentment.

Wallace Maxwell had his father's courage and patriotism, and he had won the love of a girl, Mary Morrison, poor as himself, but endowed with beauty and goodness, so that all who knew them thought them a pair well worthy of one another. She was an orphan, and they were fellow-servants to the farmer in whose cottage the widow Maxwell lived. Both had wisdom and prudence to know that it would be long before their circumstances permitted them to marry.

It happened that the leader of the English in a certain raid, the son of a rich Borderer, had been taken prisoner, and a heavy ransom paid for his release, the money having been pocketed by Sir John Charteris, who considered it a perquisite of his office. In the following raid, Wallace Maxwell was captured in his turn, and the man who had so recently paid a high price for his own son's ransom kept Wallace a close prisoner till an equal price should be paid for Wallace's release. Since there was not the least hope that either his widowed mother nor any of their friends could ever raise such a sum, the poor woman appealed to Sir John, begging him to send some of his forces after the raiders, and rescue her son. But Sir John had a grudge against young Maxwell, and contemptuously rejected her request, saying that the matter was altogether too trifling to command his attention; and the desolate mother then went and told all her tale to Mary Morrison, whose distress was no less than her own. Mary, indeed, went so far as to renew the suit to Sir John, and herself, having begged leave from her employer, went to plead with the hard-hearted Warden, who received her in very different fashion. He explained that it would be a hard task to rescue one who had rendered himself an object of vengeance to the English Borderers, and who must by now be under close surveillance. But he offered to pay the ransom, high as it was, in return for what he termed her gratitude. Mary, filled with joy, promised that all in their power should be done to show this, and prayed that Heaven should be his reward. He, however, replied that she herself had it in her power to show a more immediate thankfulness, and made it all too clear what reward he had in mind. But when she, with due modesty and courtesy, rejected every advance, he told her roughly that Wallace Maxwell might perish in a dungeon, or at the hands of his enemies, for he should never be rescued by him. Mary returned home indignant and sorrowful, and next she and the widow resolved to appeal to their kind friend, the farmer, for leave for them both, in order that they might lay their complaint before the King himself. The farmer was in full agreement; for the Warden's insolence and neglect of his duties had become the subject of general complaint, and he thought that such an appeal might be for the good of the whole countryside. King James was always easy of access to any of his subjects, and he received the woman with great kindness, promising that on his approaching visit to Annandale, their case should be attended to; and that when he sent a certain nobleman to them, they should come at once to the hearing of their case.

It was a favourite custom with the King to go about among his subjects in disguise and, when asked his name on these occasions, to give it as "The Gudeman of Ballengeich". In this character he visited Annandale, and, seeing a girl washing linen in a stream, whom he recognized as Mary Morrison, he sat down on a nearby stone, groaning as if in dire pain. Mary at once came up to offer help, and helped him to walk, leaning on her arm, to the farm. He declared that a drink of milk and a rest would soon cure his distemper, and while lying there, he contrived to learn of the general sympathy for Mary and the widow Maxwell, and the equal dislike and distrust of Sir John.

In due course the King marched back towards Dumfries, and, after passing a night in the small village of Duncow, he left his retinue there, and made his way in beggar's guise to Amisfield, where he requested the porter to procure him an immediate audience with Sir John. The reply was that Sir John was at dinner and could by no means be disturbed for two or perhaps three hours. The King gave the man a groat, and bade him tell Sir John that his business was urgent, and on receiving the same reply, produced two more groats, bidding his messenger say that in crossing the Border he had seen the English massing for an attack; and that it was Sir John's duty to fire the beacons immediately, and alarm the countryside. Sir John only replied, "If he chooses to wait two hours, I will then see whether he is a knave or a fool; but if he send such another impertinent message to me, both you and he shall have cause to regret it."

The kindly porter then offered food and ale to help the stranger pass the time until the Warden should be ready to receive him; but the King now gave him three groats, bidding him return and say that the Gudeman of Ballengeich insisted upon seeing him immediately. As the man went off on this errand, King James winded his bugle horn loudly, and, casting aside his beggar's garb, stood in his royal insignia, while his men-at-arms came galloping up in all haste. The terrified Warden stood trembling, pleading his ignorance of the King's presence, but James sternly replied that the meanest of his subjects had access to him at all times. But to give Sir John his fair chance of clearing himself of the charges brought against him, the King appointed him to attend for the hearing of his case at Hoddam Castle. He added that, if Wallace Maxwell were not produced within a week, the Warden himself should be hanged from a tree before his own window.

Meantime, the King's retinue was to be entertained at the Warden's expense, in the Warden's own castle. The King now sent the young nobleman, as he had arranged to the widow at Stirling, to bring her and Mary Morrison to him at once. When they arrived, he gave the widow a cow, worth double the price of the one stolen from her, with blankets and other presents; but even in the height of her gratitude she could not forbear asking for her son; but he sent her away in the joyful hope of seeing him again very soon.

The Warden's distress was daily increasing, but in the nick of time Wallace Maxwell was brought before him, when, allowing him no rest at all, he sent him on in hot haste to Hoddam Castle. The King now confronted Sir John with all three of his victims, and compelled him to acknowledge his guilt before them all. The Warden could do nothing but confess to it all; and the King decreed that he should establish Wallace in a fifty-acre farm, rent-free, for his lifetime and his wife's, fully stocked and furnished within three months, on pain of immediate death by hanging. Sir John submitted, and the King sent the three away with his blessing.

¶ See "The Court Cave", "The Goodman of Ballengiech".

PART 14
LOCAL LEGENDS

Some of the Local Legends hover on the brink of being Historical Traditions. Many have grown from the impact of historical events upon a quiet place: battles and the visits of kings and special privileges granted to a place. Most of those collected here, however, are strictly local. For example, the planting of a sprig of the Glastonbury Thorn at Ilminster and the flowering bush that sprang from it, "The Beasts' Thorn", is the local account of the Twelfth Night miracle of the kneeling cattle. There are many legends of the transportation of building material to account for the seemingly unsuitable position of a church, of which "The Church of Fordoun" is one. Type 766, The Sleepers under the Hill, is common all over Europe. In England it is often attached to King Arthur, but in "Canobie Dick and Thomas of Ercildoun" it has a more recent character, dating from the early fourteenth century. He takes the place often held by Merlin where the sleepers are Arthurian knights. "Crawls" is a local Godiva story where the feat accomplished is to crawl round a piece of land in the course of a winter's night. There are family traditions, such as "The Horn of Egremont", which could only be blown by the true Lord of the Castle and supernatural traditions of stone circles which had once been men, like "The Rollright Stones". There are stories of revealing dreams, of which the best-known is "The Pedlar of Swaffham", and many stories of buried treasure.

It is indeed impossible to do justice to the rich variety of local legendary matter in one short section.

THE BEASTS' THORN

Ruth L. Tongue, *Somerset Folklore*, pp. 29–30.

A pilgrim who went from Ilminster to Glastonbury was asked by the villagers to bring back some holy relic to bless the village. They were all much disappointed when he brought back a single thorn which might have been plucked from any hedge. He told them that it was part of the Crown of Thorns, but no one believed him. He planted it, however, and prayed beside it morning and evening. The strange thing about the thorn was that it began to shoot and grow at an uncanny rate, and people began to draw away from the pilgrim and look at him with suspicion. The thorn still grew, and by Christmas it was quite a little tree. The pilgrim promised that it would bloom on Christmas Day, but Christmas Day passed and nothing happened. But on Old Christmas Eve at night the whole village was wakened by a great clatter in the street. People threw on their clothes and ran to the windows, and there below them went all the sheep and cattle of the place, which had been securely shut in folds and bartons hours before. The richest farmer's master bullock was at the head of them. People tumbled out into the streets and followed their cattle. They went straight to the little thorn tree, which stood blossoming white in the moonshine. The pilgrim was kneeling there already. Just as the crowd came up the first stroke of midnight chime sounded. At that the great master bullock lowed aloud and knelt down on the frosty ground and every beast knelt with him. The stiff knees of the villagers were loosened and they knelt too, among the beasts. And that is how Ilminster knows that it has a holy thorn.

A homelier version of this was told to L. Key in Taunton in 1948. The old man who told it has since died. His experience could be dated about 1888–90:

"When I was a bwoy we did make up our minds to take a look-see on Chrissmus Eve to find if the tree did bloom and cows come to kneel to 'en. So we went along lane to Nailesbourne like, and 'twas dark, couldn't see nothing at all. Proper black, and we had no light, zee, and all to a zudden there was breathings all round us, zeemlike, whichever way we'd turn. Thic lane were vull of cattle, and we just turn and run for it. No, we never zee no thorn blossom nor I wouldn't go now if I was asked. Vull of cows thic lane was."

¶ See "The Apple-Tree Man", (A, II).

CANOBIE DICK AND
THOMAS OF ERCILDOUN

Gibbings, *Folk-Lore and Legends, Scotland*, p. 1.

Now it chanced many years since that there lived on the Borders a jolly rattling horse-cowper, who was remarkable for a reckless and fearless temper, which made him much admired, and a little dreaded amongst his neighbours. One moonlight night as he rode over Bowden Moor on the west side of the Eildon Hills, the scene of Thomas the Rhymer's prophecies, and often mentioned in his history, having a brace of horses along with him, which he had not been able to dispose of, he met a man of venerable appearance, and singularly antique dress, who, to his great surprise, asked the price of his horses and began to chaffer with him on the subject. To Canobie Dick, for so we shall call our Border dealer, a chap was a chap, and he would have sold a horse to the Devil himself, without minding his cloven hoof, and would have probably cheated Old Nick into the bargain. The stranger paid the price they agreed on, and all that puzzled Dick in the transaction was that the gold which he received was in unicorns, bonnet-pieces and other ancient coins, which would have been invaluable to collectors, but were rather troublesome in modern currency.

It was gold, however, and therefore Dick contrived to get better value for the coin than he perhaps gave to his customer. By the command of so good a merchant, he brought horses to the same spot more than once, the purchaser only stipulating that he should always come by night and alone. I do not know whether it was from mere curiosity, or whether some hope of gain mixed with it, but after Dick had sold several horses in this way, he began to complain that dry bargains were unlucky, and to hint, that since his chap must live in the neighbourhood, he ought, in the courtesy of dealing, to treat him to half a mutchkin.

"You may see my dwelling if you will," said the stranger; "but if you lose courage at what you see there, you will rue it all your life."

Dickon, however, laughed the warning to scorn, and, having alighted to secure his horse, he followed the stranger up a narrow footpath, which led them up the hills to the singular eminence stuck between the most southern and the central peaks, and called, from its resemblance to such an animal in its form, the Lucken Hare. At the foot of this eminence, which is almost as famous for witch-meetings as the neighbouning windmill of Kippilaw, Dick was somewhat startled to observe that his conductor entered the hillside by a passage or cavern of which he himself, though well acquainted with the spot, had never seen or heard.

"You may still return," said his guide, looking ominously back upon him; but Dick scorned to show the white feather and on they went. They entered a very long range of stables; in every stall stood a coal-black horse; by every horse lay a knight in coal-black armour, with a drawn sword in his hand; but all were as silent, hoof and limb, as if they had been cut out of marble. A great number of torches lent a gloomy lustre to the hall, which, like those of the Caliph Vathek, was of large dimensions. At the upper end, however, they at length arrived, where a sword and horn lay on an antique table.

"He that shall sound that horn, and draw that sword," said the stranger, who now intimated that he was the famous Thomas of Ercildoun, "shall, if his heart fail him not, be king over all broad Britain. So speaks the tongue that cannot lie.

"But all depends on courage, and much on your taking the sword or horn first."

Dick was much disposed to take the sword, but his bold spirit was quailed by the supernatural terrors of the hall, and he thought to unsheath the sword first might be construed into defiance, and give offence to the powers of the mountain.

He took the bugle with a trembling hand, and blew a feeble note, but loud enough to produce a terrible answer. Thunder rolled in stunning peals through the immense hall; horses and men started to life; the steeds snorted, stamped, ground their bits and tossed their heads; the warriors sprang to their feet, clashed their armour, and brandished their swords. Dick's terror was extreme at seeing the whole army, which had been so lately silent as the grave, in uproar, and about to rush on him. He dropped the horn, and made a feeble attempt to seize the enchanted sword; but at the same moment a voice pronounced aloud the mysterious words:

"Woe to the coward, that ever he was born,
 Who did not draw the sword before he blew the horn!"

At the same time a whirlwind of irresistible fury howled through the long hall, bore the unfortunate horse-jockey clear out of the mouth of the cavern, and precipitated him over a steep bank of loose stones, where the shepherds found him the next morning, with just breath sufficient to tell his fearful tale, after concluding which he expired.

¶ In this version of the Sleeping Army there is no King; but the tabu about touching the sword and horn in the wrong order still holds. Here Thomas of Ercildoun takes the place of Merlin.

See "The Wizard of Alderley Edge", "Potter Thompson", "King Arthur at Sewingshields".

THE CHURCH OF FORDOUN

Chambers, *Popular Rhymes of Scotland*, p. 337.

...the church of Fordoun [is] in Kincardineshire. The recently existing structure was of great antiquity, though not perhaps what the monks represented it—namely, the chapel of Palladius, the early Christian missionary. The country-people say that the site originally chosen for the building was the top of the Knock Hill, about a mile north-east from the village. After, as in the former case, the walls had been for some time regularly undone every night by unseen spirits, a voice was heard to cry:

> "Gang farther down,
> To Fordoun's town."

It is added that the new site was chosen by the throwing at random of a mason's hammer.

¶ See "The Church of Old Deer".

THE COOK AT COMBWELL

Norton Collection, III, p. 19.

In the days of the Civil War, when the country was frequently infested with travelling bands of marauders, one of these villainous gangs made an attempt on Combwell whilst the family were in church, there then being no one but the cook left in the house. According to tradition one of the robbers, disguised as a beggar-woman, appealed to the cook for admission, and the cook, being a kind-hearted woman, allowed him to enter the kitchen. He begged a piece of bread to satisfy his hunger, and was granted permission to cook it in the boiling fat in the frypan. Whilst her unwelcome visitor was stooping over the pan, the cook noticed that he was wearing boots and spurs and, with a sudden gleam of inspiration, the sinister situation burst upon her, with all its horrible possibilities.

Seizing the kitchen poker, which was the most formidable weapon near at hand, she struck him a tremendous blow upon the head, which laid him lifeless at her feet, and, rushing upstairs to the bell turret, she vigorously tugged at the bell-rope, thereby giving the alarm. The hoarse-throated clang of the bell was clearly heard in the peaceful precincts of the sacred edifice at the top of the hill, and its portent in those troublous times was only too patent that danger threatened. The male members of the family, accompanied by a band of stalwart neighbours and dependents, made all haste to the house, and so opportune was their arrival that they succeeded in dispersing the scoundrels, who in the meantime had laid siege to the house and, through the open bell turret, had, from the rising ground a short distance away, employed their time in taking pot-shots at the gallant domestic, whose presence of mind and courageous action had been the means of summoning help, which arrived in the nick of time to prevent the robbers from carrying out their nefarious designs. It was afterwards discovered that the robbers, in order to trick their pursuers in the event of their scheme failing, had had their horses' shoes removed and put on the opposite way, in order to make it appear that they were proceeding in another direction. It is stated that the head of the family, in recognition of the cook's courage, caused the bust to be executed and placed over the doorway.

" Over the entrance to the house is carved a woman's bust", Igglesden, *A Saunter through Kent*, XII, p. 42.

¶ See "The Brave Maidservant", "The Long Pack", "The Robber and the Housekeeper" (A, IV).

CRAWLS

Burne and Jackson, *Shropshire Folk-Lore*, p. 91.

Many hundred years ago there was a young lady, her father's only daughter and heiress, whom a gallant knight wooed and sought for his bride. And she loved him well, and gave him her promise. But when her father came to hear of it, he would by no means give his consent, for the knight was a younger son and landless. The young lady, though, was firm, and held to her word. One day she came and told her father that she and her true love would be married the next morning at Bromfield Church. The father was angry, as he might well be. He upbraided her for a headstrong lass, who must e'en take her own way, but of all his broad lands he vowed she would have none but what she could crawl round by morning light. She said not a word, but went quietly away. An old servant brought her a pair of leathern breeches to guard her poor knees ("else they would ha' wore out"), and thus strangely equipped she crawled round the fields all through that dark cold winter's night, and came in covered with mud to her father at his breakfast, saying that she had taken him at his word, and crawled round so much fair meadow land as reached nearly to Downton. The old man was so much delighted at his girl's brave spirit that he forgave her obstinacy, and took her back into favour. He made her heiress of all his estates, which continued to belong to her descendants for many generations, and the land she crept round during that long dreary night still bears the name of "Crawls".

¶ See "The Barefoot Pilgrimage", "Lame Haverah".

THE GOLD OF LARGO LAW [abbreviated]

Wilkie, *Bygone Fife*, p. 166.

Largo is peculiarly endowed with [such] legends...Best known is the tradition of a treasure or a gold-mine reputed to be either under or near the Law. The locality is tantalizingly vague, but that one or the other exists is proven by the fact that the sheep grazing on the hill pastures are occasionally seen to have their wool tinged yellow. The cottars know that they have been lying above hidden gold.

...While the origin of the hill is familiar, it is not so widely known that one of the tasks set by the Wizard of Balwearie to his familiars was its removal. They had only begun their labours when the happier idea of a never-ending employment of their turbulent energies occurred to Sir Michael...otherwise, surely, the gold under the Law must have been laid bare. Enough soil, as it happened, had been removed to form Norrie's Law.

...The story told around the ingle-neuk ran thus:

Once, lang syne, the shepherd of Balmain came near solving the mystery of the gold. Balmain, as everybody knows, lies at the northwestern slope of Largo Law, and the shepherd had brooded for years over the problem. He had watched the resting-places of the sheep for a clue, but it evaded him. His chance came in another way. The ghost of some forgotten denizen of the region haunted the vicinity, and was popularly believed to be possessed of the secret, but to be tongue-tied till a mortal sought of him enlightenment. Many would have fain put the question, but when the opportunity was given fear fell upon them and they fled.

Dazzling visions of future grandeur opened before the shepherd while he sat on green hillock or feal dyke with his collie at his feet, or took his way homeward after a spell at lambing-time. He had seen the dread shape more than once and quailed. But at last he took his courage in his hands, and when again the spectre stood beside him accosted it. In quavering tones he demanded what kept it from its rest. The answer was that the uncommunicated secret troubled its repose. The promise was given that if the mortal were brave enough to come to a certain part of the hill on a night indicated, precisely at eight o'clock (the tradition is exact as to the hour, though the day is not mentioned), he would learn all he ought to know.

There were, however, two conditions:

> "If Auchindowie cock disna craw,
> And the herd of Balmain his horn disna blaw,
> I'll tell ye where the gowd is in Largo Law".

The shepherd was elated. He saw himself the equal of the Laird of Largo, to say nothing of those of Montrose and Lundin. He was a man who left naught to chance. Every cock, young and old, in Auchindowie perished mysteriously; and Tammie Norrie, the cowherd, was enjoined by his colleague to refrain, on peril of his life, from blowing the horn that called the cows together for their return from the pastures.

Whether it was forgetfulness or dourness on Tammie's part that led to the catastrophe can never be known.

The shepherd was at the spot appointed. Eight o'clock was indicated by the place of the westering sun. The visitant from the world beyond stood punctually by his side.

At that moment, ere either could address the other, there floated down from the height above the notes of the cowherd's horn. Mortal and immortal were alike struck dumb by dismay and wrath, if indeed the dead suffer the emotions of the living. Then, regaining the power of utterance, the spectre pronounced doom:

> "Woe to the man that blew that horn,
> For out of that spot he shall never be borne!"

The shepherd stood alone.

No more did Tammie Norrie call the cattle home to Balmain. The blast he sounded had not re-echoed from Largo Law ere he fell, where he stood, a lifeless corpse. Nor could his body be moved. The strength went out of every arm that attempted the task, and men struggled as in a dream. So they abandoned it, and piled a cairn above the luckless cowherd.

¶ It is not certain if the ghost was summoned away by Norrie's horn, but from the killing of Norrie it seems likely. There are many features of interest in this story.
See "The Treasure of Castle Rach".

GUINEVERE'S COMB

H. Bett, *English Legends*, p. 4.

There are two high points on a ledge of rock near Sewingshields known as the King's Crag and the Queen's Crag. The legend is that King Arthur was once seated on the first and was talking to his queen, who was combing her hair. Angry at something she said, he seized a huge rock and threw it at her, where she was standing some hundreds of yards away. She caught it on her comb, and so warded off the missile, and it lies where it fell, a large block of many tons weight, with the marks of her comb still upon it.

¶ This legend is an example of the way in which people important in tradition grow in size. An example is "Macbeth's Grave" at Dunsinnon. "Cabal's Paw-mark" MOTIF: A.972.5.3. (*Indentations on rock from paws of King Arthur's dog*) is another example in Welsh tradition of Arthur's potency.
See "King Arthur at Sewingshields" and "The Silver Horseshoe" for other Arthurian legends.

THE HORN OF EGREMONT

H. Bett, *English Legends*, p. 23.

Sir Eustace de Lucy, the Lord of Egremont (in Cumberland), and his brother Hubert left home to go on a Crusade in the Holy Land. On his departure Sir Eustace blew the horn which always hung by the gateway of the castle, and which could only be sounded by the rightful Lord of Egremont, saying to his brother, "If I fall in Palestine, return and blow this horn, and take possession, that Egremont may not be without a Lucy for its Lord." When they were in the Holy Land, Hubert bribed three ruffians to seize his brother, and throw him into the Jordan.

Believing him to be dead, Hubert returned to England and took possession of the castle, but did not venture to blow the horn.

One day when he was giving a banquet he suddenly heard a blast
from the horn at the castle gate, and, knowing that only his brother as
the rightful owner could have sounded it, he started from his seat and
fled by the postern. The gate was then opened to Sir Eustace, who
resumed possession of Egremont. His brother is said to have died in a
monastery.

THE MURDER HOLE [summary]

The Book of Scottish Story, pp. 316–20.

About three hundred years ago, on the estate of Lord Cassilis between
Ayrshire and Galloway, lay a great moor, unrelieved by any trees or
vegetation.

It was rumoured that unwary travellers had been intercepted and
murdered there, and that no investigation ever revealed what had
happened to them. People living in a nearby hamlet believed that in
the dead of night they sometimes heard a sudden cry of anguish; and
a shepherd who had lost his way once declared that he had seen three
mysterious figures struggling together, until one of them, with a frightful
scream, sank suddenly into the earth. So terrifying was this place that
at last no one remained there, except one old woman and her two sons,
who were too poor to flee, as their neighbours had done. Travellers
occasionally begged a night's lodging at their cottage, rather than
continue their journey across the moor in the darkness, and even by
day no one travelled that way except in companies of at least two or
three people.

One stormy November night, a pedlar boy was overtaken by darkness
on the moor. Terrified by the solitude, he repeated to himself the
promises of Scripture, and so struggled towards the old cottage, which
he had visited the year before in a large company of travellers, and
where he felt assured of a welcome. Its light guided him from afar,
and he knocked at the door, but at first received no answer. He then
peered through a window and saw that the occupants were all at their
accustomed occupations: the old woman was scrubbing the floor and
strewing it with sand; her two sons seemed to be thrusting something
large and heavy into a great chest, which they then hastily locked. There

was an air of haste about all this which puzzled the watching boy outside.

He tapped lightly on the window, and they all started up, with consternation on their faces, and one of the men suddenly darted out at the door, seized the boy roughly by the shoulder and dragged him inside. He said, trying to laugh, "I am only the poor pedlar who visited you last year." "*Are you alone?*" cried the old woman in a harsh, deep voice. "Alone here—and alone in the whole world," replied the boy sadly. "Then you are welcome," said one of the men with a sneer. Their words filled the boy with alarm, and the confusion and desolation of the formerly neat and orderly cottage seemed to show signs of recent violence.

The curtains had been torn down from the bed to which he was shown, and though he begged for a light to burn until he fell asleep, his terror kept him long awake.

In the middle of the night he was awakened by a single cry of distress. He sat up and listened, but it was not repeated, and he would have lain down to sleep again, but suddenly his eye fell on a stream of blood slowly trickling under the door of his room. In terror he sprang to the door, and through a chink he saw that the victim outside was only a goat. But just then he overheard the voices of the two men, and their words transfixed him with horror. "I wish all the throats we cut were as easy," said one. "Did you ever hear such a noise as the old gentleman made last night?" "Ah, the Murder Hole's the thing for me," said the other. "One plunge and the fellow's dead and buried in a moment." "How do you mean to dispatch the lad in there?" asked the old woman in a harsh whisper, and one of the men silently drew his bloody knife across his throat for answer.

The terrified boy crept to his window and managed to let himself down without a sound. But as he stood wondering which way to turn, a dreadful cry rang out: "The boy has escaped—let loose the blood-hound." He ran for his life, blindly, but all too soon he heard the dreadful baying of the hound and the voices of the men in pursuit. Suddenly he stumbled and fell on a heap of rough stones which cut him in every limb, so that his blood poured over the stones. He staggered to his feet and ran on; the hound was so near that he could almost feel its breath on his back. But suddenly it smelt the blood on the stones, and, thinking the chase at an end, it lay down and refused to go further after the same scent. The boy fled on and on till morning, and when at last he reached a village, his pitiable state and his fearful story roused such wrath that three gibbets were at once set upon the moor, and before night the three villains had been captured and had confessed their guilt. The bones of their victims were later discovered, and with great difficulty brought up from the dreadful hole with its narrow aperture into which they had been thrust.

¶ There are many Burker stories after this style.

See "Burker Story" (B, VIII). Here, as in many other stories, a pedlar is the victim.

THE OLD HOUSE OF BALHARY

Our Meigle Book, p. 68.

[Above a door leading into the garden] is the old grey stone, with its curious motto and quaint spelling:

> I. shall. overcome. Invy. with. Gods. help. to. God. Be. Al. prais. Honour. and. Glorie.   1660.

Around the stone is a legend of considerable charm. The story is long, but briefly, is something like this:

In a bare old castle (mayhap the old house of Balhary) dwelt a father and son. The son, David, was a hunchback, and in consequence, was disliked and neglected by his father, who favoured a nephew, Ronald. To the castle one day, accompanied by her maid, came Lady Jean, a beautiful girl who had been placed under the guardianship of David's father. David and she became great friends; Ronald arrives on a visit, and Jean and he fall in love. David is again neglected. Came the wars of the Commonwealth, and the father and Ronald are called to the aid of Montrose. On defeat, the father had to flee to France, while Ronald, severely wounded, is brought to Jean to be nursed.

On his recovery they become engaged, and David, in bitter envy and jealously, wanders for hours into the hills. At nightfall he lands at the hut of an aged priest who comforts him. There he spends the night and dreams a dream. In it he sees Jean and Ronald and the people of the place building a castle. No matter how quickly they build up the stones it grows no bigger. David finds someone standing beside him, who says, "It is your envy and jealousy which comes between them and the building of the castle. Overcome that by raising this stone and placing it as a foundation for the castle."

Glancing at his feet, David saw a huge stone. "How can I, a poor hunchback, raise such a stone?" he said. Then he noticed its curious motto, "I shall overcome envy with God's help to God be al prais honour and glorie."

Unexpected strength came to him, and he lifted the stone and put it in its appointed place, and immediately the castle reared forth.

Next morning he went home in a different frame of mind, to find two items of news awaiting him; one, that his father could not again return, and so he made over the castle and lands to David, and the other, that owing to the very active part Ronald had played in the war he had forfeited his estates and money, and so couldn't marry Jean.

With much difficulty David persuaded them to accept the castle and lands, while he joined his father abroad. Many, many years elapsed, and feeling that his days on earth were almost numbered, he returned to his old home. He was welcomed by the two he had left and their family, the youngest of whom, his namesake, David, was a fragile, delicate youth, much as he had been. Between the two a great friendship developed, and the story of the dream was related. "Why not have the motto inscribed on a stone, and when you are gone I shall erect it to your memory?" suggested David the younger. This was done, and that is the legend of the stone, and this is its after-story.... Once a year, so it is said, a figure wearing a long cloak and a beaver hat cocked at one side with a feather appears to pay tribute. If the night be warm and he removes his cloak the outline of the poor hunchback can be seen.

OWEN PARFITT

Ruth L. Tongue, *Somerset Folklore*, p. 196.

The memory of this historical mystery still survives in Shepton Mallet. Owen Parfitt was an elderly seafaring man who returned to Shepton Mallet from no one knew where. He was supposed to be wealthy, and rumour went round that he had been a pirate. He and his sister lived together for many years until he became paralysed, and a younger relation came to look after them both. One summer day old Parfitt had been settled outside in his chair, to which he could just shuffle, when a passing neighbour told him that a seafaring man had been inquiring about an old sailor. Old Parfitt turned white, but he said nothing. Next day he was settled as usual, and his cousin went out to her shopping. When she got back his chair and rug and cushion were there, but there was no sign of Parfitt himself. The haymakers were working in the field near and had heard or seen nothing, but he was never found again. The local explanation is that he was not so lame as he pretended and that he had made off with his hoard when he heard of someone who had a right to share it. If so, he had gone off just as he was, without even changing his slippers.

¶ See Andrew Lang, *Historical Mysteries.*
The disappearance is one of the unexplained mysteries, almost as insoluble as that of the *Marie Celeste* or of the adventures of Mr Harrison of Chipping Campden, which has been examined in *The Camden Wonder.*
It is doubtful if a solution of any of them will ever be found.

THE PEDLAR OF SWAFFHAM

From Abraham de la Pryme, *Diary*, published by the Surtees Society, p. 220.

"Constant tradition says that there lived in former times, in Soffham [Swaffham] *alias* Sopham in Norfolk, a certain pedlar, who dreamed that if he went to London Bridge, and stood there, he should hear very joyful newse, which he at first sleighted, but afterwards, his dream being dubled, and trebled upon him, he resolved to try the issue of it, and accordingly went to London, and stood on the bridge there two or three days, looking about him, but heard nothing that might yield him any comfort. At last it happened that a shopkeeper there, hard by, having noted his fruitless standing, seeing that he neither sold any wares, nor asked any almes, went to him, and most earnestly begged to know what he wanted there, or what his business was; to which the pedlar honestly answered, that he had dreamed that if he came to London and stood there upon the bridge, he should hear good newse; at which the shopkeeper laught heartily, asking him if he was such a fool as to take a journey on such a silly errand, adding, 'I'll tell thee, country fellow, last night I dreamed that I was in Sopham in Norfolk, a place utterly unknown to me, where me thought behind a pedlar's house in a certain orchard, and under a great oak tree, if I digged, I should find a vast treasure! Now, think you,' says he, 'that I am such a fool to take such a long journey upon me upon the instigation of a silly dream? No, no, I'm wiser. Therefore, good fellow, learn witt from me and get you home, and mind your business.' The pedlar observing his words, what he say'd he dream'd and knowing they concenter'd in him, glad of such joyful newse, went speedily home and digged and found a prodigious great treasure, with which he grew exceedingly rich, and Sopham [Church] being for the most part fal'n down, he set on workmen and re-edify'd it most sumptuously at his own charges; and to this day there is his own statue therein, but in stone, with his pack at his back, and his dog at his heels; and his memory is also preserved by the same form or picture, in most of the old glass windows, taverns and alehouses of that town unto this day."

¶ Glyde's *Norfolk Garland*, p. 69, gives the following addition:

"The box containing the treasure had a Latin inscription on the lid, which, of course, John Chapman could not decipher. He craftily put the lid in his window, and very soon he heard some youths turn the Latin sentence into English:

'Under me doth lie,
Another much richer than I'.

"And he went to work, digging much deeper than before and found a much richer treasure than the former".

In *Transactions of the Cambridge Antiquarian Society*, III, p. 318, is another version:

"Where this stood,
Is another as good."

THE ROLLRIGHT STONES

Wright, *Folk-Lore Record*, II, pp. 165-79

There was once a king and his knights who were going to war, and it was prophesied that if ever he came in sight of Long Compton, he would be King of all England, but just as he was labouring up to the big ridge, an old witch met him, and turned him and all his men to stones, even the rebellious knights who were whispering against him. So there they stand to this day, and no one can tell the size of the army, for whoever tries to count the stones, can never count them twice the same. Many or few, they are destined to be there for ever, and ill-luck attends anyone who tries to move them. There was once a farmer who fancied one of the Whispering Knights to build into his big barn. In spite of all the neighbours could say, he yoked up his best oxen to his strongest waggon, and set to work to fetch it. It was mortal heavy, but they somehow got it on to the cart, and began the downhill way home. The oxen laboured under it as if they could hardly move, and when they had got it down to the farm-yard, they all three fell dead, and the waggon crumbled to pieces. But the farmer would have his way; he built the knight into his wall, and from that moment he never had a bit of good fortune. He had to mortgage his land and sell his stock, till in the end he had nothing left but one poor old shaky horse, and a ricketty cart that no one would buy. Then at last it came into his head what anyone could have told him, that all his misfortunes came from that stone. He pulled it out of the wall like a desperate man, and levered it on to the cart. He hitched up the old shaky horse and it stepped out like a four-year old all the way up the hill at a smart pace. The farmer dropped the stone back into its socket, and set off home again with a light heart. And after that his luck turned, and in a few years he was as rich as he had ever been. But he never meddled with old stones again.

¶ The Whispering Knights are still said to go down to the stream to drink on the night of the full moon.

Informant, Frank Pearman, Burford, 1947.

See "The Evil Wedding" (B, III), *The Wimblestone*.

THE SALE OF A WIFE [summary]

Thompson Notebooks, x.

A cobbler at Blackburn used to ill-treat his wife shockingly, though she was a very decent woman. One day he put a halter round her, and said he was going to sell her. She was ready enough. He put her up to auction and people began to bid in fun, but there was one decent old man who liked the look of her very much. He had no money, but borrowed 2s. from a shopkeeper and, when that was not enough, 2s. 6d.

He got the wife, and she said she was glad to go to him, and said, "You've got me and everything about me, I expect." He said, he didn't care for that, as long as he'd got her. But she put her hand in her bosom, and pulled out a bag with £200 in it. The old man bought a little business with it, and she was set up for life.

The people used to sing at the cobbler:

> "Oh Mister Duckworth,
> You are a cure.
> You sold your wife for beer,
> And live at [Cuckold's] Moor."

From Taimi Boswell, Oswaldtwistle, 10 January, 1915.

¶ It was widely believed in country places that if a man put a halter round his wife, and offered her in the market for half-a-crown, he would be quit of her if he could find a purchaser. An incident exemplifying this belief occurred in Burford (Oxfordshire) in the mid-nineteenth century. A man living in a house near the bridge bought a wife for half-a-crown. Public opinion was against him, and he was serenaded with "rough music". He dashed out with a pitchfork and drove some of the crowd into the river, but the feeling against him was too strong, and he had to send his wife back to her husband in the end. In this tale the purchaser was more fortunate, and the "rough music" was directed against the first husband.

Informant, Mrs Groves, Shipton-under-Wychwood, from her father, G. P. Hambridge.

SIMMER WATER*

S. O. Addy, *Household Tales*, p. 61.

A long time ago there was a village in the North Riding of Yorkshire called Simmerdale, at one end of which stood a church, and the house of a Quaker woman at the other end. It happened one day that a witch came into the village, and, beginning at the house next to the church, asked for food and drink, but her request was refused. And so she went on from house to house, without getting either food or drink, until at last she came to the Quaker woman's House. There, sitting in the porch, she was regaled with bread, meat, and beer. Having finished her repast, she rose and waved an ash twig over the village, saying:

"Simmerdale, Simmerdale, Simmerdale, sink,
Save the house of the woman who gave me to drink."

When the witch had said these words the water rose in the valley and covered the village, except the old woman's house. Simmer Water is now a peaceful lake, and on fine clear days people in the neighbourhood fancy that they can see down in its placid depths the ruins of the village and the church.

Gutch, *County Folk-Lore*, II, North Riding, etc., p. 37.

T. Whellan, *History and Topography of the City of York and the North Riding of Yorkshire*. vol. II, p. 403, gives the date of this story as "previous to the year of grace 45", and the wayfarer is not a witch, but variously given as an angel, St Paul, Joseph of Arimathea, or Our Saviour in the form of a poor old man.

¶ See "Bomere Pool".

---

* Semer Water, or Simmer Lake, is near Askrig in the North Riding.

TRAPPING THE PLAGUE

Hugh Miller, *Scenes and Legends*, p. 245.

In a central part of the churchyard of Nigg there is a rude, undressed stone, near which the sexton never ventures to open a grave. A wild apocryphal tradition connects the erection of this stone with the times of the quarantine fleet. The plague, as the story goes, was brought to the place by one of the vessels, and was slowly flying along the ground, disengaged from every vehicle of infection, in the shape of a little yellow cloud. The whole country was alarmed, and groups of people were to be seen on every eminence, watching with anxious horror the progress of the little cloud. They were relieved, however, from their fears and the plague by an ingenious man of Nigg, who, having provided himself with an immense bag of linen, fashioned somewhat in the manner of a fowler's net, cautiously approached the yellow cloud, and, with a skill which could have owed nothing to previous practice, succeeded in enclosing the whole of it in the bag. He then secured it by wrapping it up carefully, fold after fold, and fastening it down with pin after pin; and as the linen was gradually changing, as if under the hands of the dyer, from white to yellow, he consigned it to the churchyard, where it has slept ever since.

¶ There are many legends of the persistence of the plague germs. One such was current in 1926 of a piece of land in the middle of Bristol, in which plague victims had been buried, and in which the infection still persisted. The more picturesque belief was that the plague was a spirit.

See "The Plague in Edinburgh" (B, XII).

THE WIMBLESTONE

Ruth L. Tongue, *Somerset Folklore*, p. 12.

Zebedee Fry were coming home late from the hay-making above Shipham. It were full moon, for they'd worked late to finish, and the crop was late being a hill field, so he had forgot what night 'twas. He thought he saw something big and dark moving in the field where the big stone stood, but he was too bone-weary to go chasing any stray bullock. Then something huge and dark in field came rustling all alongside lane hedge, and Zebedee he up and dive into the brimmles in the ditch till it passed right along, and then he ran all a-tiptoe to reach Shipham. When he come to the field gate he duck two-double and he rush past it. But, for all that, he see this gurt stone, twelve feet and more, a-dancing to itself in the moonlight over top end of field. And where it always stood the moon were shining on a heap of gold money. But Zebedee he didn't stop for all that, not until he were safe at the inn at Shipham. They called he all sorts of fool for not getting his hand to the treasure—but nobody seemed anxious to have a try—not after he'd told them how nimble it danced round field. And nobody knows if 'twill dance again in a hundred years. Not till there's a full moon on Midsummer Night.

From a school-friend, who heard it from her Mendip great-grandmother, aged ninety.

¶ This is one of many legends of moving stones. The Whispering Knights in the Rollright Stones are said to go down and drink in the stream at midnight (Frome, *Folk-Lore*, 1895, pp. 6–51). A Cornish stone turns round three times at cock-crow (Hunt, p. 187).

PART 15
SAINTS

Most of the saints shown in this small gleaning are native to these islands, except the missionary St Augustine and St Aloys who was naturalized. English tradition claims him as a Somerset man. Small as the gallery is it shows a remarkable diversity of character, well illustrating the truth of the saying that the Christian profession develops character instead of flattening it. Some of the saints are hardly edifying characters. We have the peppery St Keverne and the thievish St Just. Some of the Saxons according to legend, appear to have had sainthood thrust upon them like King Edmund, who was dragged from his hiding-place under a hedge to be martyred, and who liked the prospect so little that he cursed the couple who betrayed him, and any newly-wed couple who crossed the bridge after them. Little St Kenelm was another involuntary martyr, as innocent as little St Hugh of the Child Ballad and of Chaucer's "Prioress's Tale". Others, however, like St Wulfric, were ascetic almost to morbidity. Legend, however, has softened their acerbities in such late, delightful stories as "St Wulfric and the Greedy Boy".

Many of the saints passed much of their time in conflict with demons and devils, and some of them were suspected of being magicians themselves. The same stories were told of St Adelme as of Jack o' Kent, Faustus, or William of Lindholm, and even St Dunstan, whose life rests on a firm historical foundation, has some magical prodigies attached to him, as well as his famous combat with the Devil.

The Celtic saints here are chiefly Cornishmen, though the undoubted fact that Ulstermen are English-speaking has made it possible to include a delightful fragment of recent oral collection about the lovable St Patrick. Some of the Cornish saints were canonized only in oral tradition, and find no place in the Calendar.

Some of the most delightful tales of both the Celtic and the Saxon saints are of their relations to animals. Of these only a few can be given; but more can be found in Helen Waddell's *Beasts and Saints*, The sources of each tale are given, but as well as these, and such early books as *The Golden Legend*, Aelfric's *Lives of the Saints* and Bede's *Ecclesiastical History*, there are a number of modern books to consult, among them Hippolyte Delehaye's *Legends of the Saints*, Helen Roeder's *Saints and Their Attributes*, and Christina Hole's *Saints in Folk-Lore*.

THE CROWZA STONES [summary]

Hunt, *Popular Romances of the West of England*, p. 262.

St Just lived at Penwith, and, finding little to do there, except to offer prayers for the tinners and fishermen, he once went to visit St Keverne in his hermitage near the Lizard headland. The two saints feasted and drank together, and St Just's envy was aroused by the beauty of the chalice from which he was drinking his rich wine. With many professions of undying friendship, he pledged St Keverne to return his visit, and took his way home.

Very soon St Keverne missed his famous cup and, after long search had been made, he could not but believe that his visitor had made away with it; so he decided to pursue him, punish him, and get the chalice back. As he passed over Crowza Down he picked up a few of the "Ironstone" pebbles which lie on its surface, put them in his pockets, and hastened on his way. Soon afterwards, he caught sight of St Just and, raging inwardly, called to him to stop.

St Just only quickened his pace a little, but made no other sign of having heard. But at last St Keverne was within a stone's-throw, and, taking a stone from his pocket, he flung it at St Just. It fell so near that the saint was alarmed and took to his heels. But as he ran he untied the cup, which he had fastened to his girdle, and dropped it to the ground. St Keverne recovered it and, being wearied he abandoned his long pursuit. But he threw all the remaining stones after the vanishing figure of St Just, one by one, and a curse with each. There the pebbles remained, entirely unlike all the other stones about them, but clearly the same as the stones at Crowza, and so heavy that none but a saint could hope to lift them. By day they have sometimes been removed, but they always return to their places by night.

¶ The Saints of Cornwall and the Celtic countries were by no means always immaculate characters. To be a hermit and a missionary was qualification enough to be counted a saint.

See *The Giant Bolster*.

MEN WITH TAILS

H. Bett, *English Myths and Traditions*, p. 86.

There are at least three local legends about the people of different places in England being blessed with tails, and the reason why. One story is that St Egwin, who was bishop of Worcester in the latter part of the seventh century, was much displeased with the blacksmiths of Alcester because they would work on Sundays, and he visited the town on purpose to persuade them to desist. But they drowned his exhortation by hammering on their anvils, whereupon the saint cursed them, and each irreverent blacksmith forthwith grew a tail.

A similar story is told of St Augustine and the men of Dorset. Caxton relates the legend thus in his version of *The Golden Legend*: "After this St Austin entered into Dorsetshire and came into a town whereas were wicked people who refused his doctrine and preaching utterly, and drove him out of the town, casting on him the tails of thornback, or like fishes; wherefore he besought Almighty God to show his judgment on them, and God sent to them a shameful token; for the children that were born after in that place had tails, as it is said, till they had repented them.

"It is said commonly that this fell at Strood in Kent, but blessed be God at this day is no such deformity."*

The third legend is concerned with Strood, and Caxton evidently confused it with his story about those who treated St Augustine so badly. It is said that the townspeople of Strood sided with Henry the Second in his quarrel with Becket, and cut off the tail of Becket's sumpter-mule as he passed through the place, whereupon the angry saint doomed their posterity to be born with tails, "binding them thereby with a perpetual reproach", as Polydore Vergil writes, "for afterward (by the will of God) it so happened that everyone which came of that kindred of men which played that naughty prank were born with tails, even as brute beasts be". The inhabitants of Strood and of the district are still jestingly called "Kentish long-tails".

Coulton, *Life in the Middle Ages*, I, p. 238.

¶ The taunt of having tails was a common accusation against the English in medieval times, and was even occasionally heard in the seventeenth century, in the epithet, "The Tailed English".

* Caxton, *Golden Legend*, III, p. 201.

253

ST ADELME [Aldhelm]

Briggs and Tongue, *Folk-Tales of England*, p. 77.

St Adelme, Abbot of Malmesbury; his father was a weaver, who as he rose early to go to worke, walking over the churchyard, when he came to the crosse something frighted him still. He spoke to his wife to goe along with him; she did, and when she came to the crosse she was struck at the botome of her belly, and conceived this Saint.

Miracle. When a boy—one Sundaye as they were at Masse he filled a barn full of little birds.

This Saint gave a bell to the Abbey, which when it was rung, had the power to make thunder and lightning cease.

The Pope, hearing of his Fame sent for him to preach at Rome; he had not above 2 daies warning to goe. Wherefore he conjured for a fleet spirit. Up comes a spirit he askes how fleet. resp: as fleet as a bird in the air. yt was not enough. Another as fleet as an arrow out of a bow not enough either. a 3rd. as swift as thought. This would doe. He commands it to take the shape of a horse, and presently it was so; a black horse on which his great saddle and footecloth was putt.

The first thing he thought on was St Pauls steeple lead: he did kick it with his foot and asked where he was, and the spirit told him etc. When he came to Rome the groom asked what he should give his horse. quoth he a peck of live coales.

This from an old man at Malmesbury.

From John Aubrey's MS. on Wiltshire, *Hypomnemata Antiquaria*, Bodleian MS. Aubrey, p. 251. Aubrey heard the tradition in 1645, from old Ambrose Brown at Malmesbury.

¶ Some similar tales are told of St Mungo, as also of less saintly characters, such as Jack o' Kent, Faustus, and such worthies as Francis Drake.

ST ALOYS AND THE LAME NAG

Briggs and Tongue, *Folk-Tales of England*, p. 78.

There were a carter 'ad a 'oss. Fine 'oss 'e were, worked wonderful 'till 'e took 'en carting stones, and they broked 'is feet dreadful. 'E 'ad a sand-crack so wide you could 'a' put a finger in it. Well! when 'e took 'en down to blacksmith, he couldn't do nothing for it. 'Ot as fire that foot was, and the butcher 'e began to get 'is axe ready. But the carter, 'e was proper proud 'o' that 'orse, real fond of it, 'e was. So 'e 'ears about St Aloys down to Wincanton, and 'e reckoned as 'ow 'e'd take cart'orse there. Well, it took 'en the best part o' two days to do the two mile, but carter 'e were determined 'oss should 'ave a chance. Well, when they got to Wincanton, St Aloys come out of 'is smithy. "Bring 'oss in 'ere," says 'e, "I'll take care of 'en, and 'ere's a bit o' zider for 'ee, and some bread and cheese." "I'm feared 'e won't stand," says carter, knowing 'ow e'd treated black-smith. "Oh! E'll be all right," says St Aloys.

So carter, 'e sits down to 'ave 'is zider and 'is bread and cheese; welcome as May, it was; and Saint, 'e just put 'is 'and on old 'oss, and then 'e go into smithy. Carter, 'e took a look and then he took another look, and 'e gollops down 'is zider. There's old 'oss, wi' a bit o' 'ay in 'is mouth, what Saint 'ad give 'im, and Saint were busy in the smithy, and 'old oss were standing there wi' three legs!

"'Ere we are, then," says the Saint, coming out, and he brings out fourth leg, and 'e claps it on, and old 'oss stands there, and 'e nuckers quietly wi' 'is bit of 'ay, and 'e worked for years arter that. Ah! that was St Aloys, that was, down to Wincanton.

Proper fine smith!

Recorded from Ruth L. Tongue, 29 September 1963, as she heard it from a carter at Wincanton in Somerset, where the legend is well known.

¶ There is a carving of St Aloys in Wincanton Church, and a fine alabaster in Nottingham Castle Museum representing the miracle. S. Baring-Gould, in his *Lives of the Saints* (xv, p. 9), says: "In art he is represented erroneously as a farrier with a horse's leg in his hand; the story going that he was one day shoeing a horse, the animal proved restive, so he took the leg off, shod it, and put it on again, without evil consequences."

The story is known in France and Germany, and is discussed by F. Saintyves in his *Saints, Successeurs des Dieux* (Paris, 1907, pp. 248–51).

St Aloys was not St Aloysius Gonzaga, but the earlier St Eligius of Noyau.

See "The Old Smith" (A, II).

ST AUGUSTINE AT LONG COMPTON

J. E. Field, *The Myth of the Pent Cuckoo*, pp. 152–3.

Long Compton has. . .[a] legend pointing to the. . .conclusion that the Briton still occupied the combe when the Saxon came here. It is not handed down in the traditions of the people, but preserved in the Chron-icles of the Yorkshire Abbey of Jervaulx—a compilation, as it supposed, of the time of King Edward III, though commonly attributed to John Brompton, who became Abbot of that house half a century later.

According to this story, St Augustine himself travelled into Oxford-shire, and came to preach "in the town called Compton", where the priest of the town complained to him that the lord of the manor refused to pay tithe of his possessions, and though he had often admonished him, and had even threatened him with excommunication, he still found him obstinate.

When Augustine had called for him and reasoned with him in vain he turned to the altar to begin the Mass, bidding all the excommunicate to depart, whereupon a corpse arose from the churchyard. Augustine asked him who he was, and he replied that he was a patron of the church before the English came and had died excommunicate, for refusing to pay his tithe; and the saint enjoined him to point out the grave of the priest who had repelled him from communion; so he in his turn arose from his grave, and bore out the truth of the story. Then at Augustine's bidding the ghost absolved the other ghost and both returned to their graves in peace, while the obstinate knight became a humble follower of the saint's teaching. At least we may gather from the tale that the memory of the Britons and their church at Long Compton had a place in the minds of the Saxon conquerors.

ST UNCUMBER

H. Bett, *English Legends*, p. 51.

[A] saint who had a connection with marital affairs, was St Wigefort, surely one of the most extraordinary saints of the Middle Ages. She was commonly known as Maid Uncumber, and her aid was invoked by wives who wished to be rid of their husbands. It is said that wild oats were usually offered to her. A sixteenth-century writer, describing the resort to various saints for help of different things, says that "if a wife were weary of her husband, she offered otes at Poules, at London, to Saint Uncumber". Another writer of the same period quotes a charm, one stanza of which runs:

If ye cannot slepe, but slumber,
Geve Otes unto Saynt Uncumber,
And Beans in a certain number
Unto Saynt Blase and Saint Blythe.*

Many altars up and down England were dedicated to this strange saint, including one in Old St Paul's in London, and one, which seems to have

* Brand, *Popular Antiquities*, III, p. 149, from Bale's *Interlude*.

been a special centre of veneration, at Chew Stoke in Somerset. There is perhaps no saint with such a variety of names. She is variously described as St Wilgefortus, Uncumber, Kummernis, Komina, Comera, Cumerana, Hulfe, Ontcommene, Ontcommer, Dignefortis, Eutropia, Reginfledis, Livrada, Liberata, and so on. The legend says that she was the daughter of a heathen king of Portugal, and she became a Christian. Commanded by her father to marry a pagan prince, she prayed that her body might be disfigured, so that she might keep her chastity. In answer to her prayer, a beard grew upon her chin, and then her father had her crucified. She is always represented as a bearded woman.

One pretty legend about St Wigefort is that a poor fiddler once played before her image, and it gave him one of its golden shoes. He was condemned to death on the charge of having stolen this from the church. He begged that he might play before the image again before he died, whereupon it kicked off its other shoe towards the fiddler, whose innocence was thus proved.

It has been suggested that Wilgefortis is from *Virgo fortis*. The more probable view is that it is derived from *Hilge Vartz* (*Heilige Fratz*, Holy Face) and that the whole legend has grown out of the fact that copies of the *Volto Santo* of Lucca were multiplied and spread through Europe. This represents Our Lord bearded with long hair hanging down to His shoulders, and clothed in a long tunic. As this was not a familiar type of crucifix, it was probably somewhere taken as the representation of a bearded and crucified woman, and so the legend arose. It does not seem to go farther back than the fifteenth century. The name "Uncumber" and its variants arose from the belief that if the saint were invoked in the hour of death you would die *ohne Kummer*, without anxiety. The feast of St Wilgefort is on the 19th of July. The Roman *Breviary* still commemorates "the holy Virgin and martyr Wilgefortes, who contended for Christian faith and chastity, and obtained a glorious triumph upon the Cross".

ST WULFRIC AND THE GREEDY BOY

Ruth L. Tongue, *Folk-Tales of England*, p. 73.

There was a poor widow with a large family and they all worked hard, even the little ones, and folk were very kind. There was always an egg or two or a sack of teddies, or a cabbage, or a bit of bacon put by to help them out. Then the farmers found work and their food for the biggest lads, and they ought to have managed, but they all went on looking so

thin as a yard of pump-water except Dicky—and he grew fat. One day
the poor widow crept to St Wulfric's cell. She'd brought him a thin little
flat oat-loaf, made from the scrapings of the meal chest. St Wulfric took
it, and the three little trots that had come with their mother burst into
tears as they saw it go.

The saint looked down at their poor little pinched faces, and whispered
gently, "Go down to the spring for me, and see what the birds have left
me." So off they toddled—half the size of the pail the baby was—but he
would go. And back they staggered with it only half full, their poor little
sticks of arms and legs couldn't lift more—but the baby's face was rosy
with joy over a big loaf with fresh butter and a crock of cream they'd
found there.

"Now, sit down and eat them," said the saint. "My birds must have
known you were coming. But I've a use for your mother's oat-cake."
Down they sat in the sunshine, and down the good food went—and after
that it was easy for the grateful widow to tell her troubles.

"'Tis our Dicky, zur; he do get his vittles all down to Varmer Mellish,
where he be bird-boy, and they do give he a-plenty. But never were such
a boy to eat, Missus Mellish say, and they be hearty trenchermen down
there. But when he do come whoame a-night he do gollop up all in the
house if I don't stop him. Then he do sneaky round when all's asleep and
there's nought for breakfusses. *And* he do get his dew-bit at farm, no
fear! All my others, they do bring a few bits of vittles whoame for me and
they little trots, but if Dicky be about 'tis all goed down his throat while
they be getting two bites in—and him so fat as a pig!"

"Tell him I want to see him," said the saint. So, after they'd picked the
saint a bunch of primroses and he'd blessed them, she took the little trots
home. They even ran a bit. Next day, a fat sulky lad came to the cell.
"I want you to take any bread you see on my shelf down to your mother,"
said the saint. "Be very quiet, for it is time I was at my prayers."

Dicky glanced at the shelf and saw his mother's oat-cake. He'd searched
for it all night! And she'd given it to an old man who knelt on a cold stone
floor—the old fool! Here he looked at the shelf again and there were two
large white cottage-loaves beside the oat-cake. Dicky grabbed them in
terror and ran for it, scared out of his wits. He was so fat he soon lost his
breath, and sat down on the turf—and the loaves smelt delicious. Nobody
would know what happened to them. The silly old saint was busy praying
and his mother wouldn't expect any food. Down Dicky's red lane went
all three loaves, yes, oat-cake and all, and my young raskill strolls off
home. He wasn't feeling at all happy inside and there were no end of queer

SAINTS

pains so he didn't go indoors, but sat down on the drashel. Out came his
mother smiling and handed him a big crust of white bread covered with
butter. "There, Dicky," she said. "You shall have a taste for being such
a good, kind boy, bringing in they three loaves from the saint. Lovely
bread 'tis, like us ate yesteddy, I did wish you others could taste." But
Dicky's hair was standing on end. "T-Three?" he gasped. "A girt big
oat-cake and two white loaves all a-buttered," she said. "I did find they
on table where you did a-put them." With that Dicky took off in terror
and never stopped till he got back to the saint's cell. St Wulfric was still
kneeling, and there on the shelf above him were a poor thin little oat-
cake and two cottage loaves. Dicky stood there and shook with fear. Then
St Wulfric stood up, "You must be hungry after your climb," he said
"Finish your bread and butter." Dicky dare not refuse, but, oh, how
terrible it was. It left him with such a taste in his mouth that he didn't eat
for days—until he was as thin as the baby had been. After that he never
made fun of saints or took more than his share. He even brought his
mother home *three* eggs one evening!

Recorded from Ruth L. Tongue, 29 September 1963, who heard the story as a child
at Hazelbury Plunkett in Somerset.

¶ Miss Tongue was told this story by an old retired clergyman of eighty-three.
He had heard it from his great-grandmother, who was seventy-three, and she had
heard it from her great-grandmother. At a rough estimate, the line of tradition
stretches back to 1681.

"Teddies" are potatoes; a "dew-bit" an early-morning snack; "drashel" is a
threshold.

USHEN AND ST PATRICK

T. G. F. Paterson, *Contributions to Ulster Folk Life, Armagh Miscellanea.*

It wus in the days of Ushen, an' Patrick wus sore tormented for ivery-
thing that he'd be buildin' on the Brague wud be down the next mornin'.
An' Ushen was jist back from the lan' of niver die, where he might have
been livin' still, only that he liked Ireland better. An' that's that.

Shure it wus on the other side of Carrickbroad it all happened. Ushen
on he's big white horse wus careerin' up the mountain when a woman with
a bag of turf—bad luck to her anyhow, for it wus the greed of her caused
it. Why cudn't she be after fillin' what she cud carry an' not be burdenin'
herself with the lazy man's load? But shure all the sorrows of Ireland
come be the weemin an' if ye ax me, they're the cause of many a heartburn
still. An' mebbe some of them are worth it an', more like, some are not.

How an' so iver, till be slicin' a long story short, shure Ushen forgot he wus safe on he's horse only so long as he didn't be after droppin' his legs on the groun', an' down he hopped, an' helped her up with the turf on her back. An' och anee, that wus the harm. Ushen soon felt the death upon him, an' down he lay upon the hillside. An' the woman, who wus mebbe the Cally Berry, or someone like her, went away.

An' Patrick wus passin' along an' he heared all about it, an' up he goes. An' says Patrick till Ushen, "It's sorry I am till see ye so wake now. Shure it's yerself can have the wish three times one before ye die now." An' Patrick talked to him of Heaven, but Ushen wasn't in much of a bother. Says he, "Are there houn's an' baygels there?" "The divil one," says Patrick. "Well I'm not going there at all," says Ushen. An' Patrick wus sore put about, for he wus takin' a likin' till him. Says he, "Tween you an' that brute of a bull on the Brague, I'm like to be breakin' my heart."

An' Ushen had a wish, says he, "Will ye bury me on Slew Gullion? An' will ye bury me high an' dry, an' clap a stone or two above me?" "Deed an' I will," says Patrick. Then says Ushen, "For me last wish I'll have me strength again till I take a look at yer bull. Give me back me strength, an' I'll rid ye of him," says he. An' Patrick says, "Rise, me boul'd boy, an' be after doin' your best."

An' Ushen went an' sarched for the bull, an' when he foun' it he struck it a mortal box in the face that knocked it as stiff as you like. An' it's buried on a mountain somewhere near till the Brague with a stone above it, like a Christian himself. An' when Patrick come till look for him, thinkin' as like as not he wud be totally destroyed, there he wus asleep in the skin of the baste. Usin' it for a blanket he wus. But shure he woke no more. An' they brought him back till oul' Slew Gullion an' buried him there. An' Patrick wus real sorry.

¶ This is a different account of the killing of the Wild Bull that harassed St Patrick from that given in "St Patrick and the Bull". Even in this broken-down version there is a touch of wistful beauty in the friendship of the Christian saint and the pagan hero.

See "St Patrick and the Bull".

PART 16
THE SUPERNATURAL

The modern researches into the field of extra-sensory perception, pursued in such books as *The Hidden Springs*, by Renée Haynes, cover very much the same ground as do the supernatural legends. The tales in this section are those which cannot be called "ghost stories" and are not precisely about witches, fairies, bogies or devils, yet have, nevertheless, no naturalistic explanation—or at least are not supposed to have such. Many of those to be found in Catherine Crowe's *Night Side of Nature* are supernatural rather than ghost stories. These tales deal with wraiths, second sight, visions of things distant in time or place, judgments and other unexplained, often inexplicable, happenings.

Wraiths are among the commonest of these, and are of various kinds. Sometimes a man will see his own double, and this is often thought to be a sign of imminent death, particularly when the real man and his shadow meet face to face. The danger of this can sometimes be averted by vigorous speech, as in the pleasant story of "The Waff", when the ominous double was fairly scolded away. Most often the wraith appears at the moment of death to friends at a distance. Sometimes the man is seen double, as in "The Doctor's Fetch", when the doctor's wife saw her husband asleep beside her and at the same time standing by the window. Sometimes the wraith is not ominous of death, but merely goes where the person wishes to go, and effects what he is unable in his own body to do. The appearance of the wraith at death is possibly a form of the same state, as in the story of the dying mother who wished vehemently to see her children once more, fell into a trance, and woke calm and comforted, having visited them and been seen by them.

Another group of stories very similar to these is about people who go back into the past or who visit distant places. Often these are seen as wraiths, as in the story of "The Dream House". Some of these experiences seem well established. The most famous of them is that recorded in *An Adventure*, which is too long and detailed to be treated in a summary and should be studied in the original book. "A Vision at Dunino" is a pleasant version of this type of tale.

The separable soul or the Escaping Soul is not unlike the wraith, but has a slightly different very primitive philosophy behind it. In these stories, which range over a wide period of time, the soul is conceived of as a tiny creature, often of a different shape from the body—a bee, a lizard, or the like—which issues out of the sleeper's mouth or ear and has adventures suitable to its size, which are remembered by the waking man as dreams. An early and often-quoted example occurs in Saxo Grammaticus, but the belief persisted until the end of the last century, and may yet be found alive somewhere.

There are also explorations into the past which concern heroes rather than places—mighty sleepers in underground caverns, or strange wanderers who come into men's houses and make brief contact with them. There are other stranger contacts still—nature spirits, dangerous creatures from the woodland or mountains, or voices calling out from the sea.

Second sight, prophetic glimpses into the future and visions of Heaven and Hell may be listed as examples of extra-sensory perception, but there are a few other, stranger legends, like "The Anchor" and other queer and freakish tales. The section covers many activities of man's spirit, from the crudest moralities to what seem like upsurgings of the unconscious itself. It is this variety which gives its interest to the whole section.

THE ANCHOR

S. Baring-Gould, *A Book of Folk-Lore*, p. 153.

On a certain feast-day in Great Britain, when the congregation came pouring out of church, they saw to their surprise an anchor let down from above the clouds, attached to a rope. The anchor caught in a tombstone; and though those above shook the cable repeatedly, they could not disengage it. Then the people heard voices above the clouds discussing apparently the propriety of sending someone down to release the flukes of the anchor, and shortly after they saw a sailor swarming down the cable.

Before he could release the anchor he was laid hold of; he gasped and collapsed, as though drowning in the heavy air about the earth. After waiting about an hour, those in the aerial vessel cut the rope, and it fell down. The anchor was hammered out into the hinges and straps of the church door, where, according to Gervase (of Tilbury) they were to be seen in his day. Unfortunately, he does not tell us the name of the place where they are to be seen.

¶ This strange early space-men story from Gervase of Tilbury [*Floruit* 1211] shows some glimmering of scientific knowledge about the relative density of the air near the earth. It is one of those strange, unmotivated and therefore rather convincing tales that are scattered through the early chronicles. An example is the story of Nicholas Pipe, the sea-man (B, V).

THE CURATE OF AXHOLME

Choice Notes from "Notes and Queries" p. 52.

At Axholme, alias Haxey, in ye Isle, one Mr Edward Vicars (curate to Mr Wm Dalby, vicar), together with one Robert Hallywell a taylor, intending on St Mark's Even at night to watch in ye church porch to see who should die in ye year following (to this purpose using divers ceremonies), they addressing themselves to the business, Vicars (being then in his chamber) wished Hallywell to be going before and he would presently follow him. Vicars fell asleep, and Hallywell (attending his coming in ye church porch), forthwith sees certain shapes presenting themselves to his view, resemblances (as he thought) of divers of his neighbours, who he did nominate; and all of them dyed the yeare following; and Vicars himself (being asleep) his phantome was seen of him also, and dyed with ye rest.

This sight made Hallywell so agast that he looks like a ghoast ever since. The lord Sheffield (hearing this relation) sent for Hallywell to receive account of it. The fellow fearing my Lord would cause him to watch the church porch againe he hid himself in the Carrs till he was almost starved. The number of those that died (whose phantomes Hallywell saw) was as I take it about fower score.

Thos. Cod, Rector Ecclie. de Laceby.
Bottesford Moors. Edward Peacock, IV, p. 470.
¶ See "St Mark's Vigil", "Midsummer Eve".

THE DART OF DEATH

Augustus Hare, *In My Solitary Life*, p. 59.

..."I have got a story quite on my mind, and I must really tell it to you." And he said that when he got to Lymington, he found Lord Warwick* ill in bed, and he [Lord Warwick] said, "I am so glad to see you, for I want to tell you such an odd thing that has happened to me. Last night I was in bed, and the room was quite dark (this old-fashioned room of the inn at Lymington which you now see). Suddenly at the foot of the bed there appeared a great light, and in the midst of the light the figure of Death just as it is seen in the Dance of Death and other old pictures— a ghastly skeleton with a scythe and a dart; and Death balanced the dart, and it flew past me, just above my shoulder, close to my head, and it seemed to go into the wall; and then the light went out and the figure vanished.

"I was as wide awake then as I am now, for I pinched myself hard to see, and I lay awake for a long time, but at last I fell asleep. When my servant came to call me in the morning, he had a very scared expression of face, and he said, 'A dreadful thing has happened in the night, and the whole household of the inn is in the greatest confusion and grief, for the landlady's daughter, who slept in the next room, and the head of whose bed is against the wall against which your head now rests, has been found dead in her bed'."

Told by Lady Waterford, who heard it from her cousin Charles, 3rd Earl of Somers, who is the narrator.

* George Guy Greville, 4th Earl of Warwick.

264

THE DREAM HOUSE

Augustus Hare, *In My Solitary Life*, p. 263.

A few years ago there was a lady living in Ireland—a Mrs Butler—clever, handsome, popular, prosperous, and perfectly happy. One morning she said to her husband, and to anyone who was staying there, "Last night I had the most wonderful night. I seemed to be spending hours in the most delightful place, in the most enchanting house I ever saw—not large, you know, but just the sort of house one might live in oneself, and oh! so perfectly, so deliciously comfortable. Then there was the loveliest conservatory, and the garden was so enchanting! I wonder if anything half so perfect can really exist."

And the next morning she said, "Well, I have been to my house again. I must have been there for hours. I sat in the library; I walked on the terrace; I examined all the bedrooms; and it is simply the most perfect house in the world." So it grew to be quite a joke in the family. People would ask Mrs Butler in the beginning if she had been to her house in the night, and often she had, and always with more intense enjoyment. She would say, "I count the hours till bedtime, that I may get back to my house!" Then gradually the current of outside life flowed in, and gave a turn to their thoughts; the house ceased to be talked about.

Two years ago the Butlers grew weary of their life in Ireland. The district was wild and disturbed. The people were insolent and ungrateful. At last they said, "We are well off. We have no children. There's no reason why we should put up with this, and we'll go and live altogether in England." So they came to London, and sent for all the house agents' lists of places within forty miles of London, and many were the places they went to see. At last they heard of a house in Hampshire. They went to it by rail, and drove from the station. As they came to the lodge, Mrs Butler said, "Do you know, this is the lodge of my house." They drove down an avenue—"But this *is* my house!" she said.

When the housekeeper came, she said, "You will think it very odd, but do you mind my showing you the house? That passage leads to the library, and through that there is a conservatory, and then through a window you enter the drawing-room," etc., and it was all so. At last, in an upstairs passage, they came upon a baize door. Mrs Butler, for the first time, looked puzzled. "But that door is not in my house," she said. "I don't understand about your house, ma'am," said the housekeeper, "but that door has only been there six weeks."

Well, the house was for sale, and the price asked was very small, and they decided at once to buy it. But when it was bought and paid for, the price had been so extraordinarily small, that they could not help a misgiving that there must be something wrong with the place. So they went to the agent of the people who had sold it, and said, "Well, now the purchase is made, and the deeds are signed, *will* you mind telling us why the price asked was so small?"

The agent had started violently when they came in, but recovered himself. Then he said to Mrs Butler, "Yes; it is quite true, the matter is quite settled, so there can be no harm in telling you now. The fact is that the house has had a great reputation for being haunted, but you, madam, need be under no apprehensions, for you are yourself the ghost!" On the nights when Mrs Butler had dreamt she was the ghost, she—her "astral body"—had been seen there.

THE ESCAPING SOUL

Norton Collection, VI. p. XXVI.

I remember some forty years ago, hearing a servant from Lincolnshire relate a story of two travellers who laid down by the roadside to rest, and one fell asleep. The other seeing a bee settle on a neighbouring wall, and go into a little hole, put the end of his staff in the hole, and so imprisoned the bee.

Wishing to pursue his journey, he endeavoured to awaken his companion, but was unable to do so, till, resuming his stick, the bee flew out to the sleeping man, and went into his ear. His companion then awoke him, remarking how soundly he had been sleeping, and asked what he had been dreaming of.

"Oh," said he, "I dreamed that you shut me up in a dark cave, and I could not awake till you let me out." The person who told me this story firmly believed that the man's soul was in the bee.

Choice Notes from "Notes and Queries", p. 269. From *F.S.*, III, p. 206.

THE GREEN LADY OF CROMARTY [shortened]

Hugh Miller, *Scenes and Legends of the North of Scotland*, pp. 70–1.

There are a few other traditions of this northern part of the country—some of them so greatly dilapidated by the waste of years, that they exist as mere fragments—which bear the palpable impress of a pagan or semi-pagan origin....

A lady dressed in green, and bearing a goblin child in her arms...used to wander in the night-time from cottage to cottage, when all the inhabitants were asleep. She would raise the latch, it is said, take up her place by the fire, fan the embers into a flame, and then wash her child in the blood of the youngest inmate of the cottage, who would be found dead the next morning. There was another wandering green lady, her contemporary, of exquisite beauty and a majestic carriage, who was regarded as the genius of the smallpox, and who, when the disease was to terminate fatally, would be seen in the grey of the morning, or as the evening was passing into the night, sitting by the bedside of her victim. I have heard wild stories, too, of an unearthly, squalid-looking thing, somewhat in the form of a woman, that used to enter farmhouses during the day, when all the inmates, except perhaps a solitary female, were engaged in the fields. More than a century ago, it is said to have entered, in the time of harvest, the house of a farmer of Navity, who had lost nearly all his cattle by disease a few weeks before. The farmer's wife, the only inmate at the time, was engaged at the fireside in cooking for the reapers; the goblin squatted itself beside her, and shivering, as if with cold, raised its dingy, dirty-looking vestments over its knees. "Why, ye nasty thing," said the woman, "hae ye killed a' our cattle?" "An' why," inquired the goblin, "did the gudeman, when he last roosed them, forget to gie them his blessing?"

Fragmentary Legends of North Cromarty.

THE HAND OF GLORY

Norton Collection, III, p. 21.

I. THE SERVANT MAID OF HIGH SPITAL

One evening, between the years 1790 and 1800, a traveller dressed in woman's clothing arrived at the Old Spital Inn, the place where the mail coach changed horses in High Spital, on Bowes Moor. The traveller begged to stay all night, but had to go away so early in the morning, that if a mouthful of food were set ready for breakfast, there was no need the family should be disturbed by her departure. The people of the house, however, arranged that a servant-maid should sit up till the stranger was out of the premises, and then went to bed themselves.

The girl lay down for a nap on the long settle by the fire, but before she shut her eyes, she took a good look at the traveller, who was sitting on the opposite side of the hearth, and espied a pair of men's trousers peeping out from under the gown. All inclination for sleep was now gone; however, with great self-command, she feigned it, closed her eyes, and even began to snore.

On this, the traveller got up, pulled out of his pocket a dead man's hand, fitted a candle to it, lighted the candle, and passed hand and candle several times before the servant-girl's face, saying as he did so, "Let those who are asleep be asleep, and let those who are awake be awake." This done, he placed the light on the table, opened the outer door, went down two or three steps which led from the house to the road, and began to whistle for his companions.

The girl (who had hitherto had presence of mind to remain perfectly quiet) now jumped up, rushed behind the ruffian, and pushed him down the steps. Then she shut the door, locked it, and ran upstairs to try to wake the family, but without success; calling, shouting, and shaking were alike in vain. The poor girl was in despair, for she heard the traveller and his comrades outside the house. So she ran down and seized a bowl of blue [i.e. skimmed milk] and threw it over the hand and candle; after which she went upstairs again, and awoke the sleepers without any difficulty. The landlord's son went to the window, and asked the men outside what they wanted. They answered that if the dead man's hand were but given to them, they would go away quietly, and do no harm to anyone.

This he refused, and fired among them, and the shot must have taken effect, for in the morning stains of blood were traced to a considerable distance.

Henderson, *Folk-Lore of the Northern Counties*, p. 241–2 (1879) 1st edn pp. 202–8.
Spring, 1861. Told by Bella Parkin, an old woman who was the daughter of the servant-maid. Stainmore, Westmorland.

II

Ibid. p. 242 The Baring-Gould Version.

Two magicians having come to lodge in a public-house with a view to robbing it, asked permission to pass the night by the fire, and obtained it. When the house was quiet, the servant-girl, suspecting mischief, crept downstairs and looked through the keyhole. She saw the men open a sack, and take out a dry, withered hand. They anointed the fingers with some unguent, and lighted them.

Each finger flamed, but the thumb they could not light; that was because one of the household was not asleep. The girl hastened to her master, but found it impossible to arouse him. She tried every other sleeper, but could not break the charmed sleep. At last, stealing down into the kitchen, while the thieves were busy over her master's strong-box, she secured the hand, blew out the flames, and at once the whole household was aroused.

Delrio. See also Thorpe's *Mythology*, III, p. 274.

III

Norton Collection, III. p. 22.

One dark night, after the house had been closed, there came a tap at the door of a lone inn, in the midst of a barren moor. The door was opened, and there stood without, shivering and shaking, a poor beggar, his rags soaked with rain, and his hands white with cold. He asked piteously for a lodging, and it was cheerfully granted him; though there was not a spare bed in the house, he could lie along on the mat before the kitchen-fire, and welcome.

All in the house went to bed except the cook, who from her kitchen could see into the large room through a small pane of glass let into the door. When everyone save the beggar was out of the room, she observed the man draw himself up from the floor, seat himself at the table, extract a brown withered human hand from his pocket, and set it upright in the candle-stick. He then anointed the fingers, and applying a match to them, they began to flame. Filled with horror, the cook rushed up the backstairs, and endeavoured to arouse her master and the men of the house; but all in vain—they slept a charmed sleep; and finding all her efforts ineffectual, she hastened downstairs again. Looking again through the small window, she observed the fingers of the hand flaming, but the thumb gave no light—this was because one of the inmates of the house was not asleep.

The beggar began collecting all the valuables of the house into a large sack, and, having taken all that was worth taking in the large room, he entered another. The moment he was gone, the cook rushed in, and seizing the candle, attempted to extinguish the flames. She blew them all in vain; she poured some drops from a beer jug over them, and that made the flames burn the brighter; she cast some water upon them, but still without putting out the light; as a last resource, she caught up a jug of milk, and dashing it over the four lambent flames, they were extinguished immediately.

Uttering a loud cry, she rushed to the door of the apartment the beggar had entered, and locked it. The whole house was aroused, and the thief secured and hung.

Baring-Gould, Henderson. Yorkshire.

¶ Milk has a magic quality against enchantments. In "Tamlane" Burd Janet quenched the burning brand into which Tamlane had been transformed in a bucket of milk.

Aubrey has also a story of the Hand of Glory.

THE SHEPHERD AND THE CROWS

E. M. Leather, *Folk-Lore of Herefordshire*, p. 168.

Years ago, on the Black Mountain above Longton, there lived a hired shepherd, who managed a little farm for his master. There were on either side of this farm two brothers, farming for their father. I can remember in my time there was terrible jealousy and animosity between the shepherds on the mountain, where the sheep all run together. I could always tell my sheep; if I whistled, they would all come running to me every one, while the strangers took no notice. A good shepherd knows his sheep, and they know him.

Well, it was worse nor ever for this man, because the brothers were together and they hated him. He stuck to his master, and they to their father. At last one day they got him alone on the mountain, and caught him, and said they would murder him. They told him there was no one about, and it would never be known. "If you kill me," he said, "the very crows will cry out and speak it."

Yet they murdered and buried him. The body was found after some time, but there was no evidence to show who the murderers were. Well, not long after that, the crows took to come wheeling round the heads of those two brothers, "crawk, crawk, crawk", there they were, all day long —when they were together, when they were apart. At last they could scarcely bear it, and one said to the other, "Brother, do you remember when we killed the poor shepherd on the mountain top there, he said the very crows would cry out against us." These words were overheard by a man in the next field, and the matter was looked into, so that in the end the brothers were both hanged for murder.

From W. Perry of Walbersham, a native of Langton, aged 80. 1903.

A VISION AT DUNINO

Wilkie, *Bygone Fife*, p. 325.

Some years ago, when many of the roads in the east of Fife were still used but by few, a visitor to the district chanced to ride from the south coast to St Andrews by that across the uplands. He had heard of Dunino Church, and knew something of its associations. He therefore resolved to make a detour to visit it. A somewhat rough track leads down to a bridge across the Pitmilly Burn, not yet united to her sister streams. Thence there diverges a broad and well-made path, cut in the hillside, and climbing among the trees to the kirk and the manse. Leaving this for the moment he continued on the level track round the flank of the hill, and saw before him on the farther side of the stream a picturesque hamlet. Some of the cottages were thatched, some tiled; but all were covered with roses and creepers. In front a strip of garden, stretching to the burn, was trimly kept, and full of old-world flowers; behind, it took on more the nature of a kail-yard. At the east end, on slightly higher ground, a smithy closed the prospect, save for the trees that shut out the farther windings of the Den.

No sound broke the stillness of the summer noon but the flow of the burn. At one or two of the doors there stood an old man in knee-breeches and broad bonnet, or a woman in a white mutch and a stuff gown, while in the entrance to the forge the smith leant motionless on his hammer....

Peace brooded like a benediction over the hollow. Half in a dream, he turned and climbed to the church, nor, as time pressed when he had seen it, did he return that way.

No sense of the abnormal had occurred to the intruder. He encountered no living thing till he had passed back to the high road. All was solitude.

A year or little more elapsed ere the wanderer came thither again. It was autumn, and tints of russet and gold were stealing into the colour of the woodlands. This time he was accompanied by a companion to whom he had told the story of his glimpse of "the most old-world hamlet in Fife". Where he had left the highway they diverged from it and, crossing the bridge, prepared to sketch the Arcady to be revealed.

The cottages were gone.

The burn flowed through the Den as when last he saw it, but its farther bank was bare. The smithy, like the cottages and those whose simple lives were passed in them, had returned to the world of dreams, and where it had stood appeared a croft, the house on which itself seemed old. The wanderer could but assure his questioning companion of the truth of his vision, and leave the riddle to be solved by other minds than his.

Both the *Statistical Accounts* state that there has been no village in the parish "within living memory"; but the population in Sir John Sinclair's day was only one-half of what it had been, and there were then thirty-one fewer inhabited houses than at an earlier date.

The author is informed on excellent authority that there were at one time at least three or four cottages and a blacksmith's shop at the place described. It is said these were taken down "some time last century".

¶ Glimpses into the past are not unheard of, though not common. The best-known example is described in *An Adventure*, by Miss Moberly and Miss Jourdain, a book which has aroused a good deal of controversy.

See *The Lord Protector*.

THE WAFF

Gutch, *County Folk-Lore*, II, *North Riding of Yorkshire*, p. 83.

Not very many years have gone by since a man of Guisborough entering a shop in this old fishy town [Whitby] saw his own wraith standing there unoccupied. He called it a "waff". Now it is unlucky in the highest degree to meet one's own double; in fact, it is commonly regarded as a sign of early death. There is but one path of safety; you must address it boldly.

The Guisborough man was well aware of this and went up without hesitation to the waff. "What's thou doing here?". he said roughly. "What's thou doing here? Thou's after no good, I'll go to bail. Get thy ways yom, wi' thee, get thy ways yom." Whereupon the waff slunk off abashed and the evil design with which it came there was brought happily to nought.

Norway, *Highways and Byways in Yorkshire*, p. 139.

¶ Scolding is often an effective way of dealing with the Devil and ghosts.

THE WANDERING JEW

Aubrey, *Miscellanies*, p. 83.

Anno 165*. At —— in the Moorlands in Staffordshire, lived a poor old man, who had been a long time lame. One Sunday, in the afternoon, he being alone, one knocked at his door: he bade him open it, and come in. The Stranger desired a cup of beer; the lame man desired him to take a dish and draw some, for he was not able to do it himself. The Stranger asked the poor man how long he had been ill? the poor man told him. Said the Stranger, "I can cure you. Take two or three balm leaves steeped in your beer for a fortnight or three weeks, and you will be restored to your health; but constantly and zealously serve God." The poor man did so, and became perfectly well. This Stranger was in a purple-shag gown, such as was not seen or known in those parts. And no body in the street after evensong did see anyone in such a coloured habit. Dr Gilbert Sheldon, since Archbishop of Canterbury, was then in the Moorlands, and justified the truth of this to Elias Ashmole, Esq., from whom I had this account, and he hath inserted it in some of his memoirs, which are in the Museum at Oxford.

¶ Aubrey's version is appended to Sternberg's notes for the sake of his pleasant narrative style, though it is summarized by Sternberg.

PART 17
WITCHES

The witchcraft beliefs are those which are most present to modern consciousness as a proper subject for folk-lore research. The automatic response of a person uninstructed in folk-studies on hearing that someone is a folklorist is to ask about witches. There is an almost morbid interest in the subject, which was illustrated by the crowded audience, many of them self-declared witches, which attended a lecture given to the Folk-Lore Society by a leading American authority on witchcraft. That the lecturer was entirely and avowedly sceptical made no difference to the fervour of his audience.

There is no doubt that witchcraft beliefs are still alive in this country, though a great deal of the interest taken in witchcraft depends upon scepticism; it is the pleasure taken in quaint, obsolete, horrific stories which would be no pleasure at all if they were believed in. Hallowe'en parties, children's games about witches, witch fairy stories would have no pleasure about them if the actual witch beliefs and witch persecutions were really present to the imagination. The humour of the witch's curse in *Ruddigore* depends on the complete scepticism of sophisticated people at the end of the last century, just as *Ruthless Rhymes for Heartless Homes* were born in the peaceful days before the First World War. That complacency is not possible to us now; our horror comics are more ruthless and brutal, and something more sinister has crept into the new fashion for witchcraft.

There are two strands in modern witch beliefs, deriving from two very different strains. The first and most widely publicized is the modern cult of self-styled witches, who claim that they are reviving, or even carrying on, a Bronze-Age fertility religion. As far as one can see—though the evasiveness of the propagandists makes it difficult to be certain—the inspiration of this is almost wholly literary and is founded on the writings of Dr Margaret Murray, herself a complete sceptic. It is an ironic thing that Reginald Scot's *Discoverie of Witchcraft*, written at the end of the sixteenth century to expose the groundlessness of the witchcraft persecutions, became a kind of textbook on witchcraft, and disseminated the beliefs it was meant to disprove. In the same way, Dr Margaret Murray's writings have provided a base and groundwork for the modern literary cult of witchcraft. Little of this will be found in the following witch legends, though there are a few lingering traditions of the Rosicrucians, a learned, mystical society of dabblers in theurgic magic, who were popularly credited with all kinds of witchcraft practices.

The real country belief in witchcraft, with its ill-will, forespelling and sympathetic magic, has left plenty of traces all over the country, and the actual belief itself is still lurking among the unsophisticated people, though no longer so explicit as it once was. This is the soil out of which the theological, intellectualized beliefs arose, which nourished them and made the witch persecutions possible. The more complicated and thoughtful features of the belief have faded in England and left only the basic assumptions on which they were founded. In Scotland, where the beliefs were more theological and nearer to those held on the Continent, and where the persecutions were more cruel, we find tales of the witches' Sabbat and more instances than in England of the diabolic compact. Tales of imps, familiars and shape-shifting are to be found everywhere. Everywhere dairy produce is tampered with, livestock are injured and human beings bewitched and visited with sickness or death. Everywhere witches are nasty people to annoy, and they are often retaliated on with unnecessary brutality. Barrett's memorat, "Witches at Hallowe'en" gives a very vivid and suggestive picture of the countryman's attitude to witchcraft in the stark surroundings of the Fen Country.

The country consciences were not over-sensitive about magical practices. Some people were content to use prayers, good thoughts, the Bible or the sign of the Cross as their defence; others resorted to magic as black as any the witches used, torturing and burning live animals with the intention of thus destroying the witches in slow fires or making them unable to urinate. Some pride and pleasure was certainly taken in the exploits of white witches and wise women, and a few of the tales about them are entertaining enough, but on the whole these stories make us realize the pressures of close proximity, when neighbours have no power to separate, however antipathetic they may be, and show us how easy it would be for ill-will to acquire supernatural powers in the minds of those who were exposed to it.

THE BLACK HEN [slightly shortened]

J. R. W. Coxhead, *The Devil in Devon*, pp. 39–40.

A great many years ago, there was a large fairy ring of particularly lush green grass in one of the meadows of a certain remote parish on the western fringe of Dartmoor, and within this magic circle a jet-black hen and chickens were occasionally to be seen at nightfall.

The vicar of the parish was an extremely keen student of sorcery, and possessed a large collection of books and manuscripts dealing with the perilous subject of black magic.

One day, while the parson was conducting a service in the village church, one of his servants happened to visit his study and, finding a large volume lying open on the table, began to read it aloud. He had read no more than half a page when the sky became dark, and the house was shaken violently by a great wind. The servant, deeply absorbed in the book, read on; and as the storm increased in fury, the door flew open, and a black hen and chicken entered the room.

The creatures were of normal size when they first appeared, but they gradually grew larger and larger, until the hen became as big as a prize bullock. At this point the vicar, who was in the midst of his sermon in the pulpit of the church, suddenly closed his discourse, and abruptly dismissed the astonished congregation, saying that he was needed at home urgently, and hoped he would arrive there in time.

When he entered his study the hen had grown so large that it was already touching the ceiling. He quickly threw down a bag of rice which stood ready in a corner of the room, and while the hen and chickens were busily engaged in picking up the grains, he had time to reverse the spell.

From *Notes and Queries*, 1st series, II, 1850, p. 512.

THE BLACKSMITH'S WIFE
OF YARROWFOOT

Douglas, *Scottish Fairy and Folk-Tales*, pp. 177–9.

Some years back, the blacksmith of Yarrowfoot had for apprentices two brothers, both steady lads, and, when bound to him, fine healthy fellows. After a few months, however, the younger of the two began to grow pale and lean, lose his appetite, and show other marks of declining health. His brother, much concerned, often questioned him as to what ailed him, but to no purpose. At last, however, the poor lad burst into an agony of tears, and confessed that he was quite worn-out, and should soon be brought to the grave through the usage of his mistress, who was in truth a witch, though none suspected it. "Every night," he sobbed out, "she comes to my bedside, puts a magic bridle on me, and changes me into a horse. Then, seated on my back, she urges me on for many a mile to the wild moors, where she and I know not what other vile creatures hold their hideous feasts. There she keeps me all night, and at early morning I carry her home. She takes off my bridle, and there I am, but so weary I can ill stand. And thus I pass my nights while you are soundly sleeping."

The elder brother at once declared he would take his chance of a night among the witches, so he put the younger one in his own place next the wall, and lay awake himself till the usual time of the witch-woman's arrival. She came, bridle in hand, and flinging it over the elder brother's head, up sprang a fine hunting horse. The lady leaped on his back, and started for the trysting-place, which on this occasion, as it chances, was the cellar of a neighbouring laird.

While she and the rest of the vile crew were regaling themselves with claret and sack, the hunter, who was left in a spare stall of the stable, rubbed and rubbed his head against the wall till he loosened the bridle, and finally got it off, on which he recovered his human form. Holding the bridle firmly in his hand, he concealed himself at the back of the stall till his mistress came within reach, when in an instant he flung the magic bridle over her head, and behold, a fine grey mare! He mounted her and dashed off, riding through hedge and ditch, till, looking down, he perceived she had lost a shoe from one of her forefeet. He took her to the first smithy that was open, had the shoe replaced, and a new one put on the other forefoot, and then rode her up and down a ploughed field till he was nearly worn out. At last he took her home, and pulled the bridle off just in time for her to creep into bed before her husband awoke, and got up for his day's work.

The honest blacksmith arose, little thinking what had been going on all night; but his wife complained of being very ill, almost dying, and begged him to send for a doctor. He accordingly aroused his apprentices; the elder one went out, and soon returned with one whom he had chanced to meet already abroad. The doctor wished to feel his patient's pulse, but she resolutely hid her hands, and refused to show them. The village

Esculapius was perplexed; but the husband, impatient at her obstinacy, pulled off the bedclothes, and found, to his horror, that horseshoes were tightly nailed to both her hands! On further examination, her sides appeared galled with kicks, the same that the apprentice had given her during his ride up and down the ploughed field.

The brothers now came forward, and related all that had passed. On the following day the witch was tried by the magistrates of Selkirk, and condemned to be burned to death on a stone at the Bullsheugh, a sentence which was promptly carried into effect. It is added that the younger apprentice was at last restored to health by eating butter made from the milk of cows fed in kirkyards, a sovereign remedy for consumption brought on through being witch-ridden.

¶ See "The Two Fellows".

THE COUNTER-CHARM [summary]

R. Blakeborough, *Wit, Character, Folk-Lore and Customs of the North Riding of Yorkshire*, p. 191.

A man living at Broughton had a spell cast on him, and went to consult a wise man, who first wished to know whom he suspected of having worked the spell. There were two possibilities: the witch Nancy Newgill and a man known to have the evil eye. If a counter-charm were worked upon the innocent suspect, it would recoil against the victim of the spell, thus adding to his sufferings; so the wise man advised him to go to both of them and accuse them openly. This he did, and was convinced that, for once, Nancy was innocent, for she looked him straight in the face, and swore a fearful oath, while the man's behaviour was so shifty that he felt safe in telling the wise man to act against him.

Just before midnight they lighted a fire of wicken wood, and while it was burning up they took a ball of clay, beat it flat with the back of an old Bible, and scooped out of it a rough figure in the shape of a man.

Into this rough mould was poured a mixture of pitch, beeswax, hog's lard, bullock's blood, and a little fat from a bullock's heart. This was melted and stirred over the wicken-wood fire, and what remained after filling the clay mould was divided into two parts. One part was thrown into water, then worked into a ball, and thrown away; the other was poured on to the fire. It flared up into a tremendous blaze, and when this had died down, the ashes were buried in the churchyard. The figure was then taken out of the mould and two small holes made in it for eyes.

Into one of these eyes a pin was driven, a charm was pronounced, and the spell was complete.

As the man was returning home to Broughton, the pain suddenly left him; and in the same night the evil-eyed man of Nunthorpe was seized with a fearful pain in the eye, and by morning that eye was blind. This story was told by one who knew all three men personally.

¶ See "The Pig and the Butcher".

THE ELDER-TREE WITCH

Ruth L. Tongue, *Forgotten Folk Tales*.

There were a farm not far from Knighton, and 'tis an unket bit of land round there, but farmer took it and he did well. His few cows give the best milk round-abouts. There wadn't any big trees to the farm, but good hedges down to the shores—and no elder bushes.

No one like elder thereabouts.

There was a tale my own great-granddad used to tell and he's a-heard 'en vrom his own girt-grand-dad about a veller as went to chop down an elder tree and it bled and chased 'en—he might h' taken thought, witches can turn into elders if they wish, but he didn't and he got a terrible chasing till he crossed running water.

Well, whether farmer believed the tale or no, there came a time when his cows was being milked unbeknown to him.

He wadn't a rich man, and he couldn't afford the loss, so he gets up by starlight and goes out to make sure his cows was in safe grazing and there was the shadow of a tree up by the hedge.

So all in a cold sweat, he drove cows to the little home pasture, but the chain was gone off the gate, and he couldn't fasten it with iron, so he put a girt stone agin it.

Come morning he tells his women-folk what had been seen and his wife she say, "Thee girt fool, did'n 'ee draw a criss-cross in the mud droo the gate?"

No, he hadn'n.

And his daughter she up and peep out the window, then she turn so pale as curd cheese, and run around cottering the inside shutters safely crying, "'Tis out in the pasture now, right among the cows."

"Oh Lord, save us!" say the wife. "What tree be it?"

"A elder!" says the girl, shivering and shaking, and the old Granny she lays the big iron shovel among the red-hot embers, and raked in a faggot of ash to make a blaze.

"Elder!" say the farmer, and he were all a-shiver too, but he were a courageous man and his cows was dear to him. "Wife, go fetch this silver button as come off my Zunday coat."

Well, she'd a-sewed'en on again but she took and snipped 'en off and brought 'en to 'en, and by time he'd a-load his gun with it the daughter she'd a-swung the cross bar down across back door and the granny she'd got the iron shovel nice and hot.

Then the wife opened vront-door a crack and he took a look. This there tree were right in among his cows now so he couldn' take a long shot.

"I'll have to get upsides with 'en," he says. "Hold the door open and let I out and in again if I has to run for it."

And his wife she done it and out he went trembling all over. But he was bound to save his cows.

Well, the elder tree were right in among they, and he had to get too close for comfort to take aim, and for the life of him he couldn't hold the gun steady and the silver button missed her.

Well she let out a yell, and so did he, and she leapt arter 'en like a stag, and he leapt too, and she come rushing arter him and went rushing vor thic open door. He were a fat old fellow, but he made the pace, and his wife she slammed door so quick she caught his coat-tails in it, but for all that she drop the iron bar safe into its socket. And there they were all safe inside.

They could hear her branches a-scrattling and a-rattling outside and her a-skreeking like a high wind. Wife and daughter they skreeked too, and farmer he bellered like a bull-calf trying to get his coat-tails free and be out to his cows again.

He had the courage, see, but not the right knowledge, or not enough of it. Then they heard her rushing round the house and rap-tapping at the shutters, but she couldn' get in, no more than they could get out— and what was to happen to the pig and the pony?

Then the old Granny she get up vrom hearth-place with a girt shovel of burning coals and she say to the girl, "Open the back door now wide," and she did, and ran back to her mother, but the old Granny she just stood there, and when the elder tree come straight at her a-leaping and a-skreeking, she just up and throw all they red hot coals at her and come in and shut the back door, then they all see blue flames flicker and hear tree crackling into cinders.

After a bit Granny she take the ashen cattle-gad and go out and thère was a girt heap of ashes cold already and they women all made a criss-cross on the ashes with the ashen gad, then they ran and opened shutters and vront door again, and Varmer were able to free his coat-tails and go out to his cows.

Then the neighbours all come, and they all rejoiced, for they said that were the end of Madam Widecombe and her coach and the gold pig who pulled it, but 'twasn't to be—she were still around, the Combwich man said, nor it wadn't the old black witch over to Steart, and then someone up and told 'em Raggy Lyddy over to Doddington had valled in her vire, and was burnded dead—so that were who 'twas.

From Mr Burton, Stolford. Somerset.

¶ In some parts of the country elders are thought to give protection against witches and fairies, and it is often said that flies will not trouble one under elders. It used to be quite widely thought, however, that if elders are cut they will bleed.

See "The One with the White Hand" (B, XII).

THE FERRYMAN [summary]

The School of Scottish Studies, Maurice Fleming from Mrs Reid.

There was a ferry, and at one time it was not safe for anyone to cross it but the ferryman himself. Everyone else was drowned. One day a shepherd came who wanted to cross to the other side to see his mother and his two sisters. The ferryman told him it was not safe, but the shepherd begged him to take him, and at last the ferryman gave him a sword, and told him to sit in the prow, and cut the waves as they came at the boat. "For three great waves will come against us," he said, "and unless you cut them they will drown the boat." So the shepherd sat in the prow, and when they were halfway across, a great wave came up, and he leant out and cut it, and it died back into the water, and let the boat pass. Then a second wave came up, and the shepherd cut that, and they got safely through. Then a third wave came up against them, far greater than either of the others, and the shepherd leaned far out, and cut into the wave, and it died back into the water, and the boat got safe to land. Then the shepherd paid the ferryman, and went up to his mother's cottage. But when he went in he found his mother and his two sisters lying on the floor, cut in two. They were the witches who had troubled the ferry.

¶ This story is usually told in Gaelic, but has been transmitted to English-speaking tinkers.

See "The Aith Man and the Finn".

FRIAR BACON

W. Carew Hazlitt, *National Tales and Legends*, p. 77-96.

1 (a)

There once lived in the West Country a rich farmer, who had an only son. The farmer's name was Bacon, and his son was called Roger, and, not because his father looked to make him a holy clerk, but for that he should get learning enough to enable him to use his wealth wisely, this Roger was put with the parson of the town where he was born, to learn his letters and to become a scholar.

But the boy discovered so rare an aptitude and so quick a wit, that his master could, after a short time, teach him no more; and as he judged it to be pity that young Bacon should lose what he had gained, he went to the farmer, and exhorted him to suffer Roger to go to Oxford, that he might shew, by taking upon him that charge, his thankfulness to God in having sent him such a son.

The father said little; but as soon as Roger came home, he asked for his books, and taking them and locking them up, gave him a cart-whip in place thereof, saying to him so: "Boy, I will have you no priest; you shall be no better learned than I; you can tell, as it is, by the almanac, when it is best to sow wheat, when barley, peas, and beans, and when the gelding season comes; and how to buy and sell I shall instruct thee anon, for fairs and markets are to me what his Mass and *Ave Maria* are to Sir John. Take this whip; it will prove more useful to you than crabbed Latin. Now do as I bid, or, by the Mass, you will rue it."

The young fellow thought this hard measure; but he made no reply, and within a short space he gave his father the slip, and entered himself in a cloister some twenty miles off, where he was heartily entertained, and continued his studies.

And, ere many years had passed he made such progress in all kinds of learning that he grew famous, and was invited to go to the University of Oxford, where he perfected himself in all the sciences, and was known for a master of the secrets of art and Nature throughout Christendom.

Now the King of England, hearing of this learned friar, and of the wonderful things which he was able to perform and to answer, sent for him at such time as he and the queen were sojourning in Oxfordshire, and he said to the king's messenger: "I pray you, thank his grace from me, and say that I am at his grace's service; but take heed lest I be at the court two hours before thee."

"Scholars, old men and travellers," answered the messenger, "may lie with authority. Scarce can I credit such a thing."

"To convince you, I could tell you the name of the wench you last lay with; but I will do both within four hours."

The gentleman departed in haste; but whether he took the wrong road or not, the friar was there before him.

The king warmly welcomed him, and told him, from what great marvels he had heard of him, that he had long desired to see him. The friar declared that report had been too flattering, and that among the sons of learning there were many worthier than himself. The king prayed him not to be too modest, and to afford him some taste of his skill; and he said that he should be unworthy of possessing either art or knowledge, did he grudge to make his grace and the queen witnesses of his ability. So he begged them to seat themselves.

Friar Bacon then waved his wand, and forthwith there arose such ravishing music that all were amazed.

"This is to please," quoth he, "the Sense of Hearing. All the other senses shall be gratified, ere I have done."

He waved his wand again, and the music waxed louder; and lo! five dancers entered, the first like a court-laundress, the second like a footman, the third like a usurer, the fourth like a prodigal, the fifth like a fool. And when they had given great content by their antics and positions, they vanished in the order in which they came. This was the indulgence of the second Sense, the Sense of Sight.

He waved his wand the third time, and the music was changed, and before them appeared a table covered with all manner of delicious fruits, many not to that season belonging, and when they had partaken fully thereof, they were suddenly removed from view. And this was the Sense of Taste.

Then the wand once more moved, and the most fragrant perfumes filled the air. And this was the Sense of Smell. And presently for the fifth and last time Friar Bacon exercised his mastery, and men of divers nations, as Russians, Polanders, Indians, Armenians, were seen bearing the richest furs, which they offered to the king and queen to handle, and for softness they surpassed all that had ever been seen of that nature. And this was the Sense of Touch.

When it happened that these wonders were at an end, Friar Bacon demanded of his majesty if there was any other thing in which he might do him service; and the king thanked him, and said no, not for that time, and he took a costly jewel from his neck, and gave it to the friar of his royal bounty. And when the friar was about to take his leave of the court, he cast his eyes round, and espied the messenger hurrying in with all speed, covered with mud, for he had ridden through quagmires and ditches, through mistaking his way.

"Be not wrath," said the friar to him. "I shall now fulfil my word that I pledged to thee." And he lifted the hangings, and there stood a kitchen-maid, with her basting-ladle in her hand.

"I trow," quoth the friar, "you have no great store of money in your purse, and I will bear the charges of your wench's journey home." And at his bidding she disappeared, and all laughed at the gentleman's greasy sweetheart.

1 (b)

Now Friar Bacon had one servant to wait upon him, and his name was Miles; and he was none of the wisest. So the friar being yet at Oxford in residence with other scholars, all were wont to fast on the Friday; and none so devout as Miles, for when his master offered him bread to eat, he would refuse it, saying that it was holier and meeter not to eat ought. But the friar knowing his craft, and that he secretly ate meat, served him well for his deceit, and it was in this manner following.

On a certain Good Friday, when the friar was accustomed to partake of bread only, he tendered some to Miles; but Miles, with a grave aspect, turned away from it, and desired leave to fast altogether. Then he left his master, and went where he had a delicate black-pudding that he had made the day before, and began to eat the same. But the friar his master so contrived by his art, that when his man had set the end of the pudding in his mouth, he might in no wise remove it again; and when he pulled and pulled, and it stirred not, he cried out for help. The friar ran to him, and taking the other end of the pudding, drew him to the hall, where all the scholars were, and showed them how Miles would not eat meat on Fridays for conscience' sake; and he tied him by the pudding for a while to one of the window-bars, where he looked like a bear fastened by his nose to a stake.

II

Friar Bacon now began to accomplish many other strange and marvellous works. Whereof one was the deliverance of a gentleman in Oxfordshire, that had been a prodigal, and had brought his estate to ruin. This gentleman scarce knew at the last how to earn bread enough to keep him during the rest of his miserable existence, and so he wandered about here and there. Then came to him one day an old penny-father, and besought him that he would say why he was in this piteous case.

The Oxfordshire gentleman told the stranger everything, and the other said that, if he would fulfil certain conditions, he would furnish him with money enough for all his creditors; and when he said that he would swear to return the money, the old man rejoined that it was not oaths he would have, but bonds.

So the gentleman met him the next morning in a wood, as they had appointed, and he was attended by two serving-men carrying money-bags. Then he dictated to him the conditions on which he would lend him what he needed; and they were, that he should discharge all his debts, and when he was no longer indebted to any man, he should become at a word the slave of the lender.

That gentleman, in the plight in which he found himself at that time, yielded to this treaty, and paid all his mortgages and chief creditors, and became richer than he had ever been before. But he was secretly troubled in his mind when he remembered how he had bound himself to the stranger, and had consented to submit to his will; and after a time the old penny-father appeared, and claimed his bond, saying, "Thou hast paid thy debts, now thou art mine." But he replied, "Nay, sir, I have not yet discharged them all." And the userer therefore waxed wrath, and transformed himself into a horrible shape, and cried, "Thou shalt not deceive me; I will come tomorrow morning, and prove to thee thy falsehood, till when I leave thee to despair." And he vanished, and the gentleman now knew that it was the devil with whom he had made that compact.

This caused him to be so sorrowful and downcast, that he would have thrown himself on his sword, and so ended his life, had not Friar Bacon happily interposed, and comforted him; and when he unfolded to the friar what had passed between the devil and himself, the friar said unto him so: "Sir, appoint to meet the devil tomorrow in the wood, and for the rest be content."

So the Oxfordshire gentleman met the devil in the wood, and the devil in sore anger upbraided him with his falsity, and commanded him to tarry no more, but to follow him.

Then the gentleman asked him whether he would suffer someone to be judge in the case, and to deliver an award; and the devil agreed thereto. Whereupon suddenly Friar Bacon was seen by the gentleman walking near at hand, and he called him, and set out how the matter was. Friar Bacon considered, and asked the gentleman whether he had ever paid anything to the devil for all his great goodness to him, and he answered that he had not. Then he told him, as he valued his life, never to do so, for he was his chief creditor; and thereupon the devil vanished with a loud cry, and the Oxfordshire gentleman thanked Friar Bacon for the great boon which he had conferred upon him in so wisely judging between them.

III

The next exploit which Friar Bacon sought to achieve proved him a loyal subject to his prince and a dear friend to England. For reflecting how often England had been invaded by Saxon and Dane and Norwegian, he laboured with a project for surrounding the whole island with a wall of brass, and to the intent that he might compass this, he first devised a head of brass which should speak. And when he could not for all his art arrive at this, he invited another great scholar, Friar Bungay by name, to aid him therein; and they both together by great study made a head of brass, yet wist not how to give it motion and speech. And at last they called to their succour a spirit, who directed them, but gave them warning that, when the head began to speak, if they heard it not ere it had finished, all their labour would be lost.

So they did as the spirit had enjoined them, and were right weary; and bidding Miles to wake them when the Head spake, they fell asleep.

Now Miles, because his master threatened him if he should not make them aware when the head spake, took his tabor and pipe, and sang ballads to keep him from nodding, as, *Cam'st thou not from Newcastle? Dainty, come thou to me,* and *It was a rich merchant-man.*

Presently the Head spake, saying, TIME IS! But Miles went on playing and singing, for the words seemed to him to import nought. Twice and thrice the Head said, TIME IS! But Miles was loath to wake his master and Friar Bungay for such a trifle; and there surely, enough, came in one of his ditties, *Dainty, come thou to me,* and he began to sing:

Time is for some to eat,
　Time is for some to sleep;
Time is for some to laugh;
　And time is for some to sleep.

Time is for some to sing,
　Time is for some to pray,
Time is for some to creep,
　That have drunk all the day.

At the end of half an hour the Head spake once more, and delivered these two words, TIME WAS! And Miles make sport of them as he had done before. Then another half hour passed, and Head uttered this sentence, TIME IS PASSED! And fell down amid flames of fire and terrible noise, whereat the two friars awoke, and found the room full of smoke.

"Did not the head speak?" asked Bacon.

"Yea, sir," replied his man, "but it spake to no purpose. I'd teach a parrot to talk better in half the time."

"Out on thee, villain!" cried his master. "Thou hast undone us both. Hadst thou roused us, all England would have been walled about with brass, and we had won everlasting renown. What did it say?"

"Very few words," answered Miles, "and I have heard wiser. It said, TIME IS!"

"Hadst thou called us then, we had been made forever."

"Then in half an hour it said, TIME WAS!"

"And thou didst not wake us then!" interposed Bungay.

"Alack, sir," answered Miles. "I was expecting him to begin some long tale, and then I would have awakened you; but anon he cried, TIME IS PASSED! and made such an uproar withal that he woke you himself."

Friar Bacon was greatly incensed at what his servant had done, and would have beaten and maybe slain him; but Friar Bungay pleaded for the fellow, and his master said, "Well, his punishment shall be, that he shall be struck dumb for a month."

So it was that England was not girded round with a brazen wall, as had nearly come to pass.

IV

Friar Bacon, this mishap notwithstanding, ever grew more famous as time passed; and it so fortuned that, when the king of England proceeded to his conquests in France, and could by no means take a certain town, but, on the contrary, sustained much loss before it he wox angry, and offered ten thousand crowns truly counted, to anyone who should conquer this town and gain it for him.

So, when proclamation had been made to such effect, and no one came to essay to do what the king desired, Friar Bacon, leaving his studies, crossed over to France, and sought admittance to the king. To whom he recalled how his grace had formerly shown him great courtesy in Oxfordshire, and he was now ready to do his pleasure.

"Bacon!" said our lord the king. "Alas! it is not art, but arms that I now require."

"Your Grace saith well," returned the Friar; "but be pleased to remember that art doth often times accomplish more than force. And speaking of art and nature, pure and simple, without any magical property, consider how ships are made without oars, and large vessels to cross the wide sea, and only one man to guide them; how chariots may be built to move with incredible force without human help to stir them; and how one may fly in the air and turn an engine; or walk in the bottom of the sea (as Alexander the Great did) and, which is more pertinent at this time, how by means of a mirror you may make one man wear the semblance of a whole army, and what is far off seem near at hand, and what is high, low, or the contrary. So Socrates did detect the dragon that lurked in the mountains, and destroyed all round. Then, as Aristotle instructed Alexander, instruments may be contrived by which venomous influences may be brought in contact with a city, and infect its inhabitants every one, even the poison of a basilisk lifted up upon the wall. These things are worth a kingdom to a wise man."

His grace gave leave to Friar Bacon to do as it liked him, and he should name his reward; and the friar caused an earthwork to be raised higher than the city wall, and desiring his grace to be in readiness the next morning to attack the town, when he should wave a flag from the earthwork, on the morrow, at nine of the clock the friar had, with certain mathematical glasses, set fire to the town hall, and while the people and the soldiers were busy in extinguishing the flames, the flag was waved, and the king took the place with little resistance.

He treated the inhabitants with such clemency, that he won the love of his brother the king of France, who, to divert him, summoned a servant of his, a German named Vandermast, to show conjuring sleights before both their graces; and the king of England, understanding what the entertainment was to be, privily sent for Friar Bacon and Friar

Bungay to come to him, that they might witness the same. But he bad them keep their counsel.

When the banquet was over, Vandermast asked the king of England if it was so that he would choose to see the spirit of any man that had formerly lived. The king said, "Yea. Above all I would see Pompey, who could brook no equal." And Vandermast made him appear as he was attired at the Battle of Pharsalia, whereat all were mightily contented.

Then Friar Bacon, all without warning given, raised the ghost of Julius Caesar, who could brook no superior, and had beaten Pompey at Pharsalia; and Vandermast, not knowing that Friar Bacon was present, said that there was someone in the hall who was skilled in magic. To whom Bacon discovered himself, and declared that he had brought Caesar to overthrow Pompey, as he did erst; and therefore Caesar engaged Pompey, and vanquished him. Which pleased all present passing well, and then both disappeared.

The king of England said to the German ambassador, that he thought his man had got the better of Vandermast; but Vandermast said that he would tell a different tale, ere all was done. "Ah!" said Friar Bacon, "my companion, Friar Bungay, shall deal with thee, sirrah; and if thou canst worst him, I will try what I may do, and not till then."

Then Friar Bungay raised the Hesperian tree, laden with golden apples, which were guarded by a fiery dragon, stretched beneath its branches. Vandermast conjured up the ghost of Hercules, and said, "This is Hercules, who in his life gathered the fruit of the tree, and made the dragon crouch at his feet; and so shall he do again."

But when Hercules offered to take the fruit, Friar Bacon raised his wand, and Hercules desisted. Vandermast threatened him and he picked it not: but he said, "Vandermast, I cannot; I am fearful; for here is great Bacon, that is more powerful than thee." Vandermast cursed Hercules, and again threatened him. But Bacon bad him not fret himself, for, since he could not persuade Hercules to do this bidding, he himself would cause him to do some service; and he commanded Hercules to take up Vandermast, and carry him back straightway to Germany.

"Alas!" cried the ambassador, "I would not have lost Vandermast at any price."

"Fear not, my lord," answered Bacon; "he hath but gone home to see his wife, and shall return to you anon."

V

Shortly after, when Friar Bacon had come again into England, a rich man of that country died, and left his estate to that one among his three sons who loved him best; and none could say who that was, for each one avowed that it was he, by reason that to him his father was most dear. So Friar Bacon was asked by the king to help him in this matter, and that learned and famous man, when the three brethren agreed to abide by his judgment, having caused the body of the father to be taken from the ground, and gotten ready three bows, and three arrows, summoned the sons to attend him, and said unto them so; "Sirs, there appeared to be no other method whereby this controversy might be concluded; therefore I have brought hither the dead body of your father, and whoever strikes him nearest to his heart shall have all his goods and lands."

The two elder brothers shot one after the other, and both hit the body, yet did not go near the heart. But the youngest refused to shoot, saying that he would liever lose his patrimony; and Friar Bacon awarded him the estate, because he showed by his loyal act that he loved his father better than the others: and all men commended the friar's wisdom therein.

Now, albeit Friar Bacon had seldom indeed taken any reward for all his great services to our lord the king, and many other, yet the report spread abroad that in his house he kept rich treasure; and certain thieves brake one night thereinat, and demanded of Miles, who admitted them, and of the friar, what money they had. The friar answered that he was poorly furnished with money; whereto they replied, these three thieves, that they must have whatso there was; and the friar gave them one hundred pounds each in a bag.

They heartily rejoiced at their good fortune; and he said to them that they should have music to boot, which still further contented them; and Miles took his tabor, and began to play thereon. Then the three thieves rose and set to dancing, and danced so lustily with their money-bags in their hands that they grew weary, but could not cease, for the friar had set a spell on them; and Miles went out of the door playing the while, and led the thieves over the fields, and over hedge and ditch, and through quagmire and pond, till they were wet to the skin, and weary to death. Then Miles stayed his hand, and they lay down as they were, and slept; and he took the money from them, and returned home to his master.

Meanwhile Vandermast was plotting how he could compass the death of Friar Bacon, to revenge the dishonour which had been cast upon him in France; and the friar, looking into his books, and finding that a great danger would befall him in the second week of the present month, unless he used some means to prevent it, devised this sleight, namely, while he read to hold a ball of brass in one hand, and beneath it a brass basin, and percase he should fall asleep, the loosing of the ball from his hand would awake him.

Now Vandermast had recently hired a Walloon soldier to come over to England, and to kill Bacon, and if he did so his reward was to be one hundred crowns; and when he arrived at Bacon's house, this Walloon soldier found Bacon dozing, yet the ball of brass still in his hand; but as he lifted the sword to slay him, the ball dropped into the basin, and Bacon awoke.

"Who art thou?" he demanded of the Walloon.

"I am a Walloon, and a soldier, and more than that, a villain; and I am come, hired by Vandermast, to kill thee."

"What is thy religion?"

"To go to an ale-house, to abstain from evil for want of employment, and to do good against my will."

"A good profession for a devil! Dost thou believe in Hell?"

"I believe in no such thing."

Then Friar Bacon raised the spirit of Julian the Apostate, with his body burning and full of wounds, whereat the soldier was almost out of his wits for fear. Friar Bacon asked the spirit wherefore he was thus tormented; and he answered, that he had been happy if he had remained a Christian, but he abjured the true faith, and now endured the doom of all unbelieving wretches.

The Walloon soldier that had come to kill the friar stood trembling all this time, and when the friar dismissed the spirit, he begged that he would instruct him in a better way of life, which the friar engaged to do; and this Walloon became a true Christian and died in the Holy War.

VI

It becomes time to relate how Friar Bacon once had a strange adventure, and helped a young man to his sweetheart, that Friar Bungay would have married to another.

An Oxfordshire gentleman had a daughter named Millisant, who was courted by a youth whose love she returned, and whose wife she desired to be; but her father was averse from that match, and would have wedded her to a rich knight.

This knight, when he perceived how loth the maiden was, went to Friar Bungay, and asked him to get her for him, either by his counsel or art; and Bungay, for that he was something covetous, promised, if he would take the lady for the air in a coach, so to direct the horses, that they should bring them to an old chapel in the wood, where they might be secretly married.

But meantime the gentleman had sought Friar Bacon, and implored him to do what he might to further his suit: and Bacon, knowing him to be virtuous and deserving, brought out a beryl, wherein he could see his best-loved and the knight in the chapel, though it was fifty miles thence, on the eve of being joined together in holy matrimony by Friar Bungay. The gentleman was overwhelmed by grief; but Bacon bad him be of good cheer, and seating himself in a chair, they were presently at the chapel door. Friar Bungay was about to join their hands, when Bacon struck him dumb, and raising a mist in the chapel, no one could see his way, but each mistook the other, and amid their bewilderment, Bacon led Millisant to the poor gentleman, and they were married by him in the chapel porch and furnished with a good store of money for their journey; and while they went their way joyfully together, the friar by his magic detained the father, and the knight, in the chapel, until they could not overtake them. And at a certain distance he prepared for them (albeit unseen) a banquet, succeeded by an antic masque of apes with music, wherein first entered three apes, and then three more, dressed in quaint coats, and then six; and all danced in merry and strange wise together, and then, when they had saluted the bridegroom and the bride, vanished.

VII

News had been brought to Vandermast, where he sojourned in Germany, that at length Friar Bacon was dead; and accordingly he came over once more into England, and met Friar Bungay in Kent, whom-of he learned that Bacon yet lived.

Now he bare no goodwill to Bungay, for that he was a friend to Bacon; and when he rose in the morning to leave his inn, he went to the stable where Bungay's horse was, and took it, leaving a spirit in its room. And when Bungay sought his horse to go on his way, he wist not what Vandermast had done, and mounted it, and in the middle of a stream it let him go, so that he perforce returned to his inn, at the door whereof he met the other, who asked him if he had been in a swimming match, and Bungay answered him again that if he had been so well posted as he was when he went to Germany, this would not have so fallen out.

Vandermast bit his lip, but said nought. And then Bungay, knowing that this German loved a wench in the house, and spared no pains to get her, shaped a spirit in her likeness, which yielded unto his advances, that he was enraptured; and when he had gone to bed, the sheet on which they lay was carried into the air, and fell into a deep pond. When Bungay saw him, he asked him how he liked the girl.

"Marry, I wish thee such another," quoth he.

"Nay, the rules of my order forbid it," he replied.

So it came to pass that these two conjurors grew more and more wroth with each other, until at last the Devil wox impatient of not having received from them the money for teaching them all their knowledge, and slew them, so that they were strangely scorched with fire amid a mighty storm of wind and rain; and the country people, finding their bodies, bestowed on them Christian burial, for that Bungay was a friar and Vandermast a stranger.

VIII

You have heard that Friar Bacon, who thus outlived both Bungay and Vandermast, possessed a wonderful glass, in which it was possible to see what was happening some fifty miles away; and this glass had been a source of great profit and pleasure to many, whom Bacon had obliged with the use thereof; till it happened that two youths, whose fathers—being neighbours—were absent from home, wished to know how they did, and besought Bacon to suffer them to look in his glass.

But those gentlemen, since their departure, had grown to be foes one to the other, and when their sons looked, they saw that their fathers were on the eve of fighting together, and as they fought, one killed the other; and this sight so fired one of the youths, whose father was slain, that he began to quarrel with his friend, and they both became so furious that they stabbed each other. Which when Friar Bacon knew, hearing the noise, he was so grieved, that he broke his mirror, the like whereof the whole world could not show; and then arrived the news of the deaths of Bungay and Vandermast, which further distressed him, so that he kept his chamber three days.

He now began to repent his wicked and vain life, spent in the service of the devil, and to turn his thoughts to Divine studies: and calling together many of his friends, he addressed them in these words:

"My good friends and fellow-students, it is not unknown to you how by my art I have attained great credit with all, and have done many wonders, as everyone knows, both king and commons. I have unlocked the secrets of nature, and have laid them open to the view of man, whereas they had been buried and lost since the days of Hermes the philosopher. I have revealed the mysteries of the stars and of every kind of life that is under the sun. Yet all this my knowledge I value so lightly, that I could wish I were ignorant; for what hath it availed me, save to keep me from the study of God, and the care of my soul, which is the immortal part of man. But I hasten to remove the cause of all my error, gentlemen." And, a fire burning in the hearth, before they could prevent him, Friar Bacon threw all his books therein, and consumed them utterly.

Then he gave away all his goods to the poor, and, building himself a cell in the church wall, withdrew from the world, and after two years space died a true, penitent sinner.

¶ In some chapbook versions Friar Bacon is said to dig his own grave with his nails. The whole story is told in Robert Greene's *Friar Bacon and Friar Bungay*, 1594.

This strange medley of motifs is an example of the traditions by which a famous man is shaped into a magician. Examples are "Virgilius", *Drake as a Wizard* (B, III, and B, VIII) St Dunstan (B, XI), *St Adelme*.

THE HARES' PARLIAMENT

N. Cooper, *Ulster Folk-Life*, 1959.

Mary and Pat lived in a nice wee house. Mary one day bought a looking-glass. When she was admiring herself in the glass she noticed that her ears were growing long and furry, and that she was getting wee-er and wee-er, and when she looked down at herself, she saw she was a hare. She ran out of the house, and started skipping about. She felt herself drawn in a certain direction and skipped along. In the meantime, Pat came into the house, and began to look for Mary; soon he spied the looking-glass. He too began to look at himself, and the same thing happened to him. Out he ran, and he also felt drawn in a certain direction. Soon he overtook Mary, and they skipped along together. They noticed that there seemed to be a great many hares all going the same way as they were. At last they arrived at a big field at Clonmallon, which was filled with hares all dancing round. So Mary and Pat danced round too. A great big hare called them all to order and began to speak. They could understand the hare's talk quite well, and it was a sort of parliament of hares.

Before long the boss hare said, "I can smell strangers. There are some hares that should not be here at all." Mary and Pat felt sort of uneasy at this, and when all the other hares turned and looked at them they turned and ran away, and all the other hares ran after them. But Mary and Pat had a good start, and got away safely and reached home. Mary went to the looking-glass to see what she looked like as a hare, and when she looked into the glass she saw that she was turning back into a woman and Pat into a man again.

Told by Mrs Mulholland, Warrenfoot.

¶ There are traditions in Oxfordshire and elsewhere of hares' parliaments, which are the meetings of the natural animals, but, in view of the magic transforming mirror, it seems almost certain that this was a gathering of witches. At Kinloch Rannoch, in Perthshire, it was believed at the end of the last century that the witches used to meet in the form of hares in the churchyard, and would scamper away in all directions if anyone passed by (Informant: Mrs J. McIntosh, *c.* 1946, who had it from her grandfather).

JAKEY BASCOMBE AND THE COB

Ruth L. Tongue, *Forgotten Folktales.*

My mother always drove our cob. She took him to market regularly, and he'd go well. He was very fast and everybody knew him, but he was so smart and good to handle she could do anything with him.

And all of a sudden he turned. He would become nappy and back away or just stand for an hour for no reason. In the end he had the dog-cart over, and broke the shafts, and mother's arm was put in plaster. They were going to have the Vet. and have him put down. Father thought he had poll evil. It was hay-carrying time, and the Vet. was too busy to come.

Grandma (she lived six miles away) was ailing, and she wanted to see mother. All the horses were working except the cob, and, of course, mother couldn't drive him. We had a very old man still doing little jobs on the farm. Father wouldn't part with him, he'd worked for us sixty-five years, and he said to Mother, "I'll drive cob vor'ee, missus. There's old putt I can put 'en in, and 'tis heavy enough to steady 'en up."

Well, mother chanced it. Father never knew till after—he'd have been furious—and old Ben drove to Grandma's without a bit of trouble.

Grandma was better, so they didn't stay too long. They wanted to get back while the cob was in the right mood, so mother was cross when old Ben went a roundabout way all through the lanes. "I knows what I be about, missus" was all he said, and they came home at a fine smart trot all the way.

When mother did tell father, he had a word with old Ben. Then he 'phoned the Vet. not to come. Mother didn't want the cob put down, so, of course, she asked why. And father said, "Did you notice which way old Ben came back?"

Mother said, "Yes. Almost in a circle."

Father said, "Going westwards?"

"Yes. It must have been."

"Well, then," said father, "Ben tells me the cob has been driven along the lower road lately, that goes past Jakey Bascombe's, and it goes wrong-handed. Ben says he reckons Jakey Bascombe won't overlook the cob any more, and his ill-wish will go back on him."

The cob worked for mother for years afterwards, and never misbehaved, but Jakey was tipped out of his putt and kicked, and laid up for a month seven days after old Ben brought mother home, "with the sun".

From the daughter of a Mendip farmer then living on the Gloucester Downs, a member of Brislington W.I., 1962. Gloucestershire.

THE LAIRD OF PITTARRO

SIR JAMES CARNEGIE

R. Chambers, *Popular Rhymes of Scotland*, p. 386.

The Earl of Southesk—better known in Mearnshire as Sir James Carnegie of Pittarro—was an expert swordsman, and vulgar fame attributed his skill in this and other sciences to the gift of supernatural power. In this tradition of Mearnshire, he is said to have studied the *black art* at Padua, a place once famed for its seminaries of magic. The Devil himself was the instructor, and he annually claimed, as the reward of his tuition, the person of a pupil at dismissing his class. To give them all a fair chance of escape, he ranged them up in a line within the school, when, on a given signal, all rushed to the door—he who was last in getting out being the devoted victim. On one of these occasions, Sir James Carnegie was the last; but, having invoked the Devil to take his shadow instead of himself, *it* being the object last behind, the Devil was caught by the *ruse* and was content to seize the shadow instead of the substance. It was afterwards remarked that Sir James never had a shadow, and that he usually walked in the shade to hide this defect. Sir James

is also remembered as a griping oppressor of the poor, which gave rise
to the following lines, and occasion to his enemies secretly to injure his
property: The Laird of Pittarro, his heart was sae narrow,
He wanna let the kaes* pike his corn-stack;
But by there came knaves, and pikit up thraves,
And what said the Laird of Pittarro to that!

Note to Lamont's diary, 1660.

MOLLY CASS AND THE NINE OF HEARTS
[summary]

R. Blakeborough, *Wit, Character, Folk-Lore and Customs of the North Riding of
Yorkshire*, p. 164.

Molly Cass lived for many years in a cottage close to Leeming Mill,
possibly in the mill itself. Abe Braithwaite, of Bedale, used to tell a
strange story of her, told by his grandfather.

Abe's grandfather, the miller and two others were playing cards in
the mill one night, and eight times in succession George Winterfield
had the nine of hearts dealt to him. At the ninth deal one of the players
laid a guinea on the table, and wagered it with Winterfield against a
shilling, that he would not receive the nine of hearts again.

Just then Au'd Molly put her head round the door, and said: "Put thy
brass in thy pocket. Thy brass is not for him, and his is not for thee."

So terrified was the man of incurring her ill-will that he at once put
back his guinea into his pocket, and Molly said, as the cards still lay on
the table: "Thou's gotten it again, George; take thy hand up and see."
And so he had. The old woman went on: "Thou's gotten it hard enough;
thou's had it eight times already. The Old 'Un's in thee now, and he'll
not leave thee till he's gotten thee altogether. Thou'st thrown away thy
chance, so I've pitched it into the Swale. The Swale's waiting to be thy
bridal bed. Go now; the longer thou waits, the longer thou'll stay."

George turned white as death, and got up, crying: "I'll wed her.
Give me another chance. I've rued all I've done." But Molly replied:
"I'm not often in the mind to give one chance, let alone two. Go thy
way. Thy bride's waiting for thee in a bed of bulrushes. Oh, what a
bridal bed!"

* *Kaes* = crows.

298

George left the mill, saying he would go at once and wed his old sweetheart. Molly shrieked after him: "Good night, George. All roads lead to the Swale to-night." And whether he lost his way in the darkness, or for some other reason, his dead body and his sweetheart's were found the next day, tangled in reeds and sedge, side by side in the water. He had never seen her alive, for she had drowned herself before he came.

For many years afterwards it was said that anyone who ventured near the spot at midnight would see the body of a girl first, and then that of a man, float by, and disappear when they joined one another among the bulrushes.

MOTHER SHIPTON [summary]

Parkinson, *Yorkshire Legends and Traditions*, 1st series, p. 151.

Most, if not all, of these stories are derived from a book published in 1684, 130 years after the reputed death of Mother Shipton, and it is uncertain how far they were the invention of the author, Richard Head.

It is said that her mother, Agatha, died in giving her birth, and that strange and horrible noises on the occasion terrified and nearly drove away all those who were present. "She was born at Knaresborough, and baptized by the Abbot of Beverley by the name of Ursula Southell. Her stature was larger than common, her body crooked, her face frightful, but her understanding extraordinary."

She was put out to nurse with a poor woman outside the town, but strange manifestations made the nurse's life well-nigh impossible. Once, when the child was about six months old, the woman left the house for a short time, and on returning found the door open and an uproar in progress. She called some neighbours to her help, but as soon as the foremost of them entered the house large yokes, in the form of a cross, were put round their necks, to detain them, and when, after a hard struggle, they cast these off, a staff was laid across their shoulders, from which an old woman clung by heels or toes.

The men of the company made their escape somehow, but the women forced their way in, and were at once compelled to take hold of the four ends of a cross, and dance round, each of them goaded by an imp like a monkey, until they were utterly exhausted. At last the priest with a band of followers, succeeded in crossing the threshold, and searching the house—the child was nowhere to be seen; but was at length discovered hanging with its cradle, both unsupported, halfway up the chimney.

As the child grew, the work of the foster-mother was invariably interfered with in mysterious ways. Chairs and tables would march upstairs, the meat would be spirited away from the table, and the child Ursula would grin and say, "Be contented. There is nothing here that will hurt you."

At school she was a prodigy: she needed no teaching of alphabet or reading; at first sight she read whatever book was shown to her. At twenty-four she was married to Toby Shipton; but little is known of their life together.

Long before her death in 1561, she foretold its day and hour. As the time drew near, she took a solemn farewell of her friends, and when it arrived she lay quietly down on her bed to await her end.

The earliest collection of her prophecies was printed about 1641; they included one to the effect that Cardinal Wolsey should never come to York with the King; in fact, he arrived within eight miles of it, but was summoned to return to the King, and died on his way to London. She is also said to have foretold the Great Fire of London and the plague, and other events of history; but it is uncertain which of the prophecies attributed to her were really hers, and which were fabricated later to fit the events.

¶ *Mother Shipton.* Mother Shipton is a kind of homely Merlin. Like him, she was the offspring of a woman and a devil, born toothed and of precocious intelligence. A play printed in 1660, *Mother Shipton,* deals with her mother's history, rather than hers. Mother Shipton is a patroness of washerwomen, and in the Eastern Counties "Mother Shipton's Day" is celebrated by laundresses with a holiday and tea-parties. More can be learned of her in *Mother Shipton Investigated,* W. H. Harrison, 1881.

THE SILVER SIXPENCE

H. Henderson, School of Scottish Studies.

There was an old farmer who had a fine herd of cattle, but they gave no milk. At last he asked a wise woman, and she said someone must be milking the cows, and he had better watch in the byre at night. So the old man lay in the byre, but always at midnight a drowsiness would come over him, and he would fall asleep. So at last he made up his mind that he must stay awake, and at midnight the byre door creaked open a little crack, and a brown hare came into the byre, and went from stall to stall. So the next night the old farmer watched again, and he took his gun, and loaded it with a silver sixpence and waited till midnight. In came the hare, and lolloped from stall to stall, and when she got to the door, the farmer took aim and fired, he only hit her front paw, but she gave a great scream, and a flood of milk came out of her, and she scampered away. The next morning the farmer went to see an old woman that lived near. The door was shut, and her granddaughter came to it. "You'll no can see Grannie," she said. "She's ill. She's hurt her hand." "That'll no prevent her seeing me," said the farmer. "An old neighbour like me." He went in, and found the old wife sitting by the fire, with her hand all bundled up.

"Let's look at your hand, Maggie woman," said the old farmer. "Maybe I can cure it." He unwrapped the bandages, and sure enough there was a wound in it, and in the middle of the wound there was a bent silver sixpence. The farmer's cows gave good milk after that.

From Jeannie Robertson.

¶ See "The Witch Hare", "Jane Wood of Basedale".

THE UNBIDDEN GUEST

J. Bowker, *Goblin Tales of Lancashire*, p. 37.

"Owd Jeremy" lived in a wretched hovel in a lane leading from the town of Clitheroe. He had the reputation of being a wizard, and claimed to be on familiar terms with the Evil One, and to be able to foretell men's destinies by his help. This cottage was furnished with all the apparatus of a wizard, and would strike awe into those who came to consult Jeremy; but in fact he was a charlatan, and had no faith in the powers he so often invoked.

For all his strange and solitary existence, Jeremy loved the world outside his home, and one day, when an inquirer had just left the cottage, he stood gazing out of the window towards Pendle, and thinking of its ancient beauty, so much more powerful and enduring than the life of a man, and as he turned back to the darkness of the cottage, he saw a stranger sitting in the clients' seat, who said to him, "Devildom first, and poetizing afterwards."

"What do you want?" said Jeremy.

"Security," said the stranger. "For five and twenty years you have been duping fools in my name, and amassing wealth for yourself, and now I want my share."

Jeremy pointed to his poverty-stricken abode, for, in spite of his reputed lore, he remained very poor, but already he suspected who his dreadful visitor was, and, rising in his agitation, he saw from the window that darkness had suddenly fallen, and a terrible clap of thunder broke over the cottage at the same moment. In panic Jeremy murmured, "What security do you seek?"

The stranger produced a written bond, and demanded Jeremy's signature, but the sturdy old man refused to sign. Then the Devil threatened that by the next day he should have a rival who would take the bread out of his mouth, and expose all his pretences and sham wisdom. But if he signed the bond, he was to have twenty-two years of life and success such as he had never dreamed of.

But still Jeremy, after deep thought stoutly refused to sign. The visitor departed, the storm abated, and the sun shone again.

But for five days no one came to Jeremy's house, and when at last he crept out to buy food, the people he passed, instead of shrinking from him in terror, called out jeering remarks, and children went on with their games, as though they had never feared him in their lives.

Next day a shower of stones broke old Jeremy's window, but no one else came to the house, and at last he cried aloud in his misery, "I wish I had another chance!"

Immediately there was a loud burst of thunder, and there sat his visitor as before, with the parchment on the table in front of him.

"Are you ready to sign?" he demanded.

"I cannot write."

The devil seized him by one finger, which he used as a pen, and made a neat X writing beside it, "Jeremiah Parsons, his mark."

He disappeared as mysteriously as he had come, and almost at once a man knocked at the door, wishing to have his future declared to him. He told Jeremy that he had first tried the new wizard's house in Clitheroe, but found it completely deserted. All fell out as the Devil had foretold. For twenty-two years Jeremy's fame continued to soar, till after one wild night, his cottage was discovered in ruins, and no trace of him remained.

¶ This tale illustrates a declension often stressed by the seventeenth-century writers on witchcraft, the steps by which a man, from using the Devil as a tool, descends to signing the diabolic contract.

See "Nancy Camel".

THE WITCH OF BERKELEY [summary]

William of Malmesbury, *Chronicle*, II, chap. 13, p. 230.

About the time of the Norman Conquest there lived a woman in the village of Berkeley who was a witch and augur, very gluttonous and luxurious, who led a life of riot and pleasure, although she was getting on in years. One day, as she was eating, her pet raven suddenly cried out loudly. At the sound the witch's knife dropped from her hand. "To-day my plough has reached its last furrow; there is nothing but grief before me from this day." No sooner had she spoken than a servant came running in with news of the death of her eldest son and all his family. This news struck her to the heart, and grief brought her to her death-bed.

When she knew that she had no hope of recovery she sent for her two surviving children, a monk and nun, both of great piety. When they had come she said to them: "My children, I have to confess to you that all my wealth has been gained by diabolical arts; all these years I have practised every wickedness, and have had no hope of salvation except in your piety. Even that has failed me now and I despair of my soul, but it may yet be that you can save my body from the Devil's clutches. Sew up my corpse in the skin of a stag, lay it on its back in a stone coffin and bind it with three great chains, curiously wrought. Let there be psalms sung for my soul for fifty nights, and masses said for fifty days. If I lie secure for three nights you may bury me on the fourth day."

With that she died, and her children did all they could to save her body from the Devil. On the first night, whilst the monks were singing their psalms, the bolted door of the church burst open, and a crowd of devils broke one of the chains. On the second night they broke another, but the third was more artfully made and resisted their efforts. On the third night, however, just before cock-crow, there was a tremendous rumbling like an earthquake, the foundations of the church shook, the door was shivered to splinters, and a great devil, more terrible than any of the rest, came up to the coffin. The monks' singing died on their lips, and their hair stood on end. The fiend called on the woman by name, and from the coffin she answered him: "I cannot come, I am chained."

"You shall be loosed," he said, and broke the massive chain like a piece of flax. He shattered the lid of the coffin with one thrust of his foot, and plucked out the woman. He led her through the door. A black charger was neighing outside, its back covered with iron hooks. He flung the woman on them and vanished with her from men's sight. But pitiable lamentations and cries for help were heard from the air for four miles.

¶ The same story in almost the same words is recorded in Ranulph's *Polychronicon*, translated by Trevisia, and also by Roger of Wendover, *Chronicle*, Bohn's Edition, I, p. 181.

See "Nancy Camel and the Devil", "The Round Square" (B, III), and other Devil tales.

WITCHES AT HALLOWE'EN

W. H. Barrett, *More Tales from the Fens*, p. 133.

I reckon I was a lad of about seven or eight when, because Mother was expecting another little one to join our already crowded house, I was sent to stay with an old aunt in one of the loneliest parts of the Fens. She had a big family, this aunt, though most of them were grown up by then, except for a boy of fifteen and a girl of twelve.

Although there wasn't another house within a mile, that didn't bother them; the farm was run by the family, and for most of the year they went to bed when it got dark and got up at daybreak.

While I was there Hallowe'en came round. In the afternoon everyone was busy putting osier twigs in front of all the doors and windows, the pigsties, stables and cow-house.

Uncle killed one of his black hens and hung it on the chicken-house door after he'd pulled out two of its wing feathers and tied them on the yard-dog's collar; then he caught the cats and shut them up in the barn. From all the talk going on, I found out that this was the night when the witches went round the fen, meeting each other and then, at the chiming of midnight, coming to some spot they'd chosen and casting spells over all the folks and animals nearby. That was why the peeled osier rods were put at all the ways into the house because no witch dared cross over them, neither would they go near black chicken feathers.

As the evening went by we all sat round the big open hearth. Aunt didn't put peat on the fire that night because witches could smell peat smoke for miles away, she said; instead, huge logs of oak were blazing away. The candles had been blown out, so the only light we had came from the fire, as we sat and listened to Aunt's stories of what witches could get up to. After supper a plate of thick slices of ham and half of a loaf of bread were stood outside on the door-stone so that, if a witch called, she wouldn't have to go away hungry because, if she did, she might start casting her spells on us. Then I was given a glass of ginger wine while my aunt and uncle and the others drank a lot of home-made botanic beer. After a while Uncle stood up and said to me:

"Come along, it's time we were up and doing."

He told me it was the custom, this night, for the oldest man and the youngest boy in the house to go round the farm an hour before midnight; so we set off. It was very queer padding along behind Uncle as he carried the lantern. All the animals seemed restless, and Uncle said they were like that because they could see and hear things that we couldn't, and they all knew what was going on.

After we'd been round the farmyard we had to visit the bees. As we went into the orchard an owl swooped over us with a loud screech, just above Uncle's head. I was scared, but Uncle got a firm grip of the thick stick he was carrying and, when the owl turned to fly over us again, he caught it such a clout that it fell down to the ground, fluttered its wings a bit and then lay still. My uncle bent down, turned it over and said:

"Well, there's one old witch who won't go home tonight."

When we got to the bee-hive, we went close up and listened to the noise going on inside; it was just like the hum of a threshing tackle on a frosty morning.

"Bor," said Uncle, "they're all worked up because they're a lot wiser than we are"; then, after tapping the hive with his stick, he bent right down to the entrance and said:

"Well done, my old beauties. I got one just now and, by the sound of it, you've got another; push her outside when you've done with her."

When we were back indoors we all sat round the fire again while Uncle told my aunt and the others what had happened while we were out.

"It looks as though some of us will be tudded [bewitched] for sure before morning," said Aunt, "if we're not careful. There's nothing, after all, to stop one of those old witches coming down the chimney and casting a spell on us."

I saw everyone backing away from the fire, and I did so too. Then Aunt got up, went over to the cupboard in the corner and came back with a big brown-paper bag.

"Whatever any old hag turns herself into," she said, "I promise I'll make her cough before she gets to the hearth. This ought to make her sneeze a bit first," and she took a handful of flowers of sulphur out of the bag and threw them on the fire. Bright blue flames and yellow smoke roared up the chimney. Aunt did this several times, even though Uncle told her not to forget that the roof was thatch, and if we were burnt out it wasn't going to be any good blaming it on any witches; but she only told him to be quiet, she knew what she was doing. This started a lot of arguing; everybody joining in till it seemed to me that the witches had been forgotten and that I was in the middle of a good old family row. Anyway, Aunt got into such a temper that she threw the whole bag on to the fire and the yellow smoke came pouring out into the room worse than ever, making us all splutter and choke.

Uncle said that two could play at that game and he went over to the cupboard and fetched out a linen bag full of the black gunpowder he used in his muzzle-loader. He'd no sooner hurled it at the back of the fire than there was a hell of a bang and we were all smothered in soot from head to foot. Well, that cleared everybody's temper and when the smoke had cleared away a bit Uncle said: "Well, I'll be damned," because lying on Auntie's lap was a jackdaw just kicking out his last gasp. And just then the old grandfather clock struck midnight.

After that we all ate a lot of thick ham sandwiches and the others drank some more botanic beer and I had another glass of ginger wine. Then Uncle said to me: "Come on, bor. We've got to make another round."

It was still very dark when we got outside, but all the animals were quiet and settled down. When we got to the orchard we found the bees quiet, too, but on the flight board, believe it or not, was a dead mouse, still warm. Uncle picked it up then went back to fetch the owl which he'd killed the time we were out before. When we were back in the house he threw the owl, the mouse and the jackdaw on the fire and said:

"Three witches on one Hallowe'en isn't a bad bag. Now, all of you get up to bed and sleep well. You won't have to worry about any witches for another twelvemonth."

Now, if you want to know where all this happened, then just walk a couple of miles from Littleport till you come to Crouchmoor Drove. Go along the drove for three miles till you come to the place called Coldharbour, and by the side of the drove you'll see a corner of a field all grown up with wild plum and nettles. That's where the farm was where I spent that Hallowe'en, and that was over seventy years ago.

¶ It is interesting to know that these ancient beliefs still had practical expression within living memory.

Curiously enough, the Motif Index does not mention Hallowe'en as the chief time of the meeting of witches, although ghosts and fairies are both mentioned as active at that time.

PART 18
MISCELLANEOUS LEGENDS

The small mixed bag that follows contains a few examples of modern legends. "The Stolen Corpse" may have been a fictional tale at first, but it has been passed from mouth to mouth in at least two continents by people who believe that they know at secondhand the lawyer who handled the case or the cousins of the people who suffered the tragic loss of their grandmother's, aunt's or godmother's body and failed to prove their right to the legacy which should have been theirs. The setting of the "The Foreign Hotel" is rather earlier, the end of the last century or the beginning of this. I myself was told it in childhood. A fictional source of this is claimed, but it is possible that it may not be the original source. It dates from the time of country house parties, when people ensured their welcome by telling each other tales, as they had done from the time of the *Pentamerone*.

The memorat is another type of Folk Tale, an unfledged legend, because it is still at first-hand. A good example of this is "Farmer Hewlett's Amends" which is of special interest because it enshrines folk practice by which, as the country people believed, legal status could be given to an illegitimate child by a mock-birth recognized in church. It is a ceremony which was much less practised than "The Sale of a Wife" (see Part 14), but like that it met a need in the country economy. "The Good Magpie" is a naturalistic version of a supernatural tale, though the conduct of the magpie might almost qualify it to count as supernatural. It is a gruesome comment on the extreme povery of the peasantry in the eighteenth and early nineteenth centuries. "The Wooden Legs" is an interesting example of a folk-tale in reverse—a negative print of "Bluebeard", as it were. It is difficult to imagine it as anything but an invention. Perhaps the narrator felt it to be unconvincing, and so added the corroborative incident of the narrator beginning to tell the tale as an after-dinner story in the presence of the hero and heroine. It is one of the tales noted by Augustus Hare, and so belongs to the period when the spoken narrative was still important.

FARMER HEWLETT'S AMENDS

Ruth L. Tongue, *Somerset Folklore*, p. 148.

This was told to me by a bed-ridden old granny somewhere near Goathurst on the Quantocks. She was repeating the tale told by her mother, who as a girl of fourteen, was a witness, of this service. I do not know where the mother's family came from—it may have been another Western county, but for its interest I have included it. It is a verbatim report except where the dialect was so archaic that an interpreter was needed. Even so, I have tried to use phrases still to be heard in casual speech. The names and locality are slightly altered in order to protect any relatives.

"There was a farmer *Hewlett* up around as were highly thought of by all. When his time came he were terrible worrited 'bout Mr *George* as he'd done wrong by. Oh dear, 'twas a gurt shock 'twas! Mr George he'd a-handled varm and stock vor his vather come twenty year and there wadn't none as folks didn't set by like Mr George, Squire and all. Well, it did sim like he were going to lose all his labour, and farm would go to a cousin over to *Taunton*. But varmer he set his mind to do right by un, and his wold Missus as had been the friend to the whole parish she come out brave and she said she'd do as he wished. So poor Mr George he just done what his Dad want. I see them come to church, and me but a maid then. And Mr George he had a loving arm to his dear mother. Then she did up and say in front of all as her and Farmer wasn't a-wed when this dear son come along. Poor old soul! She called him her dear and there wadn't a dry eye to hear her old voice. And that gurt beardy man he do croopy on hands and knees and she do pull hem of her Sunday black over'n and Parson do say the words to right'n so he should a-get farm. Parson he was so quiet as death, but his looks they proper daunted any to miscall 'en, but there wadn' no rabblement, they was too well liked. Farmer died happy—but 'ee see, my dear—old sins do come up again like weeds after a shower."

¶ This interesting survival, by which a grown man has a mock birth in order to prove himself born in wedlock, is so rare as to have no adequate motif.

THE FOREIGN HOTEL

Briggs and Tongue, *Folktales of England*, p. 98.

A lady and her daughter were travelling abroad, and arrived late at night, very tired after an exhausting journey, at the hotel where they had booked their rooms. The mother was particularly worn-out. They were put into adjoining rooms, and the daughter tumbled into bed and fell asleep at once. She slept long and heavily, and it was well on in the next day before she got up. She opened the door into her mother's room, and found it empty. And it was not the room into which they had gone the night before. The wallpaper was different, the furniture was different, and the bed was made up. She rang, and got no answer to her bell; she dressed and went downstairs.

"Can you tell me where my mother is?" she said to the woman at the reception desk.

"Your mother, mademoiselle?"

"Yes. The lady who arrived with me last night."

"But, mademoiselle, you came alone."

"We booked in; the night porter will remember; we wrote for two rooms!"

"Mademoiselle indeed wrote for two rooms, but she arrived alone."

And wherever she asked among the servants she got the same answer, until she began to think that she must be mad.

At last she went back to England and told her friends what had happened and one of them went to investigate. He went to the Consul and the police, and at last he found out the truth. The mother had been more than tired when she arrived that night, she had been in the invasion stages of cholera. No sooner had she gone to bed than she was taken violently ill; the doctor was sent for, she died, and the hotel-owners were filled with panic and decided to conceal all that had happened. The body was carried away, the furniture was taken out to be burnt, the wall was repapered, and all the staff were told to allow nothing to be guessed of what had happened. They knew that not a guest would be left to them if it was known that cholera had been in the house.

Yorkshire. K. M. Briggs from Agnes Hannam, 1915. Also heard by M. E. Luck (now Nash-Williams) at Warwick, c. 1926.

¶ Alexander Northcott traced this legend in *While Rome Burns* (New York, 1934, pp. 87–94), and got as far back as a report in *The Detroit Free Press* in 1889. Baughman gives as a reference Foster, *Collier's Magazine*, 1 January 1949. There has also been an film "So Long at the Fair."

THE GOOD MAGPIE

S. O. Addy, *Household Tales*, p. 46.

There was once a gentleman who used to ride on horseback every day. One day he had occasion to call at a house by the roadside, where a woman and her little boy lived. Whilst he was talking to the woman, he saw that she was making the oven hot, and the little boy said to him, "Mother's holing the oven to put me in."

But the gentleman thought that the boy was only joking, so he took no heed and rode away. But he had not gone far before a magpie crossed his path, and kept flying in front of his horse, and would not go away. So at last he thought that the magpie wanted him to turn back. So he rode straight back to the house, and when he got there he found that the woman had gone, and that the poor little boy was roasting in the oven.

Nottinghamshire.

¶ This is a naturalistic and modified version of a widespread tale. Grimm, no. 141, is remotely allied to this tale. No. 141 has, however, a magical foundation, and the villainess is a stepmother, not a mother.

THE STOLEN CORPSE

Briggs and Tongue, *Folktales of England*, pp. 99–100.

I

This story was told me by my cousin, who had heard it from a friend in Leeds, about a couple whom he knew, who went for a camping holiday in Spain with their car. They had taken his stepmother with them, she slept in a different tent to the others. On the morning that they struck, they were very busy, and they didn't hear anything of her for a while, and then, when they went to her tent, they found she had died, and rigor had already set in. They were in a great state, and they didn't know what to do, but they decided to roll her up in the tent, and put her on top of the car, and go to the nearest town, and go to the consul and the police. So they did this, and went to the town, and then they felt very cold and miserable, and they hadn't had a proper breakfast. So they thought they'd get a cup of coffee to revive them before they went in search of the consul. So they parked the car, and went to a small café, and had their cup of coffee, and then came back to look for the car. But it wasn't there; it had gone. So they went home to England without the car or the stepmother. But the difficulty was, they couldn't prove her will.

II

Shortly after the end of the Second World War, when money for travel was very tight, a young bride and bridegroom were anxious to spend their honeymoon abroad, but couldn't afford it. The bride's godmother said: "I should like to go to Spain. Why not come as my guests, and bring your car? We can sit lightly to each other. You can go about as you like, and I'll sit in the sun and be quiet."

So it was arranged; and they had a very happy time; but the day before they left for home the godmother had a heart attack and died. The local doctor came, and was very helpful, and said he would make all funeral arrangements for them. The girl said: "She wanted to be cremated. I know she left it in her will."

"But she can't be cremated in Spain," said the doctor. "It's illegal."

"But it was her wish. She must be!" said the girl.

They were at a deadlock for some time, but at length the doctor suggested that they should smuggle the corpse across the border to France, where cremation was legal. The hotel was very ready to co-operate, as a death in the place was bad for trade. The corpse was dressed, wrapped in shawls, and carried down to the car after dark.

At the frontier there was a sleepy guard, who didn't look too curiously into the car when they were told that madame was asleep. The passports were all in order, and they got through without incident, but for all that it had been a nerve-racking experience, and they stopped in the first town where a café was open, locked the car and went to have a drink of coffee and a roll before making inquiries about the Consul. When they got back to the car-park, the car had been stolen with the corpse inside it. They had neither time nor money to stop in France, so they went straight home.

Kentish version

1 is recorded from Winifred E. Briggs in Burford, Oxfordshire, 3 November 1963. She heard it in Canada from a cousin who had heard it in Leeds, Yorkshire. It is by way of becoming an international migratory legend. Stewart Sanderson of Leeds University is making a collection of various versions of the tale, some of them dating back twenty years. It is, however, travelling, for Laurits Bødker of Copenhagen has seen it as a newspaper story told about Poland, and Bengt Holbek, also of the

Folkedigtning Institut in Copenhagen, knew it in September 1963, having heard it from Gustav Henningsen—again about Spain—from a friend's friend. I have lately come across versions from Sussex and Kent. Richard M. Dorson heard an American variant in East Lansing, Michigan, 31 December 1963, localized in the South-West.

Other versions of the tale are rather different. A plausible one is about the German occupation of France in the Second World War. A young couple were staying with a grandmother who had a villa in the South of France. When the news of the German advance came, they prepared to escape, taking with them some particularly valuable Persian carpets, which they put in a roll on the top of the car. They were leaving early in the morning. In the night the grandmother died, and they would not leave her corpse to be insulted by the Germans, but rolled it up in the carpets. When they reached a port, they went to make enquiries about a boat, but when they got back to their locked car, they found the carpets had been stolen from the top, with the corpse inside (informant, Gerald Hardman, May 1964).

There are by now other and more extravagant variants.

THE WOODEN LEGS

Augustus Hare, *In My Solitary Life*, pp. 109–11.

There was, and there still is, living in Cadogan Place, a lady of middle age who is clever, charming, amiable, even handsome, but who has the misfortune of having—a wooden leg. Daily, for many years, she was accustomed to amble every morning on her wooden leg down Cadogan Place and to take the air in the Park.

It was her principal enjoyment.

One day she discovered that in these walks she was constantly followed by a gentleman. When she turned, he turned: where she went, he went: it was most disagreeable. She determined to put an end to it by staying at home, and for some days she did not go out at all. But she missed her walks in the Park very much, and after a time she thought her follower must have forgotten all about her, and she went out as before. The same gentleman was waiting, he followed her, and at length suddenly came up to her in the Park and presented her with a letter.

He said that, as a stranger, he must apologise for speaking to her, but that he must implore her to take the letter, and read it when she got home: it was of great importance. She took the letter, and when she got home she read it, and found that it contained a violent declaration of love and a proposal of marriage.

She was perfectly furious. She desired her lawyer to enclose the letter to the writer, and say that she could not find words to describe her sense of his ungentlemanly conduct, especially cruel to one afflicted as she was with a wooden leg.

Several years elapsed, and the lady was paying a visit to some friends in the country, when the conversation frequently turned upon a friend of the house, who was described as one of the most charming, generous, and beneficent of mankind.

So delightful was the description that the lady was quite anxious to see the original, and was enchanted when she heard that he was likely to come to the house. But when he arrived, she recognised with consternation her admirer of the Park. He did not, however, recur to their former meeting, and after a time, when she knew him well, she grew to esteem him exceedingly, and at last, when he renewed his proposal after an intimate acquaintance, she accepted him and married him.

He took her to his country-house, and for six weeks they were entirely, uncloudedly happy. Then there came a day on which he announced that he was obliged to go up to London on business. His wife could not go with him, because the house in Cadogan Place was dismantled for the summer. "I should regret this more," he said, "but that where two lives are so completely, so entirely united as ours are there ought to be the most absolute confidence on either side. Therefore, while I am away, I shall leave you my keys. Open my desk, read all my journals and letters, make yourself mistress of my whole life. Above all," he said, "there is one cupboard in my dressing-room which contains certain memorials of my past peculiarly sacred to me which I should like you to make yourself acquainted with."

The wife heard with concern of her husband's intended absence, but she was considerably buoyed up under the idea of the three days in which they were to be separated by the thought of the very interesting time she would have. She saw her husband off from the door, and as soon as she heard the wheels of his carriage die away in the distance, she clattered away as fast as she could upon her wooden leg to the dressing-room, and in a minute she was down on all fours before the cupboard he had described.

She unlocked the cupboard. It contained two shelves. On each shelf was a long parcel sewn up in canvas. She felt a tremor of horror as she looked at them, she did not know why. She lifted down the first parcel, and it had a label on the outside. She trembled so she could scarcely read it. It was inscribed: "In memory of my dear wife, Elizabeth Anne, who died on the 24th of August, 1864".

With quivering fingers, she sought for a pair of scissors, and ripped open the canvas, and it contained—a wooden leg!

With indescribable horror, she lifted down the other parcel, of the same form and size. It also bore a label: "In memory of my dearest wife, Wilhelmine, who died on the 6th of March, 1869", and it contained—another wooden leg!

Instantly she rose from her knees. "It is evident," she said, "that I am married to a Bluebeard—a monster, who *collects* wooden legs. This is not the time for sentiment. This is the time for action." And she swept her jewels and some miniatures that she had into a handbag, and she clattered away on her own wooden leg, by the back shrubberies, to the high-road—and there she saw the butcher's cart passing, and she hailed it, and was driven by the butcher to the nearest station, where she just caught the next train to London, intending to make good her escape that night to France, and to leave no trace behind her.

But she had not consulted Bradshaw, and she found she had some hours to wait in London before the tidal train started. Then she could not resist employing them in going to reproach the people at whose house she had met her husband, and she told them what she had found. To her amazement, they were not the least surprised. "Yes," they said, "yes, we thought he ought to have told you: we do not wonder you were astonished. Yes, indeed, we knew dear Elizabeth Anne very well; she was indeed a most delightful person, the most perfect of women and of wives; and when she was taken away, the whole light seemed blotted out of Arthur's life, the change was so very terrible. We thought he would never rally his spirits again; but then after two years he met dearest Wilhelmine, to whom he was first attracted by her having the same affliction which was characteristic of her predecessor. And Wilhelmine was perhaps even more a charming person than Elizabeth Anne, and made her husband's life uncloudedly happy. But she too, was alas! early snatched away, and then it was as if the whole world was cut from under Arthur's feet, until at last he met you, with the same peculiarity which was endeared to him by two lost and loved ones, and we believe that with you he has been more entirely, more uncloudedly happy than he was with either Wilhelmine or Elizabeth Anne."

And the wife was so charmed by what she heard that it gave quite a new aspect to affairs. She went home by the next train. She was there when her husband returned; and ever since they have lived perfectly happily between his house in the country and hers in Cadogan Place.

¶ Mrs de Bunsen (who told this story to A. H.) said that a cousin of hers was repeating this story when dining at the Balfours'. Suddenly he saw that his host and hostess were both telegraphing frantic signals to him, and by a great effort he turned it off. The lady of the wooden leg and her husband were both amongst the guests.

This story begins like a kind of echo of Type 312 (Bluebeard). It is indeed a kind of Bluebeard in reverse, in which the lady is given the keys of the hidden chamber, and expressly told to explore it. It is not surprising that so strange a predilection should have no motif attached to it.

About the Author

Katharine Briggs was born in 1898, one of the three daughters of Ernest Briggs, the water-colorist. She studied English at Oxford, earning her Ph.D. with a thesis on folklore in seventeenth-century literature, and became a D.Litt., Oxon., in 1969. Her writings include *The Personnel of Fairyland, The Anatomy of Puck, Folktales of England, The Fairies in Tradition and Literature,* and *An Encyclopedia of Fairies,* published by Pantheon in January 1977.

She has been president of the English Folklore Society, has taught and lectured in American universities, and has made friends in many parts of the world.